P9-BUI-647

BIO LEVIN You
Young, Josh
And give up showbiz? :

CL

33950010294517 12/14

Manatee County Public Library System
Bradenton, Florida

MANATEE COUNTY
PUBLIC LIBRARY SYSTEM
BRADENTON, FL

And Give Up
SHOWBIZ?

· ·

How Fred Levin Beat Big Tobacco,
Avoided Two Murder Prosecutions,
Became a Chief of Ghana,
Earned Boxing Manager of the Year,
and Transformed American Law

Josh Young

BenBella Books, Inc.
Dallas, TX

The events, locations, and conversations in this book, while true, are recreated from the subjects', sources', and interviewees' memories. However, the essence of the story and the feelings and emotions evoked are intended to be accurate representations. In certain instances, names, persons, organizations, and places have been changed to protect an individual's privacy.

Copyright © 2014 by Josh Young

Photos on pages 4, 7, 53, 63, 107, 149, 152, and 159 courtesy of *The Pensacola News Journal*/pnj.com

All rights reserved. No part of this book may be used or reproduced in any manner whatsoever without written permission except in the case of brief quotations embodied in critical articles or reviews.

BenBella Books, Inc.
10300 N. Central Expressway
Suite #530
Dallas, TX 75231
www.benbellabooks.com
Send feedback to feedback@benbellabooks.com

Printed in the United States of America
10 9 8 7 6 5 4 3 2 1

Library of Congress Cataloging-in-Publication Data
Young, Josh, date- author.
    And give up showbiz? : how Fred Levin beat big tobacco, avoided two murder prosecutions, became a chief of Ghana, earned boxing manager of the year, and transformed American law / by Josh Young.
        pages cm
    Includes bibliographical references and index.
    ISBN 978-1-940363-18-9 (trade cloth : alk. paper)—ISBN 978-1-940363-41-7 (electronic) 1. Levin, Fredric G. 2. Lawyers—United States—Biography. 3. Practice of law—United States.   I. Title.
    KF373.L489Y68 2014
    340.092—dc23
    [B]
            2014003377

Editing by Dorianne Perrucci
Copyediting by James Fraleigh
Proofreading by Laura Cherkas and Kristin Vorce
Indexing by Debra Bowman
Cover design by Sarah Dombrowsky
Text design and composition by Publishers' Design and Production Services, Inc.
Printed by Worzalla

Distributed by Perseus Distribution
www.perseusdistribution.com

To place orders through Perseus Distribution:
Tel: (800) 343-4499
Fax: (800) 351-5073
E-mail: orderentry@perseusbooks.com

Significant discounts for bulk sales are available. Please contact Glenn Yeffeth at glenn@benbellabooks.com or (214) 750-3628.

of and for *Fred Levin*,
Pensacola '95
Roy Neiman

sketched 2 years ago here — before
Fred Levin stopped drinking
LeRoy Neiman

ABOUT THE COVER: In 1995, Fred and his wife, Marilyn, were having dinner with their friend, the artist LeRoy Neiman, at Roberto's Ristorante at the Trump Plaza Hotel and Casino in Atlantic City. Neiman turned the menu over and sketched this picture of Fred and also one of Marilyn. Two years later, on Fred's sixtieth birthday, Neiman sent the sketch to Fred as a present. Neiman later visited Fred in Pensacola and added the inscription, "before Fred Levin stopped drinking." As with many stories in Fred's life, this one has an asterisk. Fred quit drinking hard liquor (and eventually smoking), but he still very much enjoys red wine.

For Susan Young Schwarz

Contents

· · · · · · · · · · · · · ·

Prologue

Searching for Atticus Finch

Trial lawyers are mavericks. They are self-assured. They are flamboyant. They are also full of bluster and bombast. They are vilified in life and immortalized in movies. Many of the best ones are obnoxious, overpaid egomaniacs who are despised by most people—at least until something goes wrong and those people need representation. And while it's easy to scoff at their boast, I have always admired their brio.

When I was growing up, F. Lee Bailey was one of my heroes, on par with Miami Dolphins quarterback Bob Griese and Boston Celtics swingman John Havlicek. I framed the *Time* magazine cover of Bailey that came out when he defended Patty Hearst. I read his books, saw him speak, and waited in line for his autograph. Man, was he excitement.

This led to my exploring the lives of other colorful lawyers, like Melvin Belli and Richard "Racehorse" Haynes. In prep school at Choate Rosemary Hall, I went so far as to design my own directed study class in the insanity defense. I was the only student, and it was such a slog from the touchstone 1843 *M'Naghten* case in Great Britain to the temporary insanity defense that Bailey attempted in the *Hearst* case that I abandoned the idea of a legal career.

Still, I continued to follow trial lawyers. There was no better place to watch them in action than the O. J. Simpson double murder trial in 1994 and 1995. The murders of Nicole Brown Simpson and Ronald Goldman occurred only blocks from where I had lived. Simpson was defended by a Dream Team of lawyers, led by Johnnie Cochran. With his masterful control of the courtroom, Cochran was certainly the biggest showman the public had ever seen in a real courtroom. And because the entire trial was broadcast live on CNN and recapped on every nightly newscast in the country, it was impossible to avoid.

Bailey also joined Simpson's defense team. Though Bailey was past his prime, his blasts of oratory were scintillating (despite the fact that I was rooting for the other side). Perhaps that was because he liked to knock back a couple of martinis at lunch hour, as was rumored. Only someone as confident as a trial lawyer would booze it up at lunchtime and return to court in a nationally televised trial.

But, of course, it was Cochran who dominated the trial with his Technicolor ties and silky maneuvering. He won by playing every conceivable angle and taking advantage of a colossal blunder when the prosecution asked Simpson to try on the bloody glove he had supposedly worn on the night of the murder. The glove had shrunk. "If it doesn't fit, you must acquit," Cochran famously told the jury, which, of course, they did. Love Cochran or hate him, he put on a masterful show.

Cochran was easy to follow in the years after the trial. He put his name on a national law firm called the Cochran Firm, which ran TV ads in a loop. Bailey wasn't hard to follow, either. In 1996, he was sent to prison for forty-four days for transferring millions of dollars of stock from a former client's assets to himself. In 2001, he was disbarred in Florida and reciprocally disbarred in his home state of Massachusetts. He moved to Maine, where he passed the bar exam in 2012 but was refused admission because he "[had] not met his burden of demonstrating by clear and convincing evidence that he possesses the requisite good character and fitness necessary for admission," five members of the State of Maine Board of Bar Examiners concluded.

But this news only heightened my fascination with trial lawyers, so I started doing some research. I found that the ideal of Atticus Finch, the trial attorney in Harper Lee's *To Kill a Mockingbird*, simply doesn't exist. Almost every community has a larger-than-life trial lawyer, be they a defense lawyer or plaintiff's attorney. There appeared to be very little difference between the superstar athlete and the trial lawyer, except that the trial lawyer wore a suit. Both had huge egos and relished being the center of attention.

As I was contemplating how to explore all of this in a book, I had drinks with Wayne Rogers, the actor and multifaceted businessman whose book I cowrote. "There's a wily old devil in Pensacola named Fred Levin who might be the man you're looking for," Wayne suggested. "I know his partner, and I can get you an introduction."

The name Fred Levin rang a bell. I remembered the first picture I had seen of him. I was a contributing editor at *George* magazine when John F. Kennedy Jr. was editor in chief. I was reviewing the layout for a story I had written about the catfight that erupted when Arianna Huffington implied in her syndicated column that Ambassador Larry Lawrence's widow, Shelia, was having an affair with President Bill Clinton, causing Lawrence to sue Huffington. Next to my article was "Puff Daddies," a photo essay spotlighting the lawyers who had a hand in bringing Big Tobacco to its knees. The first photograph pictured a man standing on the putting green of his estate on the Gulf of Mexico, wearing a tuxedo and sunglasses, sipping a cocktail, and flaunting a cigarette. Another picture earmarked for the teaser in the table of contents showed the same lawyer pictured shirtless standing next to his client, boxer Roy Jones Jr. "That's Fred Levin," said my editor. "He's crazy, but in a fun way."

So I went to Pensacola, Florida, and met with Levin. I told him of my affection for lawyers and mentioned that even though Johnnie Cochran had done a disservice to society by getting O. J. acquitted, I couldn't help but like his style. "I knew Johnnie," Levin said. "I helped start the Cochran Firm. Actually when we started the firm, we took out a $50 million insurance policy on Johnnie. He died two years and one day later, meaning the policy couldn't be contested. I got $5 million." He paused. "But his wife got $25 million." I would learn that was classic Fred Levin: He does something for himself, and others benefit, too.

On my next trip, I met a retired local businessman in a bar. When the well-dressed, gray-haired man asked what I was doing in Pensacola, I told him I was writing a book on Fred Levin. "Did he tell you how he got away with killing Jake Horton and Willie Junior?" the man asked, without any trace of sarcasm. He was certain that Levin was somehow responsible for killing two people in two different cover-ups, one a power company executive and the other a county commissioner. He was not alone in this belief.

The photo in *George* magazine that sparked the author's interest in Fred Levin.

I soon learned that at every turn in Levin's life, there was a twist. Levin initiated the multibillion-dollar tobacco settlement that inspired the "Puff Daddies" photo essay. But he did it by rewriting a Florida law and then getting his buddy, who was the president of the Florida Senate, to ram it through unnoticed in the middle of the night. This allowed the state of Florida to sue Big Tobacco to recover Medicaid costs spent on smokers.

Because the law that Levin wrote was upheld, Big Tobacco settled with Florida for $13 billion—and soon settled with every other state, paying out some $206 billion. As a result of the settlement and the changes required in the marketing of cigarettes, more than 100,000 American lives are saved every year—and Fred Levin personally will end up getting paid more than $180 million. It is a common theme in Fred's life: When he inadvertently does good for others, he does very well for himself.

As I dug deeper, a colorful life came into view—one that has made a difference to millions of people. Every tale seemed to have a *Rashomon* quality; that is, each part can plausibly be viewed from the extremes. Is Fred Levin a jet-setting ambulance chaser—or an advocate for those in need of justice? Even his son, Martin Levin, who practiced law alongside him for many years, lovingly calls him "a cockroach and a humanitarian." His current law partner, Mike Papantonio, said this about the trial lawyers of Fred Levin's generation: "They did huge harm to the practice of law—with their 'I won this huge verdict' and 'I'm kicking ass all over the place'—but at the same time they moved it ahead with their incredible trial skills and optimism."

It is a story chockablock with controversy. The Florida Bar Association, which should logically embrace the success of its own, has tried to disbar Fred three times, and each attempt ended up accentuating his do-gooder side. For years, the sheriff of Escambia County tried to prove Fred was a Mafia figure. Fred's critics have accused him of being involved in murdering two people, the first being Jake Horton, a friend of Fred's who died in a corporate jet crash, and the second being Escambia County Commissioner Willie Junior, an enemy of sorts who was found underneath a house with a belly full of antifreeze. Stranger still, in the same breath they accuse him of being a flamboyant self-promoter, which is worse as far as some are concerned.

His story is appealing in that the flashy parts are just slightly off the haut monde radar. His showy houses on the water are on the "Redneck Riviera" in unglamorous Pensacola, rather than in Malibu or the Hamptons. He managed the great boxer Roy Jones Jr., not the ubiquitous headline grabber Mike Tyson (whom Cochran represented at one point). He was friends with five men who came *close* to becoming president of the United States, but with no one who occupied the White House.

His story also has guts: Levin was at the forefront of establishing personal injury law in the United States and helping to push large corporations to make sweeping safety changes that have benefited every single person in this country.

But what really hooked me is that Fred Levin nailed what's so compelling about trial lawyers. He was sitting in his office, surrounded by original works of the artist LeRoy Neiman, photographs of himself with Muhammad Ali and Roy Jones Jr., and framed congratulatory letters from former Florida governor Lawton Chiles. "Without wearing the uniform, being a trial lawyer is the most exciting damn thing in the world," he said. "It's showbiz!"

ONE

Payback, Levin Style

The University of Florida Law School is a sacred institution to the lawyers in the state. No other law school in the country has produced as many presidents of the Florida Bar Association and, since 1973, of the American Bar Association. The law school has produced more governors of the state of Florida than any other. More than 250 of its graduates serve as state appellate and trial judges. So if you practice law in the state of Florida, it is likely that you, your partner, your opponent, or the judge you are arguing before—or perhaps all of the above—are Gator law school alums.

Today, a brick wall flanked by two cement columns in front of the law school at the University of Florida bears the words "Fredric G. Levin College of Law." To the uninitiated observer who has visited most any university campus, this would seem a rather innocuous, perhaps even quaint, tradition. At major universities across the country, schools and buildings have been named after distinguished alumni or wealthy donors—the Annenberg School for Communication and Journalism at USC, the Kellogg School of Management at Northwestern University, and many others. But placing *this* lawyer's name on *this* brick wall in front of *this* law school in 1999 created a firestorm filled with ironies and repercussions that were extreme even for the sun-soaked crazies in Florida.

Fred Levin standing proudly by the entrance to the University of Florida law school that bears his name.

For starters, Fred Levin would not be admitted today to the law school that bears his name. Grades and entrance exams almost entirely dictate admissions now. Fred was a mediocre student; in fact, he had to attend summer school to lift his middling GPA over 2.0 to earn his undergraduate diploma so he could enroll at law school. In those days, law schools accepted most every applicant and then weeded out the deadbeats.

When Fred entered law school in 1958, he had a reputation as a partier and a poor student. The smarter students would "dis" the dumber ones by shuffling their feet on the floor when one of the latter attempted to speak, like prison inmates protesting a bad meal. In his freshman year, Fred was one of the two most shuffled people in his class, the other being George Starke, the first African American to enter any Florida public university (prior to that year, state law had banned black students). Fred turned things around and ended up third in his class. Though the shuffling stopped, he never forgot the feeling of being mocked by his classmates.

Oddly enough, Fred never intended to put his name on the law school, but when the opportunity came along, it was too delicious for him to pass up.

Yes, Fred felt that he owed a great deal to the University of Florida Law School for educating him and teaching him to love the law. He was already a benefactor. His brother David, his law partner Lefferts Mabie, and Fred had donated some waterfront property they owned south of Tallahassee to the law school, which had sold the land for $1.2 million. In return for the gift, the law school named its dean the "Levin, Mabie and Levin Professor."

In December 1998, that professorship was held by Richard Matasar, who came to see Fred in Pensacola. Matasar and Jeff Ulmer, a fundraiser for the law school, were making the rounds of deep-pocketed donors to ask for help with the current fundraising campaign. They wanted to enlist Fred's help in asking an attorney friend of his, Bob Montgomery, to give $6 million to the law school. In exchange, they told Fred, the university was prepared to name a beautiful new building for Bob. During the meeting, one of them quipped to Fred, "Heck, tell him for $10 million we'll name the whole school for him."

The wheels immediately began turning in Fred's head. At the time, he was expecting an eight-figure check from the Florida tobacco settlement. It was a Champagne problem: Fred would soon have more money than he or his family would ever need. His mind raced through the ramifications of using some of the tobacco fee money to put his name on the University of Florida Law School. Giving the money to the law school would help with its quest to build prestige in an increasingly competitive world. Under Florida law, the school would also receive matching funds from the state, so a $10 million gift was actually worth $20 million.

But there was another angle. Putting his name on the law school would give Fred a little payback to the Florida Bar, and that might have been more appealing to him than the legacy. Fred felt that the old guard on the Florida Bar had been trying to tear him down for years. Thrice they had him brought up on formal charges and tried to have him disbarred. The first time was for gambling on football games, then going on his cable access channel, BLAB-TV, and saying he saw nothing wrong with it—despite the fact that it was a misdemeanor. The result was a slap on the wrist. The second time was for violating the ethics rule on interjecting personal statements into a trial. That stemmed from him calling his opponent's case "ridiculous" in two different trials. He was acquitted on that charge. And the third time was for him lambasting a judge's ruling. Again, he escaped.

So, after fifteen minutes of running these thoughts through his head, Fred told Matasar and Ulmer that he might give them the $10 million himself; first he needed to check with his tax lawyer. "They were stunned," Fred recalls. "It was as if I had shot both of them right between the eyes."

Fred suggested they all meet later that afternoon at Skopelos on the Bay Seafood & Steak restaurant in Pensacola to discuss the situation further. In the meantime, Matasar agreed to verify the naming arrangement with John Lombardi, the university's president.

After Fred's tax lawyer gave his okay, Fred and his son and law partner, Martin, met Matasar and Ulmer at Skopelos and sealed the deal over drinks. Matasar and Ulmer were thrilled. It was doubtful that anybody had ever contributed such a large amount of money to any school in such a short period.

Fred's gift was the largest cash contribution that the 146-year-old university had received. In return, the University of Florida law school would be known as the Fredric G. Levin College of Law, or the Levin College of Law for short—*in perpetuity*.

"The truth is that the Florida Bar and Big Tobacco were equally to thank for my $10 million donation," Fred says. "The fuddy-duddies at the Bar had perpetually irritated me with their pettiness. Big Tobacco provided the money. I was glad to give it to a school that had played such a big part in shaping my life. Really, it wasn't just my life, but my brothers' lives and my children's lives, too. To me, the funniest thing of all is that the school hadn't even targeted me for the donation, which I had essentially given on impulse."

Next came the deluge. Critics popped up from the Panhandle to the Florida Keys to Amelia Island. There was a blistering war of words in

Two big checks, thanks to the Big Tobacco settlement: $10 million to the law school, $2 million to local charities.

private and in print. Many people claimed to be horrified that the law school would put *Fred Levin's* name on it. The fact of the matter was that Fred was not one of them. Not only was he an outsider, he was an outsider who took great joy in needling the Establishment.

Some of Fred's friends believed opposition to the naming was rooted in anti-Semitism, as Matasar was also Jewish. Florida Senate President W. D. Childers (and Fred's friend) asked reporters, "Isn't it amazing that any time some honor comes to a black or a Jew, they come running out of the country clubs to complain?"

Steve Yerrid, one of the lawyers who Fred brought aboard the legal team to sue Big Tobacco, recalls receiving a phone call from an attorney who complained that Fred was Jewish. "A redneck lawyer called me up and said, 'I don't think it's right that a Jew would have a law school named after him down here. I want you to talk to Fred about taking his name off the law school.'" Yerrid told the attorney that he was disgusted by his phone call. He added: "But I have an idea. If you don't like his name on the law school, why don't you put up the fucking $10 million?" It was the last time Yerrid talked to the lawyer.

While there may be some deep-rooted truth to the anti-Semitism charges, Fred never thought it was anti-Semitism, merely anti-Levinism. "I admit that I brought some of this on myself," Fred says. "Part of this was my fault for being such a self-promoter. Part of it was animosity over my success."

At the time, Fred held the records for money awarded for the wrongful death of a housewife, the wrongful death of a wage earner, the wrongful death of a child, the wrongful death of an African American, and the highest personal injury award in Florida. Remarkably, he had won most of those verdicts in one of the most conservative areas of the country.

Many lawyers rankled at the elite political connections that Fred used to benefit his practice. The chattering class in Tallahassee would complain that Fred could pull strings at the statehouse through his connections with Governor Lawton Chiles, Florida Senate President W. D. Childers, and former governor Reubin Askew, who had cofounded the Levin law firm. At every turn, Fred encouraged the perception that he was a political power.

"Of course, when they wanted something done in the legislature, they would come to me and ask, 'Can you please talk to W. D. for us?'" Fred says. "The truth is that I wasn't a great political power broker, even though there was a perception that I was. I admit I encouraged it because it was good for my image and even better for business."

In addition to Fred's legal victories, his squabbles with the Florida Bar, and his political ties, he became ubiquitous for his other activities. He owned several restaurants and a string of women's clothing stores, and most notably, he managed Roy Jones Jr., who had become known in the world of boxing as the best pound-for-pound fighter. Jones was the World Boxing Association and World Boxing Council Light Heavyweight champion and had lost only one fight, on a controversial disqualification. Fred became so well known in boxing circles that he was approached to manage Ghana's Ike Quartey, as well as other soon-to-be champions. For his work, he was given the Rocky Marciano Award as national boxing manager of the year in 1994, and named the Boxing Writers Association of America manager of the year in 1995.

While the issue was partly that Fred was so successful in other arenas, it was mostly the way he shamelessly flaunted that success. Any time there was an HBO camera near Roy Jones Jr., Fred could be seen hugging his client or raising his arm. He had his own TV show on his own local cable channel. His picture regularly appeared in state and national magazines.

Every major newspaper in the state covered the law school naming controversy, and several took firm positions. The *Florida Times-Union* ran an editorial entitled "Law: The Name Game" on January 15, 1999, asking the university to reconsider the "hasty decision." It characterized Fred's legal record as "blemished" and called Fred "the key figure in one of the state government's worst legislative moments," referring to the law Fred had gotten changed so Big Tobacco could be sued.

In a follow-up article, headlined "New Law School Name Angers Some Alumni," several alumni declared they would no longer contribute to the law school. Former Florida Bar president Rutledge Liles told the paper: "I am in the column of being heartsick about it. There are certain things that are not for sale. The college of law has built itself a fine reputation. To come in and change the name, to me is deplorable." Next to the headline was a picture of Fred with a shit-eating grin on his face.

The *Pensacola News Journal*, however, ran an editorial lauding the gift, writing that the controversy should not detract from Fred's "extraordinary and generous gesture" that meant a brighter future for the law school.

Levin's donations are a generous gesture

We figure that if the University of Florida wants to attach Fred Levin's name to its law school in return for a $10 million donation, that's the school's decision to make. But the small controversy that erupted should not in any way detract from the extraordinary and generous gesture by Levin.

ACHIEVEMENTS

Giving back to the community through donations of time or money is what being a good citizen is all about.

At the same time, Levin's $2 million donation to the Levin and Papantonio Family Foundation, benefiting needy children in Northwest Florida, is another generous and welcome gift from the high-profile Pensacola attorney who has made a national name for himself as a litigator.

Whatever one might think about the $13 billion tobacco settlement Levin engineered for the state of Florida, or how much individual attorneys will reap — Levin stands to earn $275 million over 15 years — the fact is that it is a reality. So are Levin's donations.

Pensacola News Journal lauds Fred Levin's gift.

A *Miami Herald* article headlined "Controversy Loves Lawyer Whose Name Is on School" quoted former Florida Bar president John DeVault as saying that school officials had sent a message "that money transcends professionalism." Florida State Representative Tom Warner told the *Gainesville Sun*, "I think it's inappropriate. I am offended by it."

Fred Levin gets last laugh during the law school naming ceremony.

The letters sent back and forth between Fred's critics and the university read like a bunch of high school kids fighting it out. James Rinaman Jr., a lawyer in Jacksonville, fired off a letter to Dean Matasar saying that naming the law school after Fred "demeans the efforts of the many deans, faculty, and alumni who have worked for so many years to achieve the vision of making our college one of the top twenty law schools." He said Fred's comment in one article about spitting at the Florida Bar—a little too much, Fred now admits—"exemplifies his sneering, cynical, and selfish approach to the practice and the profession."

There was more. Rinaman went on to tell Matasar that the dean had "degraded the image and prestige" of the law school by "selling its good name to Fred Levin, a lawyer who has been castigated by the courts for abusing the rules and is notorious for commercializing the practice, thumbing his nose at the Bar, and otherwise manipulating the system." He questioned Matasar's "authority" and "hubris" to take such an action without a consensus of former deans, faculty, the alumni council, and the Board of Regents.

Rinaman now says he was angered by an interview Fred gave to the *Florida Bar News* about the gift, in which Fred underscored that part of the reason for the gift was retribution. Fred told the magazine, "I said, 'I'm going to give the money away anyway and what a wonderful gesture for the Bar to see my name there.' Maybe it's not a nice thing to say, but had the Bar not jumped on me for what I consider to be three incredible grievances, I probably would have given this money to other charities."

Admittedly, that's not the noblest way to give a gift.

But Fred had his defenders. His friend Bob Montgomery, the philanthropist and lawyer from West Palm Beach who he was supposed to help target for the donation, wrote back and said that Rinaman's letter was "revolting, ugly and offensive." He called Rinaman "a narrow-minded insurance shill" and said that Rinaman was allied with his "silk-stocking, holier-than-thou jackass friends"—this in a letter written to the president of the university.

Rollin Davis, a Pensacola lawyer and law school alum, declared: "If he gave $10 million, that's 10 million good reasons" to name the law school after him. Chesterfield Smith, a former president of the American Bar Association, called it a "magnificent act." Reubin Askew, the very popular former governor, said that it was "a tremendous thing for the law school" and called Fred "one of the most outstanding lawyers in the country." (In addition to being a founding partner of Levin's firm, Askew was a close friend of the Levin family and was the beneficiary of Fred's largesse when he was running for governor. Nevertheless, his opinion carried a great deal of weight with average Floridians.)

Naturally, Fred couldn't resist the opportunity to enter the fray. He wrote a long letter noting his accomplishments, which were considerably more extensive than those of his detractors. First, he defended himself against the Bar's charges and detailed the luminaries who had testified at his public hearing that he had done nothing unethical: Florida State University president Sandy D'Alemberte, famed attorney J. B. Spence, Southern Poverty Law Center founder Morris Dees, and the American Bar Association's ethics committee chairman, Larry Fox. Fred pointed out that both the Florida Supreme Court and the hearing's referee agreed with his witnesses. At the grievance hearing, it was noted that Fred was also the largest contributor to the United Way and cerebral palsy research in Northwest Florida. And by the way, he added, he had recently given $2 million to a foundation to benefit children in his community.

In his letter, Rinaman had asked how the university could explain to its students why the college of law was named after Fred Levin. Fred gladly provided the talking points. For starters, he pointed out that the university asked him for the contribution, not the other way around, and that it was the largest ever made to the university and the second largest to a public law school in the country. His family's long tradition at the university was plainly evident. All five Levin brothers had received degrees there, three of them law degrees. All four of Fred's children had degrees from the university as well. His daughter Marci had graduated law school with honors, and his son, Martin, was first in his law class. On his own standing, Fred sarcastically conceded, "I do not belong to any yacht club or country clubs so I apologize for not having the right social connections."

Fred went on to list a few of his accomplishments that might have been lost in the maelstrom. He had written a best-selling book on trial practice; the highly respected Chief Circuit Judge M. C. Blanchard called him the best trial lawyer in Florida's First Judicial Circuit and probably the state; he was responsible for helping to stop the overutilization of the antibiotic Chloromycetin, thus saving thousands and thousands of lives; he engineered the changes to the Florida Medicaid Recovery Act that allowed the state to recover billions from Big Tobacco; he served as chairman of two life insurance companies; he developed the cable channel BLAB-TV for live, call-in television; he managed Roy Jones Jr. and had been named boxing manager of the year by two different organizations; he had received the Perry Nichols Award as trial lawyer of the year; and he had recently been named a chief of the Republic of Ghana for his dedication to justice for all races.

He concluded by saying that even though he may not be a role model in the eyes of the *"current and past leadership of the Bar,"* in thirty-eight years of practicing law, he had never had a complaint from a client, nor had a trial judge ever insinuated that he acted unethically. "I guess," he wrote, "it really boils down to whether I would rather have a good and honorable name with the people I represent or with the Florida Bar Association," and if that was the choice—"I'm satisfied."

University of Florida president John Lombardi rose to Fred's defense in a letter to Montgomery and again thanked Fred for the gift. "The university and its law college make no apology, offer no retraction, and express no regrets about the generosity of Fred Levin or the recognition accorded that generosity," he wrote.

Reflecting on the situation all these years later, Matasar says there was no reason not to accept the money. "The Levin money was never seen as a bad gift by anybody at Florida," Matasar says. "They were consistent givers at a high amount over time. These issues from his critics were not flagged in the file, like, 'Don't take money from this guy.' As a person who is dealing only with the people in front of me and only with the things I can see they've done, Fred had done a tremendous amount of good for the university and the law school, and frankly for the State of Florida."

The gift also came with no strings attached, rare for such large contributions. "Fred Levin did not say to me on any occasion, 'Here's how I want the money invested, or how I want it spent,'" Matasar says.

The naming and dedication ceremony was held at the University of Florida in Gainesville, and the controversy over the naming was the undercurrent of the event. Reubin Askew, John Lombardi, and Richard Matasar all spoke gratefully of Fred's contribution. Representative Joe Scarborough, a former law partner of Fred's, and Fred's close friends

Morris Dees, George Starke, and Fred at the naming ceremony for the Fredric G. Levin College of Law.

W. D. Childers and Morris Dees attended, as did Fred's law school class-mate George Starke.

Fred took his turn at the microphone and struck, for him, a concilia-tory note. "I can understand the concern that some people have about naming the college Fred G. Levin or any other name," he said. "I would have felt the same way. It would have sort of bothered me. The only thing I can say is wait until the next century."

Following his speech, the new law school sign in Gator colors—blue with white letters and an orange stripe—was unveiled. Today, a duplicate of the sign hangs in Fred's office.

Marshall Criser, who had preceded Lombardi as president of the University of Florida, was critical of the arrangement but came to accept it. "I didn't like the transaction," Criser says. "But I would say also that some of the others who were critical of the decision wouldn't have made that gift or couldn't have made that gift. Fred Levin's name is on that law school, and it will be for eternity. Some of us didn't like it, but so what?"

But the ceremony wasn't the end of the controversy. Some of Fred's critics were determined not to let his name stay on the law school. Instead of focusing on Fred's run-ins with the Bar, they switched tactics and claimed the donation wasn't large enough to put anyone's name on the law school—never mind that Fred gave what the university asked. However, none of the complaints went anywhere because there was no escaping the fact that the $10 million figure was more than the university had received for other schools it had named after benefactors, and that the amount was doubled by the state.

Matasar personally met with everyone who objected. "I did what I called the 'penance tour,'" he says. "After the gift was announced, I would meet with any person in their office who had any objection and talk about how transformative the gift was. One lawyer said the following to me: 'You have to understand something, Dean. We shuffled Fred in law school, and we're shuffling him now.'"

After Governor Chiles left office, a group of lawyers took the issue to the incoming governor, Jeb Bush. They also went to the Florida legislature to push for the introduction of a bill to have the Levin name removed. But in the end, they weren't able to muster any support to return Fred's money or to erase his name from the law school.

To this day, Rinaman remains opposed to the naming. His reasons continue to be that Fred was not "a meritorious recipient," that schools should not be named for living individuals in the event that they bring disrepute by their actions, and that Fred giving the money in part to one-up the Florida Bar was uncouth.

"I don't have any personal enmity toward Fred," Rinaman says. "I don't hardly know him. But I do know of him, and I do know his track record. And I got involved in this because he said that he did this wonderful charitable thing in order to stick the Bar in the eye, and it wasn't a wonderful charitable thing anyway because he had to give it to somebody or else pay the taxes."

Though Fred's name stayed on the law school, the state did change its process for naming schools in the wake of the controversy. In March 1999, the Florida Board of Regents stripped this unilateral power from the university president and left the final say for all namings to the regents.

The fallout also resulted in casualties at the university. Due to all the publicity, as the state policy change was announced, Matasar resigned as law school dean and soon moved on to became dean of New York Law School, where he served for eleven years. He had become the scapegoat for the naming criticism.

"The university was under enormous pressure from lots of sources, and one thing the president of a university doesn't want is more trouble," Matasar says. "Having a law school that is creating trouble is not a great thing for universities. In our conversations, he, I, and the provost did what we thought was right for the university."

While Fred clearly donated the money in part to annoy his critics, there is little doubt that the donation put the law school on better footing. It immediately lifted the school's endowment to sixth among all public university law schools (behind only Michigan, Cal-Berkeley, Texas, Virginia, and Minnesota). The money was used to hire additional professors, bring down student–teacher ratios, and expand course selection. In the ensuing years, the law school, helped in part by such funding, began climbing the national list of law schools.

Today, the Levin College of Law is ranked twenty-third by *U.S. News and World Report* among all public law schools and forty-ninth overall. In terms of the criterion of "reputation," the law school is ranked by *U.S. News and World Report* as tenth among publics and twenty-sixth overall in the assessment by practicing lawyers and judges, and fifteenth among publics and thirty-fifth overall in the assessment by academics. It also is ranked fourth among all public law schools (and eighth among all law schools) in the number of graduates serving as federal district and circuit court judges. This makes Fred smile the most, because it means that any of his detractors who go to court will likely face a judge that graduated from the Levin College of Law.

The gift helped keep the law school financially stable when tough economic times arose. "History is certainly on the side of the law school making the right decision," Matasar says. "In the financial crises in the

2000s, first the dot-com bust, and then later when the economy itself tanked, the Levin gift was the difference between maintaining a good law school and not."

The law school—in part because it defended the gift that it had asked Fred to give in the wake of the vitriol against him—made a friend for life.

"I don't know what would have happened if Matasar and Ulmer would have asked for more money that day," Fred says. "Maybe I would have given it; maybe I would have thought it was too much and just helped them raise it. I do know that I continue to support the law school."

In 2006, Fred gave $2 million toward the Martin H. Levin Advocacy Center, named in honor of his son, a 1988 graduate. The center includes a full-scale courtroom where law students can experience the feeling of being in trial. In addition, his sister-in-law, Teri Levin, donated $1 million in honor of her husband, Fred's late brother Allen. The Allen and Teri Levin Advocacy Education Suite includes classrooms, offices, and practice areas for student trial and moot court teams. This is the go-to place for students who want to become trial lawyers.

The president of the university, Bernie Machen, presided over the advocacy center's dedication in March 2012. Despite the bitter aftertaste that Fred's gifts left with some, Machen was highly complimentary. "When the history of this law school is recounted fifty or a hundred years from now, Fred Levin will be known as a transformative force," he said.

Matasar agrees that what will survive is the gift. "People don't look too hard under rocks for people who have created their wealth," Matasar says. "People forget Leland Stanford's background, the Dukes' background, and the Vanderbilts' and Rockefellers'. The name survives the individual. That would be true if Fred were a rotten human and a bad guy, but Fred is a wonderful person, and he is a philanthropist, not just for education at Florida, but a supporter of his own community."

TWO

Bending the Rules to the Breaking Point

G reat trial lawyers are made in different ways. They are influenced by their upbringing; by the time and place in which they lived; and by their parents, educators, and friends. To become an effective trial lawyer, most lawyers will agree, you need a broad background. You must have some degree of smarts and plenty of common sense. You must outwork the next guy. Most difficult of all, you have to reach a point where you are respected. All of this requires a clear sense of self and an unflinching confidence.

Like most people, Fred Levin was shaped by a few key events in his childhood. These influenced his personal constitution, taught him how to bend but not break the rules, built his confidence, and, for better or worse, formed the basis for the lawyer he became.

Fredric Gerson Levin was born in 1937, the third of six boys, to Abe and Rose Levin. Fred attributes the spelling of his name to his mother's love of Fredric March, who won the Academy Award for best actor in 1932 for *Dr. Jekyll and Mr. Hyde*, which is somewhat prophetic in retrospect.

Fred has no idea where "Gerson" came from. He was so embarrassed by the odd middle name that when he applied for a Social Security card, he changed it to George.

Fred grew up in Pensacola, Florida, during World War II. At that time, as it is today, Pensacola was a huge Navy town. It was referred to as the Cradle of Naval Aviation, because most Navy pilots during that time, and notably the first person to set foot on the moon, Neil Armstrong, received their initial training in Pensacola. But Pensacola has a strange history, and the city remains in a constant struggle with itself over its relevance beyond its own borders—which some might argue also applies to Fred Levin himself.

The city was the site of one of the very first recorded European settlements on North America. In 1559, the Spanish conquistador Don Tristán de Luna y Arellano arrived in Pensacola, long before the Pilgrims landed on Plymouth Rock. Unfortunately, de Luna was a total failure. Before he could even offload his ships, most of his vessels and cargo were wiped out by a hurricane. Then, when it turned out there was no gold on land, his people mutinied. De Luna left Pensacola and returned to Spain in disgrace. It would be at least 135 years before Europeans would once again attempt a permanent settlement in Pensacola. So while Pensacola was technically the first Spanish settlement in the United States, its history carried a heavy asterisk of rejection. Over the years, it was passed back and forth, and has had five different flags fly over it: Spanish, French, British, Confederate, and now American. Oddly, Pensacola now prides itself on that fact and is nicknamed the City of Five Flags.

The Pensacola of the early 1940s was a Navy town overrun with soldiers and sailors. Fred's father owned a pawnshop downtown, where people on furlough would pawn whatever they had for partying money. Abe Levin was considered an unusually honorable pawnbroker. He would hold the pawned items far beyond the time required by law or contract, just in case the men ever returned and wanted to buy them back. He would do the same for people who had fallen on hard times, and were pawning heirlooms such as wedding rings just to get by.

His father's most famous customer was Virginia Hill, the girlfriend of Bugsy Siegel, who is popularly known as the founder of Las Vegas. Siegel was in Hill's Beverly Hills home when he was gunned down. Hill was one of the best-looking women ever to come out of Pensacola. Fred's father would tell anyone and everyone how she had purchased her luggage from him before moving to the West Coast to be with Bugsy.

Years later, Fred took his father to see the film *Bugsy*, starring Warren Beatty as Siegel and Annette Bening as Virginia Hill. "He spent the entire film looking for that damn suitcase," Fred recalls. "Sure enough, when Virginia's prop luggage came on-screen, he shouted, 'I sold her that suitcase!' And then he fell asleep."

The Levin family in 1950 (clockwise): Abe, Stanley, Rose, Herman, Fred, Allen, and Martin. David, the oldest son, is not pictured.

Fred's father worked hard, and the family had a traditional, Southern middle-class existence. They had two maids, whom Fred called Ms. Daisy and Ms. Tassie, and a yard man/butler named Mr. Willie. As the Levin family expanded with the additions of Fred's younger brothers, Stanley (1938), Martin (1941), and Allen (1944), they moved into a larger house away from the downtown area but still within the city limits.

Fred had few cares and even fewer goals. He was also a hellion. When he was five, the new Superman comic book hit the stores. He had to have it. He went to his mother, who was cooking dinner, and tugged on her apron. He demanded that she take him to the newsstand and buy the comic book. After all, it was only ten cents. But his mom was not having any of it. She told him she didn't have ten cents, nor did she have time to drive him to the newsstand. So little Freddie did what any reasonable five-year-old would do: He went and got Mom's purse, looked for ten cents, and, finding nothing, peed in her purse. Today, a first edition of that comic book is worth more than $1 million.

Upon discovering what Fred had done, his mother grabbed him and stripped his clothes off. She stuck his butt out the window and yelled at the top of her voice, "Everyone in the neighborhood come quickly and see Freddie's bare ass!"

That would be the first of many times during Fred Levin's life that he would bare his backside for the world to see.

The Levins were an anomaly in Pensacola because they were Jewish. This outsider status would follow Fred through his career, but rather than hamper him, it became a motivational force for him to take on the insiders. The city was, as it is today, Bible Belt territory. Fred grew up attending Hebrew school, having a Bar Mitzvah, attending Friday night services and Sunday school, and celebrating all Jewish holidays. His parents even kept a kosher home. "We certainly were not among the elite country club crowd, and of course, we could not be as we were Jews," Fred says.

As part of Fred's Jewish social network, he was involved with a group called the American Zionist Association. It was on the AZA's basketball team at age twelve that he was able to showcase an early talent for bending the rules to achieve a goal.

The team was heading to Mobile, Alabama, for a big Southeast tournament. Unfortunately, it had only four boys. Fred took it upon himself to make sure the team added not just another player, but a ringer. Playing pickup basketball at the YMCA, Fred had become close friends with a boy named David Cobb. He convinced David to join the Pensacola AZA team—only to make it believable, they all called him "David Cobblovitch."

The team won the tournament but made the mistake before returning to Pensacola with the trophy of showering after the championship game. One of the coaches of the other team came into the bathroom and saw David naked. The coach knew enough to know that because he was not circumcised, he was not a Jew. The team was unceremoniously stripped of the trophy.

"Of course, today the obvious question would be why did the coach enter the boys' shower area, and why was he looking at David's penis?" Fred quips. "If I thought about it during the time, I likely could have raised the issue and diverted attention from the fact that we were cheating. You would have thought the David Cobblovitch incident taught me something, but it didn't. Winning was too important to me."

At fourteen, Fred joined the YMCA basketball team. The different age groups played tournaments throughout the Southeast, and Fred was appointed coach of the twelve-and-under team. The team was decent, but it needed a stronger, taller center to win. Fred recruited a boy named David Hudson.

Unfortunately, Hudson was about two months older than the maximum age limit. No matter. Fred simply convinced the boy to say that he was born a couple of months later. Hudson was a big boy. In fact, he went on to become an All-American first-team football player at Pensacola High School, and an all–Southeastern Conference football player at the University of Florida. He wasn't that good of a basketball player, but he was imposing. Not surprisingly, Fred's team won the Southeastern twelve-and-under tournament.

One of the opposing coaches suspected that Hudson was much older than his stated age—primarily because he was starting to grow facial hair. After the championship game, the opposing coaches interrogated Hudson into confessing and pointing the finger at Fred. Another trophy gone, and Fred was again labeled a cheat.

Fred's days at the YMCA continued on a downhill trajectory. He had learned how to shoot dice, and decided that it was his duty to teach the other boys at the YMCA. One afternoon, they all gathered in the bathroom and locked the door. The adults in charge got wind of what was going on and began banging on the door. When Fred refused to open the door, they used their key and busted the game.

This appeared to be the end of Fred's YMCA career. The Powers That Be decided it was time to ban him. "Maybe there was a good reason they called it the Young Men's Christian Association," Fred says.

However, a man named Hollice Williams came to his rescue. Williams was an African American masseur for the YMCA who went on to become the first African American city councilman in Pensacola. Williams intervened, and the YMCA agreed to allow the problem Jewish child to continue to patronize the establishment. It was the beginning of a close relationship between Fred and the black community.

Being Jewish didn't mean much to Fred in elementary and middle school. Though Jews weren't able to swim or play golf at the country club, he never felt like an outcast. After attending P. K. Yonge Elementary School and Clubbs Middle School, he enrolled in Pensacola High School in 1951. Prior to high school, he hung around mostly with Jewish kids, but at PHS he expanded his social circle and was accepted by the students who came from richer families, who were better athletes, and who were more popular with the girls. The gentiles called Fred "the Happy Hebrew" and liked his way of having fun. He and his friends would drink and gamble—blackjack and poker—on Pensacola Beach. He didn't mind the moniker, and he certainly didn't feel it defined him in any way or would result in his choosing religious sides.

Pensacola High School had two fraternities, the Travares and the Rebels. The Travares had the jocks and the cool guys. David Cobb, Fred's close friend, was a Rebel. As part of Fred's continuing gambling enterprise (which didn't end after the YMCA episode), he became friends with the starting quarterback of the Pensacola High School football team, Ronnie Williams. Williams was a Travares and the superstar of the group. Not only was he unusually handsome, he was also a talented football player who went on to play quarterback alongside Burt Reynolds at Florida State University.

Williams was the big man on campus. Everyone wanted to be associated with him—including Fred. And because of that, Fred lost sight of what was important. Fred had been invited by David Cobb to join the

Rebels fraternity, and Fred had agreed. But shortly before the initiation, Williams informed Fred that Travares wanted him. Travares had been at Pensacola High School for decades, yet no Jew had ever been invited to join. Fred reneged on his promise to David Cobb, leaving his best friend hurt, and followed Williams to Travares.

His membership in Travares, and the image Fred cultivated as a gambler and partier, always walking around with a cigarette in his hand, made him popular and led to his introduction to the cool girls. While he wasn't the best-looking or most athletic guy in school, he was probably the best dancer. For this reason, many of the girls wanted him next to them on the dance floor.

"We would actually go to the black night club, Abe's 506, and dance to rock 'n' roll music," Fred says. "Despite images of the South during that time, we had absolutely no fear of being in the middle of the black side of town. Also, my Uncle Benny was running a nightclub in Gulf Breeze, which is on the other side of the Pensacola Bay Bridge. He would allow me and my friends to go there and dance and get drunk."

Fred's moves on the dance floor and his hard partying created a "fun boy" image, and this led to his dating the most beautiful girl at the high school, Ann Stephens. Her father was the county agricultural agent and an influential member of the Pensacola Country Club. Of course, the club did not allow blacks or Jews. Stephens was dating Ed Sears, a first-team All-American football player from Pensacola High School, but was also dating the son of the admiral at the Naval Air Station. Stephens' father was extremely happy about them. However, she wanted to date Fred.

"There was no way I could go up to the door to pick her up for a date because her father would see me," Fred says. "So I would lie on the floorboard of the backseat of a car and have my buddy, Y. B. Patterson, another hotshot football player who also went on to play at the University of Florida, go to the door and pick her up."

Fred's true source of happiness, however, was hanging out with his friends, drinking and gambling. His father helped run the dog track. Fred loved gambling on the dogs, but his father would not allow him and his friends in the establishment because they were underage. Forced to stay outside, they found people to place bets for them. One of Fred's friends, Jack Gardner, always bet on the same dog, Alibi Mike. The name stuck, and from that point forward everyone called Jack "Alibi."

In addition to dating and gambling, there was plenty of other action for the guys. "Although all the high school guys wanted to have sex, the high school girls generally were not willing, at least none that I knew," he says. "However, there were several African American women in the area we frequented who you could pay for sex. We didn't know their names so we called them by the automobile they drove. In other words, 'I was with Buick last night.' 'Yeah, I had Pontiac.'"

Though Fred spent more time in high school cutting up than studying or playing sports, he managed to graduate. "Looking back, it's interesting to think now that only the top students in their class with top SAT scores can become a freshman at this state university," Fred says. "When I entered, all you needed to do was graduate from high school, which I barely accomplished."

After high school, he headed off to the University of Florida, which his brother David had attended. He moved into an apartment in Gainesville with his friends Claude Bailey, David Cobb, and "Alibi" Gardner. Fred's goal was to continue partying and having a good time, but there he would again face obstacles because he was Jewish.

When it came time to join a fraternity, Fred expected to be rushed by Sigma Alpha Epsilon like the rest of the partying crowd. Unfortunately, Fred was told by his buddies that a Jew couldn't be in Sigma, which was all white and all Protestant. At first, Fred was annoyed, but then he realized he might be getting some sort of karmic payback for his high school transgression.

"The first thing that went through my mind was, 'I don't believe I could do this if I were them. I would take a stand,'" he says. "But then I remembered that I hadn't taken a stand on the Rebels and the Travares fraternities in high school. I had jumped ship myself. Now the tables were turned. For the first time in my life, I was forced to reflect on my own actions."

The Pensacola guys in Sigma were eager to help Fred. They connected him with Tau Epsilon Phi, a Jewish fraternity that was friendly with Sigma. They consoled him that it was the coolest Jewish fraternity. But there was no mistaking that the guy who had been the cool insider was now the outsider.

The next day, Fred went to Tau House, which was a few doors down from Sigma House. He was expecting to be greeted by the "cool Jews."

He entered the house and made himself a name tag. He circulated, but no one said a word to him. Finally, he approached the group that looked like the big shots and introduced himself. One of them dismissively told him to line up for a hamburger. He went for the hamburger and sat down alone. No one approached as he ate.

After about an hour of being ignored, Fred gave up and walked back to his apartment. The route took him past Sigma House. He could see his buddies in there drinking and celebrating at a party that he couldn't attend. Fred was devastated. He was certain that his social career at the University of Florida was wiped out and that he was going to be a nobody, the worst thing in the world for someone who had always associated himself with the big men on campus.

That evening, Fred's friend "Alibi" Gardner came to him and told him that he had been rushed by Sigma Chi, the fraternity next door to Pi Lambda Phi, another Jewish fraternity. Gardner said that he talked up Fred with the Pi Lams, and they wanted to meet him.

"Sometimes I wonder what a change there would have been in my life had I become a TEP rather than a Pi Lam," Fred says. "I went to the Pi Lam house, which was like a scene from the movie *Animal House*. These were the poor Jews, who were vulgar, loud, and anti-feminists because most girls would have nothing to do with them. Alibi told them what a great guy I was, and they treated me like a superstar."

Just like that, Fred was back. He pledged Pi Lam, and the experience ultimately gave him an insight into Jews as achievers. The members were leaders in academics and great athletes as well. The fraternity turned out to be where Fred made lifelong friends—Fred Vigodsky, who became his business partner, and Jack Graff, who became one of his law partners—and it was also how he met his wife.

"None of that would've happened if SAE hadn't banned Jews, or if even just one of the TEPs had been civil to me," he says. "Had either of those circumstances been different, I would have joined one of those two fraternities. Instead, because of those rejections, my life changed."

One night in sophomore year, Fred Vigodsky told him that he had met the most gorgeous Jewish sorority girl named Marilyn and he wanted to introduce Fred to her. Better yet, Vigodsky said, she wanted to meet Fred.

"He hadn't lied," Fred says. "She was the most gorgeous woman I had ever met." She had an angelic face framed by beautiful, flowing black hair.

Fred Vigodsky (far left), Fred (second from left), and friends hanging out in Mexico in 1957.

There was a major problem, however. Vigodsky didn't tell Fred that he was one of numerous guys there that night to meet Marilyn. Fred stood in line, waiting his turn, and finally Vigodsky introduced Fred to Marilyn. Unfortunately, all of Fred's bravado vanished in that moment, and he could barely utter a word. He sulked away in shame.

A few weeks later, Vigodsky convinced him to call Marilyn and ask her out. To Fred's surprise, she accepted. However, she added that her social calendar was quite full and she should be available for a date in approximately eight weeks. So Fred did the only thing he could: He waited.

Finally, the big night came, and Jack Graff and Fred double-dated. They took the ladies to a local hangout, and Fred immediately started drinking. As he became more intoxicated, Marilyn mentioned that she thought he needed to stop drinking, which only made him drink more. Heavily intoxicated, and guessing this would be his last date with Marilyn, he decided he would attempt to hypnotize her in the back of his car into wanting to have sex. Unfortunately, Fred knew nothing about hypnotism. He waved his finger back and forth in front of her face and chanted, but Marilyn brushed him off as being totally drunk, which he was.

"Hypnosis proved a lot more difficult in the back of a 1956 Pontiac than I had seen demonstrated on stage," Fred says. "Marilyn would have none of it, and the date ended in humiliation."

Even Graff, who could trade party circuit stories with Fred, was horrified by the evening. Incredibly, and to both of their surprise, Marilyn wanted to continue to date Fred. "I think she saw me as the bad boy that she could work on taming," Fred says.

U of F was like a playground for Fred. He spent most of his time drinking, gambling, smoking cigarettes, partying at the fraternities, and going to football games. Occasionally, he would drop in on a class. His grades reflected his lack of effort.

By Fred's junior year, gambling had become an obsession. Vigodsky and Fred often would drive to Jacksonville to the dog track, making a stop at a whorehouse on the way back. They would also bet on football and baseball games, but they were betting more than they were winning. It finally reached a point where they owed one bookie a sizeable sum. They decided to return to Pensacola and tell Fred's brother David that Fred had knocked up a girl and needed money for an abortion.

David bought the story and loaned Fred $600. Unfortunately, on the way back to Gainesville, the two stopped at a dog track and lost the money. It then became Fred Vigodsky's turn to go to his father for the money to pay the bookie. Taking Fred's lead, he told his father the same story. It worked again, and this time they paid off the bookie.

But that wasn't the end of their gambling exploits. By this time, Fred's younger brother Stanley was at University of Florida, and a member of the same fraternity. Fred came up with the idea of setting up a dice table in the fraternity house and dragged Stanley and Fred Vigodsky in as his partners. Unfortunately, about that time university police arrested a guy who had stolen a bunch of student credit cards. He told the university that the reason he did this was because he owed gambling debts to Fred and his partners. The three were brought up before the disciplinary committee. Stanley agreed to take the rap, and Fred received a private reprimand. Stanley was kicked out of school for a year, though Fred claims he wanted a year off anyway.

By the end of Fred's senior year in 1958, he didn't want to leave U of F, so he hatched a plan to buy himself another three years of partying. He would attend law school and then join his brother David's firm. However, there was one problem: Fred needed a 2.0 GPA to get into law school, and he didn't have it. Amazingly, in those days, anyone with a 2.0 or above could get into law school. Fred went to summer school, raised his GPA just over the precipice, and entered law school.

Law school would open Fred's eyes to a new world and bring focus to a life that had none. Though he had originally enrolled because college was so much fun that he didn't want to leave, he was hit with a quick dose of reality in the opening assembly. There were 360 new students gathered to hear Henry Fenn, the dean of the law school.

Before Dean Fenn stood up to deliver his remarks, a sideshow ensued. The auditorium doors opened. Federal marshals entered, surrounding a young man named George Starke, the first African American to enter any public university in Florida.

"I didn't understand all the details of what was going on, but I remember looking at George," Fred recalls. "He was dressed in a suit, while the rest of us were dressed like a bunch of bums in cutoffs and T-shirts."

Then Dean Fenn delivered a reality check. He told the group: "Look to your left and look to your right. If your class is average, neither of those guys will be here when you graduate."

Fred felt sick to his stomach. His first thought was, "Shit, these guys are a whole lot smarter than I am." At least a third of them were magna cum laude. Because the school wasn't that large, Fred's reputation had preceded him. Everyone in the room knew that he was a goofball, a party boy, a gambler, and a lousy student. So from day one, Fred studied like crazy for the first time in his life.

"I was certain they were going to kick my ass out of school," Fred says. "I didn't know what I would do with my life if I flunked out."

Even the dean predicted Fred would never graduate. After Fred was in law school for several weeks, he got a call saying that his younger brother Martin's health was quickly deteriorating. Martin had been fighting leukemia for months, but he now appeared near the end. Fred told Dean Fenn that he needed to go home. The dean pulled out his undergraduate file and told Fred, very coldly, "You know, with your grades and everything, you might just as well stay home."

Stanley, Marilyn, Fred Vigodsky, and Fred loaded themselves into his Plymouth station wagon for the trip home. By the time they reached Pensacola, Martin had passed away. Nothing would ever be the same in the Levin family.

"I had never seen my father cry before, but at the funeral, he sobbed uncontrollably," Fred remembers. "From that moment on, I don't believe I ever saw my mother smile again—until the day my son was born and we named him Martin in my brother's honor."

Despite Dean Fenn's advice, Fred didn't stay home. He returned to law school full of purpose. He kept studying hard and asking questions. At first, he found the law extremely difficult and remote. There were no clear-cut answers, and there always seemed to be equally plausible sides to everything.

But slowly, he began to understand the law and the logic. Things fell into place, and he started to fall in love with the law. Instead of being the class clown, he became a good student. He began to understand the background and the beauty of the law. He would walk around campus for hours by himself studying in his mind why law was the way it was.

"For the first time in my life, I started a program that I continue to this day," he says. "From the moment I wake up, I am constantly working on something—a case, a business project, football statistics, something to keep my brain working."

In those days, law school strictly followed the Socratic method. Students were assigned cases to read, and the professor would call on them in class and drill them with questions. There were some students who perceived themselves as smarter than others. As mentioned earlier, to express their disdain for the lesser students, the smarter students would shuffle their feet on the floor. The two people who were most shuffled by far were George Starke and Fred Levin. They shuffled George because he was black, and they shuffled Fred because they thought he was dumb.

In the library, everyone had study partners—except George and Fred. They would both sit alone, but not together. "I felt bad for George," Fred says. "The students would call him names. Even some of the professors were in on it. But I didn't have the guts to befriend him."

When the first semester ended, the grades were posted. Fred Levin was first in the class. Everything immediately changed. The shuffling stopped, and most students wanted to be his study partner. One day when Fred was in the library, George Starke entered. The students started shuffling him, and he took his usual seat away from everyone else. For some reason, Fred stood up, walked across the room, and sat down next to George.

"George," Fred asked, "do you need any help?"

"I sure do," George answered.

"Then you're my new study partner," Fred informed him.

This changed the dynamic of the entire class. "The interesting thing was that, as time went by, more and more students sat with George and me," Fred says. "Pretty soon, the majority of the law students were with us, leaving a handful of racists by themselves."

Fred's success that first semester gave him a glimpse into his future. For the first time, he realized he could be recognized for something besides being a goofball—and the other students realized it, too. Instead of shuffling when Fred Levin spoke, there was nothing but writing—everyone was taking notes.

For the next three years, Fred kept his foot on the accelerator. He worked harder than he ever had. His relationship with Marilyn progressed, and law school and Marilyn became the only two things in his life. Marilyn and Fred married the summer after his first year of law school and lived in a small apartment on campus.

Fred once again had become the big man on campus. This time, however, it was because he was excelling in academics, winning numerous book awards (top in a course), serving on the law review, publishing legal articles, and competing for the first spot in the class.

The newlyweds abstained from partying. Over Christmas and New Year's, Fred stayed at school and studied. He didn't attend a single football game during the entire three years he was in law school. When Marilyn was in labor with their first child, Fred held her hand with one hand and a law book in the other so he could study.

Fred continued tutoring George Starke, but academically, Starke was not doing well. At one point, he was on the verge of flunking out, and he desperately needed to pass an upcoming exam. Fred told him to meet at his apartment so they could study the material, but Fred ran late. When he arrived, George was sitting on the front steps.

"I asked him whether he knocked on the door, and whether Marilyn had answered," Fred says. "He said yes, and that Marilyn was so kind and

Fred and his bride, Marilyn, on their wedding day.

had invited him in to wait and have something to eat. George explained to me that he refused because it was not appropriate for a black man to enter the home of a white woman when her husband was not present."

Starke and Fred stayed up most of the night studying. There was no doubt in Fred's mind that his friend was going to pass the exam. The day after the exam Fred called him to see how he thought he had done. Starke explained that he forgot to set his alarm, and slept through the exam. He failed the class, and eventually left school. It was the last time Fred saw George Starke for thirty-five years.

Years later, Fred was delivering the keynote speech at the fiftieth anniversary of the first black graduate from the University of Florida. George Starke was there and told Fred that he had fudged the story. He did not sleep through the exam—he showed up ten minutes late, and the professor would not let him take the exam.

When it came time to graduate in 1961, Fred finished third in the class, but only because he was beaten by two transfer students. His class was unusually talented, as evidenced by the fact that it included a future governor, a future attorney general, and a state Supreme Court justice. Fred had finished first of the 60 who remained from the original 360— not bad for a kid who had partied his entire life before law school and had been told just three years earlier not to worry about staying around because he had no chance of graduating.

Fred's plan was to return to Pensacola for a year; work for his brother David and David's partner, Reubin Askew, at their firm; pass the Bar exam; then go to New York University to study tax law, a nice, quiet field.

"I was scared to death of speaking before a group, all because I had messed up my Bar Mitzvah speech when I was a kid," he says. "Under no circumstances was I going to become a trial lawyer."

That would change, too.

THREE

Chasing the Ambulance

Personal injury law dates to Biblical times. In those days, people who harmed others were often forced to pay with the exact punishment—in other words, an eye for an eye. As laws evolved and societies became more civilized, the justice system became rooted in the concept that people or companies must conduct themselves and their business in a way that will not harm others. If a person or company injured a third party and that injury was documented as a result of a breach of duty, then the injured party would be entitled to reasonable compensation.

The practice of personal injury law as we know it today was in its infancy in 1961, when Fred Levin graduated from law school. There were no lawyers with their pictures on billboards seeking out people injured in car accidents or from slipping on a waxed floor. There were no ads on TV with *Star Trek* star William Shatner soliciting cases for people who have been harmed by taking bad drugs. No one called personal injury lawyers "ambulance chasers," because there were no lawyers chasing ambulances.

The fact is, personal injury cases at that time were not financially lucrative. Consequently, none of the big law firms took them. They were handled by the little guy, the sole practitioner, and they were the lowest rung of the legal practice.

The nascent field of personal injury law found Fred's brother David because he was Jewish. Though he had graduated second in his law school class from the University of Florida, David could not find a job in the conservative Pensacola firms that represented the utility companies and banks. These firms did not hire Jews, so David was forced to strike out on his own.

In 1955, David established his own firm. Three years later, his close friend Reubin Askew joined as a partner. Named Levin & Askew, the firm consisted of the two of them and a secretary. Because the established firms had the corporate business, Jewish lawyers were forced to handle low-level cases, such as divorce, criminal law, foreclosures, and soon personal injury.

"People made remarks to me about going into a firm with Jewish people," Askew recalls. "I just told them I wanted to be with the best."

The situation was very much like that of the Jewish lawyers in New York who practiced mergers and acquisitions law in the 1940s because it was considered dirty work and the big firms wouldn't touch it. Those lawyers, notably Joe Flom, became so proficient that when M&A evolved into a lucrative field, they had a huge head start over the old-school firms. Because of this, companies came to them first, and they made out like bandits. Flom's firm later grew to a worldwide power earning more than $1 billion a year.

After graduating from law school in the spring of 1961, Fred returned to Pensacola and went to work at Levin & Askew. After all, the reason he had gone to law school in the first place (other than to stay at University of Florida after college) was because this job was waiting for him. He started out doing research for cases and handling uncontested divorces.

"I was earning $400 a month, which was good money in those days, especially in Pensacola," he says. "Things were going smoothly, and I was very comfortable with my workload. If a couple wanted a divorce, I'd file the paperwork with the courthouse and move on to the next case."

But then one day a lady walked into the office and said she wanted a divorce. In those days, the firm charged $50 for an uncontested divorce and $170 for a contested divorce. Hers would be a contested divorce, she volunteered. When Fred asked to what degree, she mentioned that her husband had threatened to kill her lawyer.

"That ended my divorce law career," Fred says. "I went and told David that I was going to become a tax lawyer."

Part of Fred's fear of becoming a trial lawyer was that he hated speaking in public. He had avoided speaking in front of groups through college and law school. But a short time after ending his divorce law career, Fred took a case that ended up landing him in court.

A woman named Angeliki Theodore lived in a brick home on Scenic Highway outside of Pensacola. Her house had sustained fire damage and her insurer, Travelers Insurance Company, offered her $17,000 for repairs. But she wanted more, so she hired Fred to represent her. The arrangement was that Fred would receive a percentage of anything he collected over $17,000.

When Travelers refused to budge off the settlement offer, Fred started working up a case against the company. Eventually, he filed a lawsuit, asking for a nonjury trial. Though petrified of speaking before a group, he figured he could handle explaining the case to a judge.

Then one afternoon his phone rang. It was Bert Lane, Travelers' lawyer. He was a legend in Florida legal circles.

"People claimed that the best trial lawyer in the area was Bert Lane when he was sober, and the second best trial lawyer in the area was Bert Lane when he was drunk," Fred says.

Lane offered to settle the case for $18,000. He then warned, "If you don't take it, Fred, I've got to ask for a jury trial."

That figure was perfectly acceptable to Fred. He hung up with Bert Lane and called Theodore and begged her to take the $18,000. He immediately volunteered to waive his fee. He was so terrified of having to address a jury that he was willing to finish off her case for free just to escape speaking in public. But she was determined to get $22,000 and refused to settle.

Fred was stuck. He had to go to court.

"For days, I couldn't sleep," he says. "I was scared to death of a trial before a jury. The only reason I went into law was because my brother was a lawyer who had an established practice that I could join. I never once perceived of myself as being a litigator. But then I started working on the case, doing the research, examining the angles, and I started to feel as if I were back in law school."

The case was heard in federal court. As everyone took their places, the bailiffs and the court reporters were mumbling under their breath about how this young lawyer, Fred Levin, was going to get whipped. Everyone knew it was his first case, and he was going up against the local hotshot, Bert Lane. The place was packed to see the old lion slaughter the young upstart.

But it didn't happen that way. Fred was so well prepared that he knew everything about the case. He had coached his witnesses on what to expect from Lane. He delivered a seamless presentation. The jury felt like both his client and Fred were one of them, and they wanted to help them out.

The jury came back with a verdict for Angeliki Theodore and an award of $45,000. On top of that, the judge awarded Fred a $5,000 fee, payable by Travelers. He had earned more on one case than he could make in an entire year of handling divorce cases. Better still, nobody was threatening to kill him.

The case was a lesson that provided Fred with a framework for being a trial lawyer. "The case taught me that if you prepare well, you can compete with the best," he says.

From that case forward, Fred followed the same principles. "When a plaintiff's lawyer is preparing for a trial, the most important thing is to figure out what is the best case for the defense," he explains. "That determines where the plaintiff's lawyer can attack and how he should present his case. For this reason, I always try to keep the other side talking before we go to trial.

"If we are discussing a possible settlement, I can learn what they think are their strong points," he continues. "They might say that they will kill me on this point or they have this piece of damning evidence. This allows me to see their cards, so I know how to play my hand."

He always plans his closing argument first, so he can work backward and build his case. For both his opening and closing arguments, he writes outlines and practices them until he is comfortable, but he doesn't memorize the arguments, so he can stay flexible. To this day, he still gets a little nervous before he speaks, though he is no longer the guy who was mortally afraid of speaking when he started as a lawyer. Interestingly, in normal conversation, Fred often speaks in fragments and meandering half thoughts, but in the courtroom, he is known for his clarity.

"The key is being prepared," he says. "That gives me plenty of material to discuss at length, as well as the ability to ad-lib if things don't go my way. When I cross-examine an expert witness, I might ask questions that don't seem particularly related. That's part of my strategy. I ask those questions because I know where I want to go in closing arguments, and I pick things that will fit into my closing.

"I also keep track of the cheap shots the other side takes during the trial," he adds. "Then, in the rebuttal during closing arguments, I remind the jury of the cheap shots and say, 'You don't say these things to someone if you feel you are in the right.'"

Beating Bert Lane in his first case provided Fred a huge boost of confidence, and changed his attitude about his career. As Clarence Darrow once said, "The only real lawyers are trial lawyers, and trial lawyers try cases to juries." Fred was on his way to becoming a real lawyer. Now all he needed was a big case to make a name for himself.

The case came when a woman called Fred and said that her son had died of aplastic anemia after he was treated with Chloromycetin. Aplastic anemia, a blood disease, is a serious, often fatal side effect of the drug. She said that she had heard of someone else who had died in similar circumstances, and wanted to know if she had a case against the manufacturer.

Fred took the case. "I had a close family tie with Chloromycetin," he recalls. "My brother Martin had taken it for acne as a kid before he died of leukemia in 1958, and my mother often wondered if Chloromycetin had contributed to his death. It was time for me to find out more about this drug."

Chloromycetin had burst onto the scene in 1949. Deemed a wonder drug and a "miracle antibiotic," it was a synthetic antibiotic that could cure numerous problems, particularly infections. The drug was very well known, partly because the manufacturer, Parke-Davis, spent huge sums of money to market it directly to doctors, something that had never been done before.

The more research Fred did, the more fascinated he became. On the positive side, Chloromycetin was very effective at battling Rocky Mountain spotted fever (for which it was the drug of choice) and other illnesses. But as he dug into the medical statistics, he learned that one out of every thousand people who took the drug during that time period died. Not only was aplastic anemia a side effect; so was leukemia, which had killed his brother. That gave him a personal stake in the case.

Fred took the woman's case to trial, where he asked for punitive damages. It was a bold move. At that time, no other lawyer had ever sought punitive damages against a drug company for producing prescription medication. The company's lawyers fought back hard, arguing that exposure to punitive damages could force Parke-Davis to withdraw the drug from the market. But the judge ruled in Fred's favor.

In the end, Fred didn't win any punitive damages, and the compensatory award was hardly enough to make a dent in Parke-Davis' profits. But a combination of the judge upholding Fred's request at trial, the fear of punitive damages in future cases, and other research developments on the drug eventually resulted in the company dramatically cutting production and changing the recommended use of Chloromycetin.

To this day, the drug can be used solely for serious infections, and then only if it's closely monitored. That means it is now mostly used only in hospitals in the United States; unfortunately, the drug is still commonly available in some underdeveloped countries. Undoubtedly, thousands of Americans are alive today because the drug was effectively shelved. This was a real-life victory, as opposed to merely a legal victory, and it set the stage for people wronged by drug companies to ask for punitive damages. It has had the very real impact of controlling the distribution of a drug that had been proven to kill people in certain situations, and of taking it off the market in this country except in special prescription circumstances.

Fred Levin had scored his first major victory for victims' rights.

In the days when Fred was a young lawyer, Pensacola followed its deep Southern roots when it came to tolerance on race and religion. No matter how successful a Jew was in business, he was not allowed to set foot in the country club. In the tradition of the Southern aristocratic mentality, blacks were viewed as inferior even if they were accomplished in their fields. Discrimination seemed to be in the water.

After Fred had practiced law for a few years, he noticed that no black lawyers were members of the Society of the Bar of the First Judicial Circuit, even though there were two practicing in Pensacola: Nathaniel Dedmond and Charlie Wilson. Both were very good lawyers and more than qualified to be members. Fred recommended to the society that they admit Nathaniel Dedmond, who handled mostly criminal cases. Controversy swirled immediately.

Before the meeting was held to vote on the nomination, the situation became so racially charged that some of the members' wives tried to cancel the vote. "One of them actually called my wife," Fred says. "She asked, 'Marilyn, in the Bar Auxiliary, how would you like to be sitting next to Nathaniel Dedmond's wife?' Without missing a beat, she said, 'Wow, that would be great. Can you make this happen for me?' I was so proud of Marilyn."

At the meeting, Dedmond never stood a chance. The elite and most respected old-school lawyers in the community all stood up in opposition. This was the early 1960s, when the nation was dealing with the infancy of the Civil Rights movement. Making things even tenser, this was the Deep South, just twenty miles from the Alabama state line. The society overwhelmingly voted down Dedmond's nomination.

Then they turned on Fred. It happened around Christmas, at a meeting at the Mustin Beach Officers Club for the election of officers. All the major officers had been selected without opposition. A category came up for someone who had been a lawyer less than five years. Fred's name was placed in nomination.

Because Fred was the only nominee at that point, the president moved for election by acclamation, the normal process. At that point, someone stood up and said, "I'd like to nominate Frank Bozeman," another young lawyer. The president declared they would take up a discussion of the two candidates. He asked Fred and Bozeman to step outside during deliberations.

The two men left the room. Bozeman told Fred that he didn't know why someone would put forward his name. He said that he had no real interest in the position. When they called the two candidates back into the room, everyone was clapping and offering Bozeman congratulations.

"I was floored," Fred says. "I didn't even get the votes of all the members of my own firm. Ultimately, the experience made me a better lawyer. It heightened my competitive streak. To this day, I relish the idea of somebody taking cheap shots at me or trying to undercut me. I thrive off that and am usually able to turn it around for my client's benefit."

And although that was the first and last time Fred ran for anything, it wasn't the last time he would cross swords with the Florida legal establishment.

Levin & Askew gained statewide political notoriety when its founding partner, Reubin Askew, was elected to the Florida State Senate in 1962. (He remained a partner in the firm while serving in the legislature.) Then, in 1970, he ran for governor.

When Askew declared for governor, he was not given much of a chance, despite the fact that he was by then president of the Senate. Pensacola was in the sticks, far from the state's political and financial strongholds. There was no political machine to provide him with backing, just a small law firm that was trying to make a name for itself. He was running against the incumbent Republican governor, Claude R. Kirk Jr., who ridiculed Askew as "a momma's boy who wouldn't have the courage to stand up under the fire of the legislators."

The Levin & Askew firm in 1970. Fred is to the left in the bottom row. David Levin is second from the left in the top row. Reubin Askew, the next governor of Florida, is third from the left in the top row.

Fred and his brother David supported their law partner by raising money and putting up their own money. Despite the fact that the Levins had virtually no experience in politics, there was something about Askew that led them to believe that he was the right man in the right place.

"They were undying supporters, like two brothers would be," Askew recalls.

When the campaigning got under way, Askew's poll numbers were dismal. He questioned whether he should continue. He was even asked to run as lieutenant governor on another candidate's ticket, but the Levin brothers encouraged him to push ahead. Against long odds, Askew won. Twenty years after being elected president of the student body at Florida State University, he became the thirty-seventh governor of Florida.

Askew's election shined a bright spotlight on the law firm. People began asking who were these Levin brothers who had helped elect a governor from little ol' Pensacola. In many circles, the Levin brothers were regarded as the new power brokers in Florida politics.

"It was funny how people kept thinking David and I were political kingmakers," Fred says. "We supported Reubin, and David was part of Reubin's administration, but people seemed to think we were more important than we actually were. I encouraged them to keep thinking we were political power brokers. It was good for business."

With his law partner in the governor's office, Fred assumed he would finally be accepted among the aristocratic community in Pensacola. He was wrong. Like the African Americans in the community, Fred still was on the outside looking in, despite his money and political power. He had never been a society person, and he still would not be.

In his youth, Jews were not allowed to participate in all facets of life, such as joining the Pensacola Country Club. After he had reached his newly found fame, Fred went shopping for a nicer house for his wife and four children. A large house owned by the estate of one of the most powerful historic families from Pensacola came on the market. The home was near the front entrance to the country club.

When Fred began looking at the house, the neighbors sent a delegation to his office and asked if it was really the house for him. The delegation was led by the stepfather of Fred's son Martin's best friend, who also happened to be the son of David Cobb, Fred's best friend in high school. Cobb had passed away many years earlier in an automobile accident.

The delegation asked Fred to imagine what his kids were going to feel like when they looked over the fence and saw all the kids playing tennis and swimming at the country club, but they would not be allowed to participate because they could not become members. Fred got their drift.

"The next day I called and told them that I had given it a lot of thought and they were right," Fred says. "I told them I had decided not to buy the house for myself, but rather I was seriously considering making it a Jewish progressive club. I told them my daddy lived alone and I wanted him to have some place to play gin rummy with his Jewish friends. The group apparently was horrified. The next thing I knew many in the group pooled their money and bought the home."

CHAPTER

FOUR

The Case That Landed Fred Levin in *US* Magazine

I n the late 1970s and early 1980s, corporate liability was not a prevalent concept. Corporations could act with willful disregard, and often did. The jury—that group of citizens judging a case brought by one of their peers—had to rise up and do what the government was not doing, and send a message to Big Business that it could not act callously and recklessly toward people. It was the job of the trial lawyer to ensure that the victims had the best chance of succeeding.

Yet there were a few critical plaintiff protection cases in the country that, in different yet complementary ways, altered the landscape of personal injury law and made corporate callousness a cornerstone of verdicts for years. One of those was the 1980 case *Thorshov v. Louisville & Nashville Railroad Company*, which Fred handled. The stage for the *Thorshov* case was set by larger actions against Ford over its Pinto car, and against the Kerr-McGee energy company for the treatment of a chemical plant worker named Karen Silkwood.

In the early 1970s, Ford received reports that when the Pinto was rear-ended, the fuel-tank filler pipe was susceptible to breaking and puncturing the fuel tank. This resulted in fires in some accidents, calling the safety of the car into question. The Center for Auto Safety asked the National Transportation Safety Board to recall the Pinto in 1974, but three years passed with no action taken by the government.

The turning point came in 1977. An article in the investigative magazine *Mother Jones* revealed that internal Ford documents showed that the company knew of the fuel tank issue and actually had a better fuel tank it could have used. However, that tank was more expensive and impinged on the Pinto's design. Worse, the magazine reported that Ford had conducted a cost–benefit analysis comparing the $11 per car cost to repair the fuel tanks to the amount of legal settlements from injury and death, and concluded that sticking with the faulty fuel tank would be cheaper. The document became a symbol of profit-grubbing Ford executives.

Not long after the damning article, Ford was hit with a $125 million punitive damage award by a jury in the case of *Grimshaw v. Ford Motor Company* in Orange County, California, in addition to $2.5 million in compensatory damages. The jurors justified the high award because Ford had sold the Pinto knowing that such injuries were inevitable, and therefore reasoned that the punitive damages should exceed the $124 million Ford had earned selling the cars. The appeals court upheld the compensatory damages, but reduced the punitive damages to $3.5 million. Still, the result forced Ford in 1978 to recall 1.5 million Pintos, as well as 30,000 Mercury Bobcats with similar issues, thus saving countless injuries and lives.

The Karen Silkwood story was another example of gross corporate malfeasance. Silkwood, whose story was later told in the eponymous 1983 movie starring Meryl Streep, worked as a chemical technician making plutonium pellets for nuclear reactor fuel rods at the Kerr-McGee Cimarron Fuel Fabrication Site plant in Oklahoma. Silkwood claimed the plant's unsafe working conditions were contaminating the workers with plutonium. She started a quest to protect workers' safety. After leaving a union meeting in 1974, on her way to deliver evidence to two *New York Times* reporters, she died in a mysterious auto accident.

Silkwood's relatives sued Kerr-McGee, claiming her body had been poisoned by harmful amounts of plutonium. The case came to trial in 1979 with Gerry Spence representing the family. The jury agreed with the claim, awarding $505,000 in compensatory damages and $10 million in punitive damages. After a series of appeals, including the US Supreme Court affirming the original decision, Kerr-McGee settled out of court for $1.38 million. Though the company admitted no liability, the case sent a clear message that such actions were unacceptable.

And then in 1980 came the *Thorshov* case, which Fred Levin handled. It didn't have the same name recognition as the Ford Pinto case and the Silkwood story, but it was every bit as important.

The *Thorshov* story began on November 9, 1977. Dr. Jon Thorshov, a thirty-eight-year-old physician at the Medical Center Clinic in Pensacola, had come home early that evening and taken his twenty-eight-year-old wife, Lloyda, his four-year-old daughter, Daisy, and his one-year-old son, GamGee, for some early Christmas shopping. When they returned home at about 5 P.M., it was raining, so Jon relaxed with a beer and played with GamGee. Lloyda tuned the radio to WMEZ, the easy listening station, and cooked the family dinner. Around 6 P.M., the hamburgers were in the oven, the vegetables on the stove. The family heard a train approaching the Escambia Bay trestle just above Gull Point, where they lived.

The massive freight train was L&N No. 407 on its nightly run to Chattahoochee. In addition to feed, lumber, and automobiles, sixteen of the train cars were carrying the hazardous material anhydrous ammonia. When the train hit the curve at Gull Point, two locomotives and thirty-five of its cars derailed while twenty-two others jackknifed. A horrendous pileup ensued, and two of the cars loaded with anhydrous ammonia were punctured, sending the toxic gas into the air, engulfing the Thorshovs' home.

Hearing the horrific crash and smelling the fumes, Jon grabbed his daughter, and his wife grabbed their son. As the ammonia smell was pouring over them, they ran out of the house to the family truck. Jon threw the truck in reverse, but it quickly stalled because of the lack of oxygen caused by the ammonia. They bolted from the truck, clutching their children, and tried to run for their lives. Within a few yards, both parents were overcome by the ammonia. They collapsed.

By this time, rescue workers had been called. The firemen strapped air packs on their backs and began saving people in the path of the ammonia vapors. When they reached the Thorshov home, they found no one there. As they searched the grounds, they discovered Daisy and rushed her to the hospital. They continued to search, knowing that it was unlikely a small girl had been left alone. Next they found GamGee, and finally Jon and Lloyda, and put them in ambulances.

In all, 1,000 people were evacuated and 46 were injured, but none of the others suffered like the Thorshov family. Jon Thorshov died on the way to the hospital. Lloyda survived for seventy-five days on a ventilator and then died. Miraculously, both children lived, though GamGee suffered permanent lung damage.

Dr. Thorshov's parents came to Pensacola looking for a lawyer to help them seek justice. They had the names of three lawyers, one of whom was Fred Levin. On a Saturday, they called all three. Fred was in New Orleans, but he returned their call the next day.

They met with Fred in his office on Monday and talked about the tragedy and how Fred would approach the case. "They seemed impressed that one of my partners, D. L. Middlebrooks, was a former federal judge, and our founding partner, Reubin Askew, had been governor," Fred says. "However, I later learned they chose us because I was the only lawyer who returned their phone call."

Fred and his firm started investigating as soon as they were given the case. Neither Fred nor anyone at the firm knew anything about train derailments, but effective lawyers must be fast studies.

The first thing they learned was that derailments for L&N trains were common in Escambia County. In the previous two years, L&N had logged seventeen derailments within fifty miles of the Gull Point accident site. Incredibly, one of the previous derailments had resulted in an anhydrous ammonia tank car rupturing—virtually the same thing that happened in this derailment. Though no one was seriously injured in the earlier accident, several people were hospitalized. From that accident until the Thorshov tragedy, L&N averaged one derailment a month.

The firm's investigators also quickly realized there were many defects in the tracks that had not been repaired after the derailments. They immediately photographed the tracks around Gull Point. It turned out the law firm's investigators were literally steps ahead of the L&N workers that were fixing the tracks—trying to cover their tracks, if you will.

"On the surface, this was the ultimate dream case," Fred says. "There were substantial damages, virtually indisputable liability, and the defendants had deep pockets. Of course, even the best of cases has drawbacks."

The jury pool in Pensacola was conservative, and therefore not naturally inclined to award large damages to a wealthy doctor (relatively speaking) and his beautiful wife. Pensacola was also a railroad town, and L&N employed several hundred people in the area. So while the plaintiffs' witnesses would be highly educated experts, the railroads' were apt to be laypeople whose primary qualification was that they had a lot in common with the jurors.

L&N had also hired Bert Lane and his firm to represent them. In fact, the railroad had to coax Lane out of retirement for one last case. Lane was well liked in Pensacola because he came off like a local yokel done good. Fred had taken on Lane many times—notably in his first case—and Fred felt that Lane always tried to lord his success over him, despite the fact that Fred had beaten him on every case they tried against each other.

But the most complicated aspect was that the case was highly technical. The facts of the accident were complex and difficult to grasp in their entirety. Fred would also need to introduce expert witnesses to explain how the damages were to be calculated if he proved his case. This meant the jury would be hearing how much it should award before it decided if the railroad was even liable.

Another potential tripwire was that federal regulations required a railroad to accept every car sent over its line. The two cars that spilled the ammonia were not owned by L&N. Furthermore, the cars did not have shields on their ends to prevent punctures because the federal government did not require them in 1977. That law was changed in 1980, and L&N could claim that had the law been in place, the spill would never have happened. Though this wasn't a legal argument, it was a practical one and offered a potential escape hatch for the jury.

Preparedness was critical. Fred was working with his partners D. L. Middlebrooks and Dan Scarritt. The firm logged 10,000 legal hours and, equally important, 3,000 investigative hours. They conducted copious research and hired independent experts to testify about the details of the accident. Oddly, the defense didn't hire any experts, but instead chose to let railroad employees explain how the accident happened.

Prior to the trial, Fred turned down a $2 million settlement offer. At the time, that was an astronomical sum for a settlement. But Fred convinced his clients that they would win more at trial. "This was either an extreme act of guts or one of sheer stupidity," he says. "Aside from the guaranteed fees we would have received, it could have wiped out the firm had we been sued for malpractice. And, of course, a trial is *always* a crapshoot—but I loved shooting craps."

The wrongful death action *Thorshov v. Louisville & Nashville Railroad Company* went to trial in February 1980. It was the biggest case of Fred Levin's career to date. He had overcome his fear of speaking in front of a jury, he felt ready to rise to the challenge—and there was a lot of money to be made.

"My job in opening statements was to acknowledge the disadvantages of our case and highlight its advantages," he says. "My goal was to destroy the entire defense case with my opening statement"—a tactic he would use again and again in his career.

Fred started out by congratulating the jury for its service, which is fairly standard. But he went a step further. The panel contained eight members, the largest ever for a Florida civil case. Fred pointed this out so the jurors understood they would be deciding a monumental case. He then told them, "The opening statement itself is not evidence, and it is not law; it's lawyer talk." This was an effort to defuse Bert Lane's thunder in his opening statement.

Then he delved into the case. He explained that this case was only for the death of the parents and not for the injuries to the children. However, there was a fine point to be grasped: The case also involved the condition of the children prior to the accident. This was important because the son, GamGee, had prior medical issues that would have required his parents to care for and support him well into his adult life.

To remove thoughts of a sympathy verdict—always a must at these types of trials—he distinguished between the emotional response to two orphaned kids and the law. He explained that law required the jury to award damages not for sympathy, but for the fair value of what was taken from them.

This was a critical point. Fred told them that had Dr. Jon Thorshov not been killed, he would have earned more than $20 million over his lifetime, a figure that would be explained by an economics professor. Mentioning a dollar amount in the opening statement was a risk, but Fred felt it was a must. The jury would never be able to ignore the publicity of the "multimillion-dollar case." He then told the jury that he was going to ask for $12 million that was taken from the children by their father's death.

"Pensacola being a working-class community, I knew it would be hard for jurors to get their arms around such a huge sum of money," he says. "So I told the jury that children don't need that kind of money, and we know they don't need that kind of money. But the law said that they should award what they believe has been taken."

Fred explained the burden of proof was his, at 51 percent. He used a football analogy, that he only needed to win the game 21–20, not 21–0, and emphasized that he did not have to prove anything "beyond a reasonable doubt" because that is only the test for a criminal case.

Now it was time to tell the jury the story of the two lives lost. Fred took great care to tailor the Thorshovs' story to his audience. The couple had met while Jon was in the Air Force and Lloyda was an X-ray technician. Jon was shipped to Germany after they met, but he returned three weeks later on leave and asked for Lloyda's hand in marriage. This is the fairy tale version; typically, as the jurors knew from living in a military town, the officer never returns. Fred hoped Jon's return to the woman he loved would help him with one particular juror, an attractive, single woman in her twenties.

The Thorshovs were eventually married and had two children. Jon was then recruited to work in the Medical Center Clinic in Pensacola, and they bought the house overlooking Gull Point. The family was very tight-knit, and the parents only spent one night apart. They did everything together. One of their favorite activities was watching the trains near their house.

Fred pointed out that they were all in excellent health, except for GamGee, who suffered from kidney problems. This would be a central point even though the children were not the plaintiffs, because GamGee was expected to require care and financial support into his adult years due to health issues unrelated to the railroad derailment.

The goal was to paint a Norman Rockwell picture of their lives at the time of the derailment. "I cannot imagine that they felt that they were ever safer in their lives than they were at that particular moment, nor could they have felt that they could be any happier than they were at that particular moment," he told the jury.

He delivered a narrative of L&N and its record dating back to the installation of the track. He drew the tracks on a whiteboard to help the jury picture what had happened. On the route of the tracks, he highlighted three places, all of which had been the sites of major derailments.

There were several relevant points about L&N's history. In the 1960s, a company called Seaboard Coast Line Railroad (SCL) started buying up L&N, and by early 1972, it had complete control. This was a critical date because Fred's team had discovered that maintenance spending on the tracks had dropped substantially from 1972 until 1977. This became an important theme in Fred's case—and one that the defense didn't understand until it was too late.

Fred then went into derailments and how they occur. There were twelve things that can cause a train to derail: heavy train, wide gauge, bad ties, loose spikes, light cars in front, long car–short car in front, superelevation, superelevation runoff, 131-pound rail, six-axle locomotive, speed limits, and braking in a curve. He wrote all twelve on a whiteboard and explained each one in practical terms. Many of these points would be recurring themes to show that L&N was at fault for the derailment. "As long as the list was, I needed to establish it so I could return to it," he explains.

L&N employees had been called before the National Transportation Safety Board after the derailment. The employees had testified that the speed and braking-in-a-curve rules were simply guidelines that were only followed in mountainous areas, but not in Pensacola.

"Of course, this was ridiculous and callous, and I wanted the jury to keep that in mind when I told them that L&N averaged one derailment per month in our area," Fred says.

Fred told the jury that inexplicably no one on the train crew had tried to help the Thorshovs. In fact, after the spill, the crew jumped in the engine car and took off because they knew that ammonia fumes could quickly kill. They all testified in their depositions that they did not try to reach any of the homes nearby because they did not have air packs and oxygen masks. The reason: L&N refused to spend the money on those safety tools.

To hammer home the profit-first philosophy at L&N, Fred finished with the concept of per diem. On that train run, L&N would have to pay a $10,000 per diem unless it was able to offload the cars by midnight. Thus, he wanted the jury to infer that L&N was an unsafe railroad whose owners were more concerned about profit than safety and were in a constant hurry to pump up its bottom line.

With the table set and L&N's poor track record laid bare, Fred went into great detail about the accident that led to the deaths of Dr. Jon and Lloyda Thorshov and the twelve issues that cause derailments. He hammered away that money and L&N's refusal to spend it on safety were the underlying cause of many of the violations. L&N knew the railroad ties were so bad in that section that they violated minimum federal standards, but they didn't fix them because it would have cost money. L&N knew the first two light cars were connected in violation of federal regulations, but again, it would have cost money to realign the train, so they didn't bother.

Fred next gave the jury a thumbnail of the witnesses. "I painted all the L&N witnesses with black hats and ours with white hats," he says.

The worst was an L&N company vice president. In his deposition, the executive testified that he had personally come to Pensacola from Jacksonville and inspected the track. He proclaimed it in perfect condition. But what the guy didn't know was that between the time of the derailment and his examination of the track, Fred's investigators had photographed the bad track just ahead of the repair crews. Fred promised to put him on the stand and have him look at their pictures of the track. In essence, he was going to have L&N's own witness testify against the railroad.

Perhaps the most important part of his opening was the final section on damages. Because it was the most difficult part of the case, he needed to explain it up front. After the closing arguments, each jury member would receive a special jury form. He posted the form on the board.

The first step would be to determine if L&N was negligent. For that to happen, the jury needed only to find that L&N committed one of the twelve violations by 51 percent of the evidence. Next would be damages to property (for which there would be testimony), followed by medical and funeral expenses, which were $45,000 for Lloyda and $2,000 for Jon.

The big-ticket item was the amount of money Jon would have accumulated. If he had lived out his life, how much would he have earned, saved, and invested, and how much of that would have been left for his children? In determining this figure, Fred explained to the jurors that an economist would give them exact figures. The important factor here was the claim that GamGee would be a dependent his entire life based on his previous condition.

Fred told the jury that L&N had also listed three economists as witnesses. He openly challenged Bert Lane to put them on the stand if they disagreed with his economists, and told the jury not to rely on Lane telling them that the plaintiff's economists were wrong.

"I suspected—correctly, as it turned out—that Lane would not call his own economists," Fred says. "I wanted to be able to say in my closing that L&N must have agreed with ours because they offered no rebuttal."

In closing, Fred told them that the judge would give them an opportunity to do what the government couldn't do: to control the L&N railroad. "Now, they didn't want Jon Thorshov and Lloyda Thorshov to die, but they knew somebody was going to, somebody was going to get seriously injured out there," he concluded. "But the L&N said, 'We are willing to take that gamble,' and I think you will find that Jon and Lloyda Thorshov lost that gamble."

"For all intents and purposes, the case was over after my opening statement," Fred says. "Not only were we far better prepared than the defense, I had used my opening to portray L&N as callous and money grubbing, and I had turned the defense's best ammunition in our favor. During the trial, we systematically proved what I had detailed in my opening. The defense, however, proved nothing they said in their opening."

Bert Lane tried to ruffle Fred before closing arguments. The two were outside the courtroom talking. Fred was wearing a Countess Mara tie, with the initials CM on it. Lane pointed at the CM and asked Fred, "What does that say in Yiddish?" Fred smiled and replied, "It says I'm going to go out there and kick your ass in closing arguments." And he did.

"Imagine this accident never happened," Fred began to the jury. "It is Jon's birthday today and his wife would be baking him a cake. But that is a dream, and the reality is we are in court."

Fred told the jury that it is "probably one of the most important cases ever tried in this country," which told them that they needed to step up and send a clear message. He drove home that he did not want a sympathy verdict. Had that been the case, he said that he would have put the kids in the courtroom and had the grandparents testify about their grief. He did not do that because he wanted the jury to decide the case based on the law.

Fred went down the jury form, point by point. Compensatory damages were to replace what was taken from the two children. "Negligence," he explained, "is the failure to use reasonable care." It seemed clear that L&N had not used reasonable care based on the evidence.

If the jury answered "yes," the next step was to determine whether the kids were dependent for twenty-two years or for life. Fred reminded them that doctors had testified that if GamGee's lungs didn't improve, the boy would be a pulmonary cripple for life. The jury also had to determine the value of what was taken from the children. Fred laid out the numbers, which came to $3 million per child.

Fred then told the jury that punitive damages were imperative in this case. What L&N did was "disgusting" and "sickening." Aside from the ten failures of basic operating conditions, he asked them to consider that the L&N troubleshooter who arrived hours after the accident, at the time when three of the Thorshovs were in critical condition, went directly to Gull Point to measure the superelevation. Rather than check on the victims—which he never did—he was only concerned with liability.

Lane delivered his closing: "Now there are a lot of things I haven't responded to, and as I say again, I won't respond to rabbit tracks," he said at one point. "And you haven't got time for me to follow rabbit tracks anyway. All you want to do is get on with your determination of who was responsible for the injuries to the family and what amount of money should be paid for it."

The jury came back with an $18 million verdict ($8 million compensatory and $10 million punitive), the largest compensatory verdict in the nation at the time. "It just floored Bert—and pretty much everyone else, too," Fred recalls.

The events of the appeals process had a tremendous and lasting impact on the legal profession. Fred proposed that the case be settled using a structured settlement. In a structured settlement, the defendant establishes a fund to pay the plaintiff over time. At the time, virtually no companies did structured settlements, and only a few trial lawyers had attempted them. But Fred thought it made perfect sense in this case for all sides.

The children didn't need millions of dollars in a lump sum, Fred reasoned. Damages in personal injury cases were tax free due to a 1977 IRS ruling, so there would be no up-front tax on the payout. However, if the children did receive the money and invest it, the proceeds of the investments would be subject to income tax, which was a whopping 70 percent at that time. Consequently, a 15 percent yield on the money would be whittled down to around 4.5 percent. There was also the chance that something could go wrong with the investments.

Fred proposed that L&N pay $11.5 million, not the $18 million awarded by the jury, and pay out that sum over time, a proposal that was ultimately accepted by all sides. The first thing this did was end the appeals process and get his clients and his firm paid. The way this worked was that L&N paid the money to IBAR Inc., a Los Angeles company specializing in this field, which assumed the liability. IBAR then purchased two annuities for the children, paid out $1.5 million for litigation costs and current expenses for the children, and set up a trust for the attorney's fees. The two annuities IBAR purchased from Life Insurance Co. of North America cost $7 million and guaranteed an 8 percent return for thirty years. This meant the Thorshov children would receive $52 million tax free, because damages were not subject to taxes.

After the first $1.5 million, the payout to the children was $1.2 million per year for the first five years, $500,000 for years six to ten, and then an additional $100,000 a year at five-year intervals until they reached $900,000 per year in years twenty-six to thirty. At the end of year thirty, there was a final lump sum payout of $27 million in November 2011. From the insurance company's point of view this payout made sense because, at that time, Treasury bonds were selling for 12 percent, thereby allowing the insurance company to cover its costs and make a profit on the transaction.

Forbes published an article about the arrangement Fred devised. The magazine declared: "When a company balks over an $18 million wrongful death award and then agrees to a $52 million long-term settlement, get ready for some fancy legal and financial footwork."

But the bigger gamble was that Fred also structured the attorney fees, a risky move that was not widely used at the time. Attorney fees in personal injury cases were taxable. This would have been a disaster, because at the tax rates in those days the firm's tax bill would have been $2 million in the first year, even though it would have collected only $1 million.

The IRS could have ruled that, as a corporation, the firm was entitled to take the full $6 million up front and therefore had to pay taxes on the

The Pensacola

A Gannett Newspaper

6 Sections   Pensacola, Florida, Wednesday Morning, December 10, 1980

L&N signs away $52 million in derailment suit

By CRAIG WATERS
Journal Staff Writer

A record-shattering $52.15 million settlement was signed Tuesday in a lawsuit brought by the representatives of two children orphaned in the disastrous 1977 derailment of a Louisville & Nashville train near Gull Point.

Daisy Thorshov, 8, and her brother GamGee, 4, will become millionaires on Jan. 12 when the first of 30 annual payments will be made to them by the

The payments are meant to punish L&N and to compensate the children for the loss of their father, Medical Center Clinic pathologist Dr. Jon Thorshov, 37, and their mother Lloyda, 28. Both parents died after inhaling deadly anhydrous ammonia fumes that spewed from overturned tankers on Nov. 9, 1977, in one of Pensacola's worst manmade disasters.

Daisy and GamGee Thorshov currently live with their mother's parents, Mr. And Mrs. Lloyd Hutchins of Rangely, Colo. They have suffered some eye and breathing difficulties from inhaling fumes in the derailment, but their attorneys said they are in good health now.

The children will receive an initial payment of $1.5 million in January, followed by yearly payments that vary according to a formula. At the end of 30 years, a final lump sum of $27 million will be paid, bringing the total to $52.15 million. Attorneys' fees and expenses will be deducted from this amount.

The settlement follows about four months of negotiations with L&N's Tallahassee attorneys. Talks centered on the legal complications of the train derail-

Fred's eye-popping courtroom victory in *Thorshov v. Louisville & Nashville Railroad Company* made legal history.

full amount in the first year. Instead, the agency concluded that the Levin firm would only be taxed on the money when it was collected.

"It was a hell of a gamble because it was very technical and carried a potential IRS land mine, but it worked very well," Martin Levin says.

Fred structured the firm's one-third fee to be paid out $1 million per year for five years, and $2 million at the end of twenty-five years. This accomplished two things: First, it gave his firm an additional $1 million overall. Second, the money would be compounding; therefore, if the interest rate was 10 percent, at the end of year one that payment would be worth $1.1 million. If, however, the IRS had taxed the firm 40 percent on that 10 percent interest, the Levin firm would have $1.06 million. Fred's idea allowed interest to accumulate on the full amount, and it also deferred the firm's tax bill, which worked out well because tax rates decreased over time.

Fred told *Forbes* that this was the wave of the future. Indeed, it turned out to be. In the end, the IRS agreed that the full amount of attorney's fees was not taxable up front. It made perfect sense because they were paying out less than they earned, much like a bank does when it loans money at a higher rate than the one at which it borrows the money from the Federal Reserve Bank. Now, lawyers and insurance companies structure nearly all large settlements for both plaintiff's money and attorney's fees.

Clearly, Fred had seen the future in this area. Shortly after the trial, he was invited to give the keynote address at an insurance convention where companies were exploring structured settlements as part of their business model. At first, however, none of the large insurance companies wanted anything to do with structured settlements. Fred, who was the chairman of the board of Orange State Life Insurance Company, was certain this area was going to explode and become hugely profitable for insurance companies. Orange wasn't big enough to execute the idea, so Fred got in touch with AIG, then and now one of the largest insurance companies in the world. They were interested and promised to send two representatives to meet with Fred and discuss doing business together.

"But like so many things, for some reason I never followed through," Fred says. "Had I, the sky would have been the limit, because less than five years later every major insurance company was using structured settlements."

Perhaps Fred never followed through on starting that division with AIG because he was busy basking in his success. He certainly received plenty of attention after the *Thorshov* case. The largest compensatory verdict in the nation had led to the largest legal settlement in history, and to put it bluntly, Fred became a national celebrity in the legal profession. It wasn't something he shied away from, either.

The reach was so wide that *US* magazine did a story on Fred in its swimsuit preview issue. On the cover were Randi Oakes from *CHiPs*, Morgan Fairchild from *Flamingo Road*, and Donna Mills from *Knots Landing*. Inside was a half-page picture of Fred Levin standing in front of an L&N railcar under the headline "I'll Sue."

"My attitude was all publicity was good publicity," Fred says. "I was given some advice when I first started practicing law by a lawyer named Shakey Latham. He told me that it doesn't make any difference what they

After his huge verdict against L&N, Fred bought matching Mercedes for his three teenage children.

say about you in the press; it's the name recognition you are after, so just make sure they spell your name right. That advice was significant in my career, because it put my name out there."

W. D. Childers, Fred's close friend who was president of the Florida State Senate, gave him a scrapbook of newspaper clippings discussing the *Thorshov* case that Childers titled "Made for Movies." Fred put it front and center on his office coffee table. Another friend gave him a gold lighter inscribed, "$6,000,000 Man," in reference to Fred's attorney's fee on the *Thorshov* case and the hit 1970s television show by the same name starring Lee Majors as a bionic man.

Fred told a reporter from Miami that clients seek him out because he wins. At that point, Fred hadn't lost a jury trial. One reporter quoted him telling another reporter, "Be sure and use the part about where W. D. Childers tells me I'm the world's best lawyer . . . 'cause it's probably true."

Fred Levin certainly thought it was.

CHAPTER FIVE

Winning Over
Everybody

There was no single moment when the floodgates opened and trial lawyers became so plentiful they were dubbed "ambulance chasers." Large
damage awards like the one Fred Levin won in the *Thorshov* case certainly
made the field appear highly lucrative. Because the US Supreme Court
had approved legal advertising in 1978, lawyers volunteering to help the
injured were everywhere. The initial venue of choice was the local phone
book, followed by billboards and eventually television.

The result of the large jury awards was the proliferation of personal
injury law firms that were often just one lawyer in a room with an ad and
a phone number. The basic tactic of these lawyers was to advertise for
cases, then attempt to settle the cases without a trial that they were not
equipped to win, or refer the cases to a lawyer who could actually try them.

As easy as this seems, it was actually far more difficult in practice
due to IRS regulations, which some lawyers learned the expensive way.
IRS rules prevented law firms from deducting the expenses they incurred
in working up a case until it was concluded. For example, if a firm spent
$100,000 developing a case for trial and it dragged on for two or three

years, those expenses could not be deducted from law firm revenue until the case was settled. This would result in law firms appearing to make more money in any one year than they actually did, and then paying taxes on money they had not yet received. For a lawyer accustomed to being paid by the hour, this became suffocating financially because the cases took longer and he or she had to spend money without being able to deduct the costs for tax purposes.

But some lawyers were becoming wealthy, and the more prominent cases, such as the Ford Pinto, Karen Silkwood, and *Thorshov* cases, also were making an impact on public safety. Corporations began to realize for the first time that they could be held accountable for extremely large damages for negligence. In the Ford case, the initial jury award, though reduced, had stripped the company of all its profits made from the Pinto. The Silkwood case put worker safety in the spotlight and pulled unions together to push their members' employers to make conditions safe or face huge financial penalties in the courts. The sheer size of the *Thorshov* verdict—the largest wrongful death compensatory damage verdict at the time—sent up a cautionary flare that made railroads around the country address safety problems and repair faulty tracks far more quickly and effectively, no doubt averting injuries and saving lives.

After the *Thorshov* case, Fred had a string of other victories that solidified his reputation. By 1981, he had secured four verdicts in Escambia County, Florida, in excess of $1 million. Yet for every three cases that appeared to be about money, there was one that ended up being solely about principle.

One case Fred handled involved a young black woman killed in an auto accident. "The defense lawyer said, 'We'll pay you $250,000 and that's more than any nigger is worth,'" Fred recalls. Fred rejected the offer and won $1 million at trial. At the time, it was the largest amount ever awarded for the life of a black person, and a touchstone victory given that it occurred in the South, where racial prejudices were ingrained in much of the culture.

Fred's firm, called Levin, Warfield, Middlebrooks, Mabie & Magie, had twenty-two lawyers, and it had become a reflection of Fred's personality. The firm spent $1 million—a shocking sum at that time, particularly in Pensacola—to decorate its five-floor offices. The place was anything but understated. The rose-colored hallways were lined with crystal chandeliers and had lavender carpet, a motif that was condescingly described as "early bordello" by Bert Lane and his team. Fred's office had Tudor-style furniture, with a massive oak desk as the centerpiece. The walls were adorned in English tapestries and prints of foxhunts. The offices had a sauna, a gym with a weight room, an elaborate dining room where lunch was prepared daily for the lawyers by a chef, and a bar that opened at 5 P.M. There was a barbershop, where haircuts and manicures were available twice a month. The goal of keeping the lawyers in the office was that they would be more productive.

"Maybe we were over the top, but we were on the rise," Fred says. "Here I was sitting in the backwater town of Pensacola, and everything seemed to be coming to me. In the Deep South, people were anti-Semitic, but they always were taught if you need a lawyer or a doctor, make sure you get a Jewish one. The difference between me and others is that I haven't forgotten where I came from. I am a very empathetic person. I tear up when I see the flag. There are things that are very inconsistent with the asshole image I get."

Inevitably, as Fred tried to maximize his status, controversy found him and he developed his share of enemies—not unlike other outgoing trial lawyers across the country. One thing was certain: It was soon clear that Fred Levin was operating on a different level than any ambulance chaser—and most successful lawyers, as well.

One of the more fortuitous and controversial relationships in Fred's life was his friendship with W. D. Childers, the president of the Florida Senate. But the fact that these two men became friends changed the lives of an overwhelming number of people in the state of Florida, even as it led to endless gossip, backstabbing, and newspaper articles over a twenty-year period. It was a relationship that Fred's critics would try to use against him time and time again.

Childers was a Pensacola native. Initially, Fred regarded him as a stuffed shirt. When Childers ran for reelection to the state Senate in 1976, Fred was one of the few financial supporters of his opponent, Chris Hentz. Childers won a whopping 90 percent of the vote, which told Fred that Childers was going to be his senator for some time.

Fred first met Childers in 1978. Childers asked Fred to speak out against a proposed bill that would eliminate pain and suffering awards. Fred gave an hour-long speech and made a compelling case to keep the law in place. In a legislative effort led by Childers, the bill was ultimately defeated. Afterward, Childers called Fred into his office and asked him if he thought Chris Hentz could have pulled that off. Touché.

As Childers rose to president of the Senate, he picked up his fair share of enemies along the way. In 1980, people started whispering that Childers had benefited from a state land-purchase deal in southwest Escambia County. This was problematic for Pensacola because Childers was not only the president-elect of the Senate, he was also the city's main source of political power. A grand jury investigation began, with rampant speculation about what would happen to him.

Though Fred didn't know Childers very well at the time, the senator asked Fred to represent him. Childers told Fred that he had been recommended by Dempsey Barron of Panama City, a state senator who was the most powerful man in the Florida legislature. Barron was a bare-knuckles politician in the mold of Huey Long.

"At the time, I was flattered," Fred says. "However, I started thinking otherwise after I saw how tricky Barron could be."

The more Fred learned, the more he began to wonder if Barron had encouraged Childers to hire Fred because Barron secretly figured that, since Fred was primarily a civil trial lawyer, he wouldn't understand the nuances of criminal law in the case and would mess up. If Fred blew the case, it would bode well for Barron because it would eliminate Childers, his now out-of-favor protégé who was slowly gaining more and more power on his own.

During the case preparation, things looked bleak for Childers at every turn. One day when Fred and Childers were preparing his defense, they took two chairs to the beach. It was a sunny afternoon, and people were out playing Frisbee. Out of nowhere, a small cloud appeared over them and started raining on their paperwork. "We looked up at the sky and down the beach," Fred recalls. "It wasn't raining anywhere else but on our small patch of the beach. Childers shook his head, looking utterly defeated."

As Fred forged ahead with the defense, he felt certain that Childers had done nothing wrong. Fred convinced him to take a lie-detector test before a statewide grand jury. This was a radical move, far from what the typical lawyer would recommend. All the criminal lawyers were telling Fred that he was crazy. The test was unpredictable, they said, and if Childers didn't pass, he would really be behind the eight ball.

But Childers passed the lie-detector test, which Fred used to blaze a path to victory. Instead of an indictment, the case ended with Childers receiving a presentment, or formal order, from the grand jury stating that everyone in politics should be as honest as W. D. Childers. It was a truly remarkable turn of events, and it cemented Childers' friendship with Fred.

On New Year's Day, Fred and Childers went to the Sugar Bowl together. During the trip, Childers asked Fred if he would serve as his special counsel. Childers wanted a lawyer to review the actions he took as Senate president to avoid the appearance of impropriety, as well as to run interference with all the requests that his office received. Fred gladly accepted his offer to become special counsel to the Senate president. The salary was $1 per year—but Fred did receive Senate letterhead and business cards embossed with the state seal. This again shined the political spotlight on the Levin firm, as David Levin had done when he served as a special counsel to Governor Reubin Askew.

"After I wrestled W. D. out from under the grand jury investigation, he told me, 'Whatever you want in the legislature, I will do my best to make it happen,'" Fred says.

It was an uncommon backroom gesture from a politician to a lawyer with so many possible interests before the legislature, but Childers made good on his promise.

One day, Fred was on the phone explaining to a woman why she couldn't sue for pain and suffering even though her son, a medical school student, had been killed by a drunk driver. At that time, the law allowed the victim's family to sue only for funeral expenses because he was over twenty-one. Childers happened to overhear the conversation. He was amazed that the law was written so restrictively, and he asked how it could be straightened out.

Fred went to work and drafted a bill called the Florida Wrongful Death Act that would allow survivors—even parents of married children—to collect for pain and suffering, as well as funeral expenses. He sent it to Childers, who took it to the Senate floor for passage.

Dempsey Barron opposed the bill and tried but failed to block the legislation. Barron relied heavily on the insurance companies for campaign contributions and was a former partner in a law firm that represented them. The legislative fight over the bill led to a major break in relations between Barron and Childers.

While Barron was in Colorado, Childers (as Senate president) was preparing the list of people he would appoint as chairmen of Senate committees, positions that carried significant political power. A Barron aide confronted Childers and told him to not make the selections public until he first showed them to her. That was what Dempsey wanted, she told him. The woman wasn't merely an aide; she was Barron's girlfriend and soon to be his wife.

"W. D. was upset that he would have to run the appointments by Barron," Fred recalls. "I told him he was right and such a demand was ridiculous. So Childers released the names publicly, and all hell broke loose."

Things grew more tense when the Florida Wrongful Death Act passed in 1981, with a strong push from Childers. The law made it possible for parents of children under twenty-five to sue for mental pain and suffering upon the wrongful death of a child. Under the previous law, the parents could recover only if the child was younger than twenty-one, and could not recover at any age (even under twenty-one) if the child was married. The new law became the most liberal wrongful death act in the country, and made Fred Levin a lot of money.

In 1983, Fred won a $3.5 million jury award in a case where a teenager was killed in a 1981 auto accident due to an improperly attached tire. The teen's mother and father were each awarded $1.75 million. At that time, it was the largest judgment in a case of wrongful death of a child in the United States.

Fred argues the law was about justice. "Did the parents deserve to be compensated for pain and suffering?" he says. "I believed they did. Imagine their horror. They had trusted a mechanic to properly service the wheels on their truck. While the truck was hauling a trailer on the interstate with their son in the trailer, a wheel of the truck dislodged, causing the truck and the trailer to flip over. Their son was killed, and their daughter survived."

Fred won another case using the new law in 1985. He won a $4.3 million jury verdict for a widow and the parents of a twenty-three-year-old man who was electrocuted due to the negligence of the local electric company. In the judgment, the parents were awarded $1 million—the first award of its kind to parents of a married adult.

In this case, a power pole had fallen and its loose, hot wires were dangling on a wire fence. Though the power company had known the pole was down for two hours, it did not shut off the electricity or repair the pole.

The man, who was legally hunting in the area with friends, touched the fence and was killed instantly. "Imagine if you were his parents receiving that phone call," Fred says.

So while the Florida Wrongful Death Act was profitable for Fred Levin and his law firm, it also provided relief for people in Florida who were anguished when their children died due to negligence.

But others saw things differently. There were numerous stories that Fred had undue influence on W. D. Childers. It reached the point where one state senator became so incensed with Fred's position that he proposed a $78 budget amendment to buy Fred a one-way ticket home. (Incidentally, a vote was never taken.)

Senators complained that they couldn't have private conversations with Childers because Fred was always in his office. A state representative told the *Pensacola News Journal* that Fred thought he was "God" and that he was "power mad."

The most vitriol came from Dempsey Barron. He told the *Pensacola News Journal* that Fred had "replaced [him] as Childers' best friend." He continued: "Fred has all the money in the world and so now he wants to be

The Lawyer and the Legislator: The press scrutinizes the cozy relationship between Fred and Florida Senate President W. D. Childers.

a power over here in Tallahassee. He's around the senate all the time now, giving Senator Childers advice, some of which I think is bad, and passing out business cards just like they print for senators, identifying himself as Senate Special Counsel."

"Though I plead guilty to passing out the fancy business cards, I certainly wasn't controlling W. D.," Fred says.

During the budget negotiations in the summer of 1981, Barron and Childers nearly came to blows. Barron blamed Fred.

"At one point, I was sitting in W. D.'s office—he wasn't there—and Dempsey barged in and started yelling at me," Fred says. "He stood over me, screaming that the Senate was a great collegial body and I had 'fucked it up.' About that point, W. D. returned. He sat down and started cleaning his nails with a knife, ignoring Barron's tirade."

That was the end of Childers' relationship with Barron, who put together a coalition of Republicans and Democrats bent on dumping Childers as Senate president, and it was the beginning of the escalation of Barron's incredible animosity toward Fred. Barron called trial lawyers "the bloodsuckingest people I've ever known." Fred, in turn, pointed out to the *Tampa Tribune's Floridian* magazine that "Barron's philosophy is that if the rules don't fit what he wants to do, then to hell with the rules."

Dempsey Barron hadn't seen the last of Fred Levin.

Fred finally saw an opening to take down Barron in 1988. Barron, who by then had served thirty-two years in the Senate, had tried at every turn to ruin W. D. Childers. Barron was the lord of the Florida Senate, which he called "my Senate." He led the powerful Senate Rules Committee and cast an intimidating presence over all the body's proceedings. Those who defied him, like Childers, found themselves in the legislative wilderness. To defeat Barron, Fred first needed a candidate to run against him in the Democratic primary, as the general election results were certain to follow the primary.

Fred called Max Bruner, a former superintendent of schools who was very popular in Barron's district. He told Bruner that he could raise $100,000 for him to run against Barron (who was then sitting on a $122,000 war chest). Bruner demurred, saying he was busy running two motels in Fort Walton Beach. Instead, he suggested his thirty-one-year-old son, Vince, an attorney.

ANDY CLINGEMPEEL PHOTOGRAPH   NOVEMBER 1988 ▽ FLORIDA TREND **51**

Florida Trend highlights Fred Levin for taking down Dempsey Barron.

Fred met with Vince and was impressed. Vince was a clean-cut churchgoer and a former football star at Florida State University. He was married to a very attractive woman and had a photogenic family. In short, he was everything a candidate needs to be. Fred then drove Vince to Tallahassee to meet with the Academy of Florida Trial Lawyers and drum up support.

"It turned out they were not only afraid to challenge Barron, they decided to kiss up to him," Fred says. "They didn't want to be seen as supporting Fred Levin's candidate."

A few weeks after that meeting, Barron cut a deal with the trial lawyers. In exchange for the Academy of Florida Trial Lawyers agreeing not to back a candidate against him, Barron promised not to introduce any more anti-lawyer bills during the current legislative session.

Fred was incensed. He set out to find a different coalition to support Vince Bruner. "Most people thought there was as good a chance of Vince Bruner winning as there was a blizzard hitting the Panhandle of Florida," Fred says.

But Fred helped bring together a coalition of independent-minded attorneys, including J. B. Spence, Al Cone, Bob Kerrigan, and Wes Pittman. The group raised $200,000 for Bruner, which was a formidable sum in 1988 for a state race. Bruner hired political professionals, cut glitzy commercials, and ended up beating Barron by two thousand votes.

The gunning down of the "Red Barron" made news across the country and was even written about in Alaska. It was as if Huey Long had been defeated. And there was Fred Levin, front and center, in another Florida political story.

As a result of the publicity Fred was receiving, a publisher asked him to write a book for law students. The publisher wanted a book that focused solely on opening statements that it could market using Fred's increasingly famous name. Fred wrote it longhand during a family vacation. He spent all of his time working, so a vacation was hardly an exception. He loved his family and provided for them very well, but work came first, second, and third.

The book was titled *Effective Opening Statements: The Attorney's Master Key to Courtroom Victory*. The book provides weapons for the trial lawyer in what Fred calls the most critical part of the trial. He talks about how to use subtle personal appeals to individual jurors, ways to reel in the jury's attention to a critical part of the case, and how to dramatize the client's situation and make the jury invest in them. It also contains practical advice that seems obvious but is often overlooked, such as how to dress, where to stand, how to convey importance, and the tone of voice to be used at the different junctures of the opening statement.

There was a section on how to work in damage requests, as Fred had done in the *Thorshov* case, and make them sound justified rather than excessive. "Often times, it is incredibly difficult for juries to wrap their heads around figures in the millions, far above what they will ever know, so if this is handled correctly in the opening, a lawyer can actually condition the jury to accept the figures he presents," Fred explains.

He also introduced a newly formulated concept: winning over everyone in the courtroom. In addition to convincing the jury, his tactic was to convince the judge, as well as the opposing party and their counsel, of the plaintiff's point of view on the case. "Strange as it may sound, it is possible, and if a lawyer can win over the entire courtroom, he will almost never lose," Fred says.

At the end of the book, Fred says that he wrote it because "there's no other calling within our profession that can give the ultimate 'turn-on' as when you are sitting in that courtroom and hear the words, 'We the jury find for the plaintiff and assess damages at . . .'"

The first edition was printed in 1983, when many lawyers didn't yet realize something that Fred understood: After the jury hears opening statements, most jurors make up their minds and don't change their opinions for the rest of the trial.

In the appendix, the book reprinted the opening statements from two of Fred's cases, as well as those of the defense attorneys. Like a professor grading a paper, Fred critiqued what had helped and what had hurt each side. "These examples are great learning tools, because they show a law student how to present a case and explain it in common words, not lawyer words," he says.

Of course, Fred used the *Thorshov* opening statement, since he believed it had won the case. He also used the opening statement from the case of a Pensacola child named Chad Tolan, who was severely brain-damaged and left a "vegetable" after a Kmart pharmacist gave his mother ten times the recommended amount of a prescribed drug. Chad's case resulted in a $2.15 million verdict, a huge amount at that time for a child. "It was a case where I probably had the jury at 'Good morning,'" Fred says.

The most important consequence of all the publicity Fred was receiving was that he was invited to join the Inner Circle of Advocates, a group of highly respected trial attorneys. Joining the Inner Circle led to relationships with several prominent attorneys. It was there that Fred befriended Johnnie Cochran, the controversial lawyer who later defended O. J. Simpson.

When Fred first met Johnnie Cochran, Cochran had just been installed in the Inner Circle of Advocates. Fred ran into him in the hallway of the hotel at the annual meeting and introduced himself. At the time, there was a boxing connection, as Cochran was representing Mike Tyson and Fred was handling Roy Jones Jr. Cochran flashed his megawatt smile and said, "I know who you are." The two chatted about boxing and struck up a friendship.

Like everyone, Fred followed the O. J. Simpson case. "From my perspective, he had won an acquittal of the double murder charge against O. J. by playing the race card very effectively—and ultimately regretted it," Fred says. "On a smaller scale, I knew how that felt because I had done it on a case I handled in the early 1960s."

Fred's case involved a prominent black preacher named Reverend H. K. Matthews. The preacher was driving to an NAACP meeting when Fred's client pulled out from a stop sign and Matthews smashed into him. This was in the days of contributory negligence, which meant if a client was even 1 percent at fault, he couldn't collect any damages. Therefore, winning such a case had a high bar.

Throughout the trial, Fred kept repeating that the reverend was speeding "on his way to an NAACP meeting." The jury was all white, and the trial was shortly after *Brown v. Board of Education*, which had hit a raw nerve across most of the South. Fred played right into their sentiments and won the case.

"For days, I felt like a horrible human being, and to this day, that win remains one of the real downers in my professional life," Fred says. "Years later, I ran into Reverend Matthews and apologized. He accepted, and we actually became friends."

Fred ended up being present when Cochran and O. J. Simpson ran into each other for the first time after the trial. It occurred at a boxing match in Miami in February 2002. Fred had invited Cochran as his guest to the fight with his friends, former congressman and 1996 Republican vice presidential nominee Jack Kemp and Dallas Mavericks president Terdema Ussery. The group was sitting ringside in the same row as several celebrities, including Barry Bonds, the great baseball slugger who had just broken the Major League Baseball home run record. Minutes before the fight, a commotion erupted nearby. O. J. Simpson was entering with two blondes in tow.

It had been almost seven years since Cochran's skillful courtroom tactics—which some called smarmy and underhanded—had gotten Simpson acquitted of the killing of his ex-wife, Nicole Brown Simpson, and her friend, Ronald Goldman. Because the trial was televised gavel to gavel on CNN and had such a bizarre cast of characters (and a shocking verdict, based on the evidence), it had made Johnnie Cochran the most famous lawyer in America.

Ussery says he elbowed Cochran and pointed out Simpson. "I thought Cochran would be happy to see O. J. Simpson, his most famous client," Ussery recalls. "Cochran didn't want to have anything to do with him. He's telling me, 'If he comes down here, I don't want him to know I'm here.' All of a sudden, O. J. shouts out, 'There's my lawyer!'"

Both Ussery and Fred moved in front of Cochran to keep Simpson away from him. But before Simpson could try to make his way over to Cochran, he spotted Barry Bonds and let loose on him. "It was a weird tirade that was very, very loud, and very, very obnoxious," Ussery recalls.

"O. J. took one look at Barry Bonds and launched into a rant," Fred says. "'That home run record should have been mine! I was a home run hitter and I was better than you!' Bonds shook him off, but O. J. wouldn't quit. 'No, no, I mean it!' he yelled even louder. 'You know I was a better hitter than you.' He just kept at him."

Ussery explained to Cochran that he was president of the Mavericks and couldn't be seen in the same camera shot on HBO as Simpson; therefore he was going to leave the arena.

"It was almost surreal when you saw the personalities that came together," Ussery says. "It was one of those weird moments none of us will forget. I asked Johnnie, 'Do you want to see him?' He said, 'Hell no, I haven't spoken to him since the trial, and I don't want to talk to him.' That told me a lot."

Ussery slipped out, but Jack Kemp didn't seem to mind O. J., as Kemp's political career had ended at that point. The actor Steven Seagal was sitting behind Fred. "He leaned over and told me, 'If there's any trouble, don't worry . . . I'm carrying heat,'" Fred says. "To confirm this fact, he pulled his jacket back, revealing a gun tucked into his waistband."

"Johnnie wanted absolutely nothing to do with O. J.," Fred says. "Johnnie later told me that was the first time he had seen O. J. since the trial, and yet he didn't even so much as nod to O. J. My take is that Johnnie thought O. J. was guilty, and even though his successful defense was a cornerstone of his career, it was something that troubled him."

Months later, Ussery had an in-depth conversation with Cochran about the O. J. Simpson verdict over lunch in Dallas. A lawyer himself, Ussery felt it would be disrespectful to ask Cochran point-blank if he felt that O. J. was guilty. But Ussery says as a result of that night at the fight, he became curious.

"I was shocked that he didn't want to have anything to do with him," Ussery says. "I asked him when he and I were alone, and he told me something very profound, which I have never forgotten. Johnnie said, 'I haven't talked to him since the trial and I don't have any need to talk to him.'"

Ussery told Cochran that he understood. He recalls it getting quiet as they kept eating. Cochran told Ussery to ask him anything he wanted, but Ussery demurred. Cochran then answered the question that Ussery wouldn't directly ask: whether or not he believed O. J. Simpson was guilty.

"Johnnie said, 'The answer to your question is, his character is going to eventually answer the question for those who are curious as to whether or not he did it. So what I would say to you is watch him. Eventually—because character is something that you cannot suppress long term—your question is going to be answered if you just watch him,'" Ussery says, relating the conversation.

In 2008, three years after Johnnie Cochran died, O. J. Simpson was found guilty of several felonies stemming from a memorabilia scheme. Among other charges, Simpson was convicted of armed robbery and kidnapping. He was sentenced to thirty-three years in prison.

Everywhere Fred went with Cochran, people approached Johnnie. The morning after the fight in Miami, Kemp, Ussery, and Cochran took Fred's corporate jet to the Super Bowl in New Orleans. On the walk from the hotel to the stadium, every third person gave a friendly shout-out to Cochran. Through his connections, Kemp had secured tickets on the fifty-yard line, just above the lower walkway. "During the game we couldn't see a thing because of all the people coming up to Jack but mostly to Johnnie," Fred says.

Cochran and Fred eventually went into business together. Keith Givens, an attorney then based in Alabama, came to Fred with the idea of doing a national law firm using Johnnie Cochran's name. Givens also recruited plaintiff's lawyer John Morgan and his firm. They created two firms, one based in Memphis and one in Washington, DC, called the Cochran Firm. The catchy slogan was "Johnnie Cochran, America's lawyer. The Cochran firm, America's law firm."

At the time, Fred had a close relationship with a top life insurance executive in Oklahoma City. Because the firm needed Cochran for advertising, Fred proposed they take out "key man" life insurance on him, which

Fred and John Morgan, longtime friends and business partners.

compensates a business for financial losses if an important member dies or becomes incapacitated. The insurance executive sold them a $50 million term life insurance policy.

Cochran wasn't so sure about the arrangement. Referring to the firm's private jet, he quipped: "I don't like the idea of four white guys controlling my aircraft and having $50 million of life insurance on me."

The premiums were roughly $1 million per year for the policy, which could be converted to whole life so that the payers would eventually see their money back. Under the terms, if Cochran died, his widow would receive $25 million, his law partners and Keith Givens would collect $15 million, John Morgan would get $5 million, and Fred Levin would receive $5 million.

After the policy was purchased, Cochran developed brain cancer. He died two years and one day after the policy went into effect, meaning that the policy could not be contested because the two-year anniversary had passed. The policy paid out accordingly, and the Cochran Firm has since expanded to more than a dozen cities. Though not active, Fred's firm retains a share in the Washington, DC, branch of the firm.

CHAPTER
SIX

"Home Sweet Home"

F red Levin, the hotshot lawyer, the politically connected operator, the manager of the only boxer in a century to win both the middleweight and heavyweight championships, the friend of five men who were serious candidates for president of the United States, was, not to put too fine a point on it, a lousy family man. He was far more concerned with his image and status in society than being named Father of the Year, and he utilized his home as an extension of his public persona. For him, the person with the biggest and most elaborate house is the one to be admired. He or she is the one who has succeeded, and the one that others want to be associated with. Such a person's home is an ideal place to facilitate self-promotion for business by throwing over-the-top parties for politicians, charities, and business colleagues.

Today, Fred owns two large homes and a penthouse condo. All are on the water, and all are within a three-mile radius. He lives in one of the homes, which is decorated like a boutique Las Vegas hotel. Named the Carriage House, it's on the Bayou Texar outside of downtown Pensacola and has three elaborate bars and a massive fire pit. It was made for entertaining. The most outrageous room is what used to be the garage. Now, it's a bar. The room's centerpiece is a Rolls-Royce convertible that Aristotle Onassis bought for Jackie Kennedy Onassis. The trunk has been converted to a Champagne bar, complete with crystal glasses. Next to the Rolls is a bronze of Jackie O.

The Carriage House has several historical display cases. One contains the Nobel Peace Prize won by Fred's friend Betty Williams in 1976 for work she did to bring peace after centuries of conflict in Northern Ireland. There is also a case with memorabilia from Oskar Schindler, the German businessman who saved 1,200 Jews from extermination by the Nazis in World War II. His life was made famous in Steven Spielberg's film *Schindler's List*.

Across the Bayou Texar, Fred is remodeling a house that his son once owned. The house will have a Viking theme to the front, and the interior will be ornate, with lots of art and other icebreakers to stimulate conversation. The aperitif room will have a French Louis XIV look, with a portrait of Fred, naturally. The garage will be decorated as if it were the *Titanic*, and it will feature a vintage Renault, of which only two were made. One went down with the ship; the other will be in Fred's garage. In the movie *Titanic*, the Renault is the car steamed up by Leonardo DiCaprio and Kate Winslet.

Fred has never even slept in his penthouse condo, Triton, which is located at the Portofino resort that his brother Allen developed on Pensacola Beach. The penthouse boasts an extraordinarily large Chihuly chandelier, a rare 1929 Danish piano, a Picasso drawing, a waterfall bar, a moving circular bed, and a panoramic view of the Gulf of Mexico from twenty-one floors up. For Fred, the homes are solely about the show, the business, and the enjoyment of others.

Fred's fascination with homes began in 1967, when he had been practicing law for just six years and was not yet wealthy. He decided to purchase one of the biggest homes in Pensacola—on credit, of course. The home was extremely large for its time. It sat on more than two acres, and had a tennis court, swimming pool, elevator, and more than 100 feet of shoreline. It was far more money than Fred could afford, and the house far larger than the family needed, but it was Fred's way of showing the legal community and the town that he existed.

At the time Fred and his wife, Marilyn, moved into their new home, they had three children: Marci (age seven), Debra (age five), and Martin (age three). Two years later, their fourth child, Kim, was born. The children's early childhood years were ideal. Marilyn was the storybook mother. She adored her children. She treated them as young adults, holding very candid and mature conversations in which the children were permitted to ask any questions and openly discuss their fears and concerns. She was a magnificent cook. She made sure every Jewish holiday and even some Christian ones were lavishly celebrated. She drove the children to school, took them clothes shopping and grocery shopping, and arranged extracurricular activities, which were many and diverse.

Fred and Marilyn in Las Vegas in 1986.

Marilyn taught her children that the most important thing in life was always to treat everyone they encountered with the same compassion they would show each other, no matter their race, religion, sexuality, nationality, gender, or economic status. She was one of the first in the country to openly embrace and care for AIDS victims, during a time when any contact was considered a death sentence. She took in several troubled teens to live in her house, even while caring for her own children. She was also active in the Jewish community, running the gift shop at the B'nai Israel Synagogue and serving as president of the Pensacola chapter of Hadassah.

Fred took very little part in raising the children. Part of the reason he neglected them was that there was always something more fun going on elsewhere, but part of it was also the memory of the only basketball game of Martin's that he attended.

Because Martin had begged him to come, Fred agreed. "Martin was going on and on, 'Daddy, you've got to come and see me play,'" Fred remembers. "I said, 'I've got important things to do, like drinks with the boys.' He told me it was the championship game so I finally agreed to go."

Everyone in the gym knew who Fred was. Aside from his legal practice, he had four kids in the small private school, and he had bought the team's uniforms. Fred sat with the other parents. As the game progressed, Fred became more and more agitated as Martin rode the bench. The coach detected his irritation, so with Martin's team leading by just one point with twenty seconds remaining in the game, the coach put Martin in the game.

A jump ball ensued. The referee tossed the ball up, and both teams swatted at it, trying to gain possession. The ball bounced from player to player and then landed in Martin's hands. Martin charged up the court and laid the ball in the basket just before the buzzer sounded. Martin turned to his father and gave him two thumbs way up.

The problem was that Martin had scored in the wrong basket, and the other team had won the game by one point. The crowd rained a chorus of boos on Martin. Mortified, Fred got up and walked out of the gym.

"That really was a turning point for Dad," Martin says. "He was at a crossroads in life. He was feeling guilty about not being a family man. He had to make a decision: Is it family, or is it law? He thought about it and thought about it. He smoked a lot of cigarettes and did a lot of shots of Crown Royal. He decided, 'I choose family.' The next day he comes to the famous basketball game and when I scored for the wrong team, he said, 'Fuck this family bullshit. The rest of my life will be devoted to law.' He owes all his success to me."

While Fred and Martin love joking about this story, which as they say in Hollywood is "based on actual events," the truth is that Fred always saw his sole responsibility as providing for the family financially, as his father had done. It was up to Marilyn to raise the children. Fred's job was to make the money, and the more money he provided the family, the better a father he was. Fred would leave home before the kids would get up for school, and return home around 7:30 at night for dinner, virtually always extremely intoxicated.

The upside was that Fred was a very happy drunk. He would come home singing and joking, and interact with the children in a very child-like manner, which generally involved a lot of farting and dancing with Marilyn and the girls to loud music. To young kids, it was humorous, endearing, and memorable. After dinner, Fred would play with his kids for a half hour, and then go upstairs to watch TV and pass out.

On occasional weekends Fred would spend time at home, after working for half a day, but only if his friends were coming over to watch football. On game day, Fred Vigodsky (whom the kids called Uncle Fred), Bob Williams (whom the kids called Uncle Bob), Allen Levin (Fred's brother and closest friend), and occasionally Dean Baird (whom the kids called Uncle Dean) would come to the house. None of these individuals (other than Allen) were true uncles, but they were so close to the family that the children referenced them in this manner. Baird not only was not an uncle, he actually was Fred's bookie. The reason everyone was watching football was because they all had thousands of dollars riding on the games.

Because Fred would find the children irritating while he had money riding on the games, most often he would find ways to get them out of the room—for example, by giving them money or buying them something that would cause them to play outside. The kids didn't mind because they had a large home, yard, tennis court, and pool to occupy their energy and imagination, and Fred Vigodsky would bring over his kids (Holly, Brett, and Craig), who were around the same ages as Fred's. It usually was a fun time for both families.

Once night fell, the loveable Fred would once again appear. At five o'clock he would begin drinking, and the grill would be fired up for incredible feasts, usually involving three-inch-thick steaks. Marilyn and Fred's wife, Brenda, would cook everything for the meal other than the meat, while Fred and Vigodsky did the grilling and consumed large amounts of alcohol. The Levin and Vigodsky children would continue playing until dinner was served.

For the children this seemed like an ideal time. They wanted for nothing. They lived in a safe and secure environment where they knew they were loved, and they admired their parents. Unfortunately, this fantasy-type existence would come to an abrupt end in 1975.

That year, Marilyn began experiencing stomachaches that progressed to unbearable pain. She went to numerous doctors, but none could diagnose the problem. Today, they know the condition as irritable bowel syndrome, but at that time they simply informed Marilyn that she was having psychological issues. Fred believed the doctors over Marilyn. He felt he had no choice. They were the experts, and he took Marilyn to the best medical professionals available, who recommended Marilyn undergo psychiatric therapy.

Marilyn knew it was not psychosomatic. She began self-medicating with alcohol and narcotics, and her dependence on both became extreme as the years progressed. By 1980, Marilyn was often inebriated. During her binges, she would stay in her room sleeping most of the day, and act out in fits of rage at night, especially when Fred would come home drunk, which was most every night.

Marilyn was not always incapacitated, however. Just as quickly as her drinking binges could start, they also could subside. She would once again return to making handmade gift baskets for abused children, which would include clothing, candy, toys, and items that Marilyn would handcraft, such as yarn dolls. She also was popular among various teenage friends of the children. Marilyn would counsel the teenagers, who often did not feel comfortable communicating with their own parents or others. These teenagers typically came from unstable homes or had substance abuse or mental issues.

While Fred wasn't around much, when he was home he generally made it memorable. Fred had a twisted sense of humor, which the children loved. The problem was, people outside the home often didn't understand Fred's brand of humor.

Each time the family believed Marilyn had possibly overcome her medical issues with proper counseling and a change of medicine, she would suddenly revert back to binge drinking and consumption of powerful prescription narcotics. Marilyn's condition first began deteriorating

The Levin family in 1976 (left to right): Kim, Martin, Marilyn, Fred, Marci, and Debbie.

around the time Marci left for college. When Marci returned home, she was stunned by her mother's condition.

Marci always had been the disciplined one of the children. She saw her role as a motherly figure to her younger siblings, making sure boundaries were respected inside and outside the home, to the best of her ability. As Marilyn's condition worsened, Marci often was the one responsible for driving her siblings to school and appointments, and for performing many of the household chores such as grocery shopping. Marci was a take-charge-type person who would analyze situations objectively with a unique ability to block out much of the emotional baggage.

With Marci away from home during the school year, Debra assumed the role of the mother figure. Unlike Marci, however, Debra didn't desire this kind of position. Debbie (as her siblings call her) was a noncon-frontational child, and she started acting as if she lived on an island on which no one else existed other than her two younger siblings. She would chauffeur them to school and appointments and occasionally grocery-shop.

Debbie was able to block out the noise by focusing on the fact that she also would be gone soon, and by maintaining an immense self-confidence that she would make it on her own, if necessary. She didn't need interaction with her peers, nor did she crave their acceptance. The only time Debbie showed the emotion of a typical high school girl was when she was cheerleading, where she shined. Like her sister Marci, Debbie abstained from cigarettes, alcohol, and drugs, and still does to this day.

When Debbie left for college in 1980, Martin and Kim remained at home. Martin attempted to handle the situation differently from either Marci or Debbie. He believed his home life and societal ills could be resolved by everyone in society becoming friends and helping one another. He naïvely thought this would result in a "pay-it-forward"–type chain that could bring world peace. No matter the person, Martin attempted to befriend him or her and seek acceptance.

Martin had transferred from a small private school to a large, inner-city public school (Booker T. Washington High School) his sophomore year. Taking a cue from his father's school days, he aspired to be the most popular kid in school. He hung with the blacks, whites, Jews, Christians, academics, athletes, politicians, and even druggies. To each group he acted as if he were one of them, without exception.

He became student body president, and vice president of all student councils in the state of Florida. He was nominated as one of the top soccer goalkeepers in Florida, and he was voted by his senior class as most likely to succeed. Yet he also was a heavy drinker, marijuana smoker, and drug user who often found himself in compromising and dangerous situations. Nevertheless, he ended up graduating third in a class of 400.

One morning during Martin's senior year at high school, Martin caught his father before school. He explained that it was career day and he was supposed to dress up to emulate the profession he most admired. Fred instructed Martin to dress up as a member of the Ku Klux Klan, as Fred thought everyone at the school (which was half African American) would think that was funny.

Martin complied. He wasn't trying to be mean or prejudiced; he had lived with his father's humor his entire life and had grown to believe everyone would naturally think it was funny. Martin was wrong. Upon seeing his KKK costume, kids literally were screaming and running in the halls of the school. Martin was called to the principal's office. The principal, Sherman Robinson, an African American and former All-American football player, asked Martin, "What the hell is going through your mind, son?" To which Martin replied, "I'm sorry, Mr. Robinson, but you know I hate those damn Jews!"

Even Mr. Robinson had to laugh. He told Martin to take off the outfit and get back to class. When Martin explained to Fred what had occurred, Fred couldn't stop laughing. He then provided his typically poignant and fatherly advice: "Well, you were the idiot for listening to me. I hope you learned your lesson. Never trust anyone, including your daddy."

Kim, by far, had it the worst of the children because she never really got to know her mother before alcohol or drugs, and thus never experienced the motherly bond so important in early childhood. There also was a large age difference between Kim and her three siblings. Even Martin was five years older than her; when Martin left for college, Kim could not drive, and she was just beginning to experience puberty. She realized she had to fend for herself.

Being only thirteen and having no means of transportation or adult supervision, Kim discovered the best way to accomplish her goals was to hang out with much older kids who had cars and lived a partying lifestyle, which Kim quickly adopted. At a time when fake identification was easy to come by and the drinking age was eighteen, Kim had little difficulty getting into bars or acquiring drugs. Like her siblings, as soon as she graduated from high school, she took off for college to get out of Pensacola.

By this time, Marilyn was virtually incapacitated, and certainly was in no position to raise Kim. The relationship between Fred and Marilyn had also deteriorated to such a point that nighttime seemed like a scene out of the movie *The War of the Roses*.

"When I first got to know Marilyn, she was functioning," explains Phillip Morris, a longtime household employee who became Marilyn's closest friend. "That was right at that same time that Fred was on the springboard from being the big man to the great man. Around that time, Marilyn became reclusive and then nocturnal so she would not have to deal with the house staff during the day. She would get out of bed just before Fred got home for dinner. She'd ready herself and have dinner with Fred. She slowly but consistently became more dysfunctional and seldom went out in public."

Incredibly, after leaving home, each of the children not only survived, but also thrived. Marci and Debbie went to Tulane University, where they received economics degrees. Marci then went to the University of Florida College of Law, where she graduated in the top 10 percent of her class, and became one of the leading authorities on juvenile justice in the state of Florida. Marci is now a circuit court judge in Pensacola, where she and her husband, Ross (also a judge), raised their two children, Jackie and Brenton, in the very house where all the events occurred when Marilyn was at her worst. Jackie is now a registered nurse in New Orleans in the process of receiving her doctorate as a nurse practitioner, with a specialty of working with adolescents with psychiatric disorders. Brenton is in his second year of law school at the University of Florida's Levin College of Law, and has the distinction of being one of the very few Caucasians in the country who is a member of Kappa Alpha Psi, the predominantly African American college fraternity founded in 1911.

After graduating from Tulane, Debbie went on to earn her master's in business administration from the University of Florida. She pursued a career in teaching computers, and now devotes her time to charities that grant wishes to terminally ill children. Like her sisters, Debbie lives in the Florida Panhandle, spending much of her time with her son, Jake, who is an accomplished musician based in California, and hanging out with her best friend and younger sister, Kim.

After high school, Martin attended Stanford University, where he earned top honors in economics, and then went on to graduate first in his law school class at the University of Florida College of Law. After serving as a judicial clerk in federal court in Miami for one year, he returned to Pensacola, where he joined his father's firm, eventually rising to president. While he still enjoys drinking socially, his excessive partying and drug days are decades behind him. Instead, he has become the kind of devoted family man that his father was not to his wife, Terri, and boys, Dustin and Jayden.

Kim received her degree in psychology from Florida State University, and began living all over Florida with her husband, Gary, who climbed the corporate ladder in hospitality management. They eventually settled in Destin, Florida, not far from Pensacola. Kim gave up partying decades ago, and rarely drinks alcohol. Instead, she spends her time volunteering in wildlife rescue and overseeing a 500-acre farm that Marci, Debbie, and Kim own jointly near Pensacola along the Blackwater River, which is the only pristine white sand river remaining in the United States. The sisters each have large, modern cottages on the property, along with pigs, donkeys, goats, cattle, a fish pond, and a horse. Kim's son, Tyler, is the full-time operator and caretaker of the farm, and Kim's daughter, Alex, is in the final year of earning her degree in pre–veterinary medicine from Louisiana State University, and will be seeking her postgraduate degree in veterinary medicine.

After the children left home, Marilyn became progressively worse, rarely (if ever) leaving the house. She had been temporarily institutionalized numerous times without success. Finally, her situation reached the point where a circuit judge in Pensacola ruled that he was giving Marilyn one more chance by sending her down to an inpatient treatment facility in Miami.

It was 1989, and Martin was living in Miami, working as a lawyer in the federal court system. He was listed as Marilyn's contact. One day while at work, Martin received a call from the facility stating that Marilyn had left the facility and could not be located. The police had been called, but their search was not productive.

Martin left work and went home, hoping to hear from his mom. Late that night, he received a call. It was from a man who inquired whether Marilyn was Martin's mother. The man said that Marilyn was sitting on his front porch in Miami's Liberty City neighborhood, which had been the scene of race riots just months earlier. He provided Martin with his address, and Martin proceeded to the location.

Driving an expensive sports car, Martin headed into Liberty City in the middle of the night. He pulled up to the man's home and saw his mother sitting on the porch. The man came out and said, "I tried to get your mother to come inside, but she said it was not appropriate." Martin could not help but think of the juxtaposition of George Starke waiting on Marilyn's porch for Fred to return home during law school.

Martin drove his mother to his small apartment in downtown Miami. Marilyn entered the room and immediately asked for alcohol. Martin lied, saying he had none. Marilyn then went to a medicine cabinet, drank a bottle of NyQuil, and passed out.

The next day, the police arrived and took Marilyn back to the facility. She went peacefully, and even thanked the officers for the ride. That would be the last time the family would ever see Marilyn consume alcohol, other than possibly a sip or two in a social setting. When Marilyn returned to Pensacola, her drinking days were over. She would still consume prescribed narcotics, but she was no longer the angry person who refused to communicate with her family.

Marilyn once again became part of the family after returning from Miami, almost immediately traveling to Tampa to help care for Marci's firstborn child. Marilyn also began showing genuine interest in others again, spending time talking to and counseling household staff, strangers, and family members about their issues. She would fill her large home with candy jars so that no matter where the grandkids would go, there would be candy. She would build arts and crafts with them, and challenge her children and grandchildren to endless games of Scrabble and Pac-Man. It was the happiest the children had seen her since their early childhood.

Fred and Marilyn moved out of the home that had been the source of years of turmoil, and into a 20,000-square-foot home on 300 feet of waterfront.

Named the Phoenix, the house was the largest in Pensacola, and it had a gracious master bedroom suite, which was the size of the average house in the area. Fred hired a staff of fifteen to manage the house, two of whom (Marcella Rhyne and Bonnie Bryant) became Marilyn's caretakers, but more importantly very close friends of hers.

A few years after the Levins moved into the Phoenix, Phillip Morris returned to Pensacola after more than a decade away. Morris became Marilyn's closest friend. He lived at the home with Fred and Marilyn, helping to care for Marilyn, who in return became his most reliable and trusted therapist as Phillip tried to cope with the loss of his long-term partner to AIDS. "She brought me through a very tough time," Morris says.

Although she had the largest home in Pensacola, money meant nothing to Marilyn. She didn't care about anything material. Fred was still rarely home as he now was enjoying the fame of his career and spending his nights out drinking. He had so little interest in involving himself in family functions that of thirteen graduations his children had, Fred attended just one.

To make up for his lack of attention to Marilyn, Fred bought her elaborate gifts (including a $500,000 sapphire necklace), but she would merely smile, thank him, and put them aside. She never wore any of them. He also paid $500,000 to have Marilyn's name put on the Gulf Coast Kid's House (a safe haven for abused children). She never even went inside the building, but she was touched that there now was a place to provide care for these children.

The one gift she treasured was a blue facsimile Fabergé egg with an "M" on it that Fred gave her one Mother's Day. There was a small picture frame on the egg and Fred wrote inside the frame: "Happy Mother's Day. Love, Fred." Actually, she didn't care about the expensive collectible, just that little, itty-bitty stamp of a note.

"You have to realize how simple she was," Fred says. "All she ever wanted was a husband who would come home and say, 'Darling, I love you,' and throw her in the sack. She didn't care about clothes or jewelry. She came from a very simple background. Her mother even made her clothes. Marilyn mentioned to me how embarrassed she was on her prom when the boy came to pick her up and commented that Marilyn's dress looked like the draperies. The reason for this was that her mother had actually used some of the draperies to make the dress."

All she wanted was to spend time with Fred, hold his hand, and dance, as she and Fred did so well in their younger days. All Fred wanted to do was party, drink, get publicity, watch television in bed, pass out, and then start all over. He loved Marilyn dearly, but he still was more interested in satisfying his insatiable ego. "I was the worst husband in the world, and I was well into myself," he admits.

In something of a metaphor, in 2004 when Hurricane Ivan was bearing down on the Gulf Coast, Fred left town with his brother Allen; Allen's wife, Teri; and Fred Vigodsky and his wife. They went to a hotel in Lake Mary, Florida, which was owned by John Morgan, who had cofounded the Cochran Firm with Fred. Marilyn did not want to travel—or to leave the comfort of the master suite where she spent her days—so she stayed in Pensacola with Phillip Morris and the staff.

Morgan remembers how casual Fred was about the hurricane. He would call and check on Marilyn, and then it was off to cocktails and dinner. "The hurricane was blowing his life apart," Morgan says. "It destroyed his house and left his law firm in tatters. He was never worried about

Fred and Marilyn in 1970.

his house. It was always, 'What are we going to do for lunch, what are we going to do for dinner?' I would not have been able to eat. We'd be at Del Frisco's finishing off some steaks and he'd say, 'What do you think about us going to TooJay's for lunch tomorrow?' He took it so stoically and matter-of-factly."

Back home, Marilyn refused to leave the Phoenix. The Category 3 storm was bearing down on Pensacola. Waves from the Gulf of Mexico were cascading over the elevated swimming pool. Marilyn and the staff had a hurricane party, drinking chocolate martinis and watching the storm surge rise. It took a few visits from the local police to convince the group that this was going to be a severe storm situation and that staying at the house simply wasn't an option. Finally, at the last minute, as the winds starting blowing apart the house, Marilyn reluctantly relented.

"I carried her to the car," Morris recalls. "As soon as we crossed the Three Mile Bridge [connecting the beaches to the mainland], the sheriff closed it down."

Hurricane Ivan wiped out the Phoenix. The 20,000-square-foot house could not be repaired. Water penetrated the stucco walls, and the roof was ripped off. The grounds were in tatters. The putting green was blown into the bay. The damage was so bad that the house had to be torn down. Fred did not rebuild, but to this day, he still owns the property.

Over time, Marilyn's past alcohol and drug abuse seemed to catch up with her. She began suffering from early-stage dementia and occasional severe hallucinations. Once again she was becoming bedridden, but the difference this time was that she was in a very peaceful place, often smiling and loving the company of her husband, children, and grandchildren. She was not irate or bitter.

Marilyn unexpectedly died on Super Bowl Sunday in 2011. She had not been feeling well for several days prior. The previous Friday night, an ambulance was called to the home for the paramedics to take her to the hospital. As they were wheeling Marilyn out on a stretcher, she pulled Fred over to her side.

"Tell me you love me," she said to him.

"Of course, I love you," Fred replied.

That was their very last conversation. Fred visited the hospital on Saturday, but Marilyn had been taken off all medication and was completely out of it. On Sunday morning on his way to a Super Bowl party, Fred stopped by the hospital to see her. As he drove up, the hospital called his cell phone to say she had gone into cardiac arrest. By the time Fred arrived in her hospital room, Marilyn was dead.

By the time of Marilyn's death, the children and Fred had learned to accept that Marilyn had done her best with her illness and the lack of proper medical care available at the time. Marilyn's funeral was held on a rainy morning in a small Jewish cemetery in Pensacola in front of family and close friends. On behalf of the children, Martin gave the eulogy, in which he did not even reference his mother's troubled past, and he summed up his mother with the following lines:

> Race, religion, education, wealth, and social status were meaningless distinctions to Mom, because she understood they were not distinctions. She understood we all are humans facing the same basic pleasures and pain, and everything else we pretend is of importance is superfluous. It was this innate insight in human nature that Mom possessed that allowed her to communicate with, counsel, and attempt to help anyone in need. She was a believer and an encourager. In her eyes, people were better than they often were, and could achieve more than they likely could, but Mom's wisdom and sincerity convinced you both were true.

After the eulogy, and as customary in the Jewish religion, Fred and each of the children took a shovelful of dirt and placed it on top of Marilyn's casket as she was being lowered into her grave. They each said they loved her, and they returned to Fred's home. On the way there, Fred reflected critically on himself:

> Marilyn never wanted anything other than to be loved. She didn't ask for any of the fame and fortune, and didn't want it. She just wanted me to be there and believe her and support her. All I wanted is to be a superstar in everything, everything except family. I fucked up her life. Had she been married to the guy who owned the gas station, I don't think she would have had all the damn problems she had, and would have lived a happy life.

The children disagree.

"Mom was extremely proud of Dad," says Debbie. "Despite all of the ups and downs, they remained married and lived together for more than fifty-one years."

"Mom absolutely adored Dad, despite his flaws as a husband and father," Marci adds. "She allowed Daddy to be the 'showboat,' while she was relegated to merely an admirer instead of the 'copartner' that she was. Outsiders would see things differently and were constantly telling her how lucky she was, when in fact, Daddy was lucky to have her as not many women would put up with what she had to go through, but her love was strong and made us all the better for knowing and loving her. Daddy would have found it difficult to have a family and a lively practice if she had not given up part of her life for him. She was happy to do it and only wanted to have him for a 'little bit.' Fate intervened and at the time that she could have had him and he wanted a more sedentary life, it was not to be. Such is life and love!"

"Mom kept meticulous scrapbooks of every newspaper article, magazine article, and other accolade that mentioned Dad's name or showed his picture," Kim says. "She would keep small mementos such as matches or napkins from dinners, trips, and nights out, all pressed in scrapbooks in chronological order. When we found these dozens of scrapbooks shortly before Mom died, it was obvious that Mom had been keeping them not only before and after the times she suffered from severe alcohol and drug abuse, but also during the times when everyone believed her to be completely incapacitated."

It turns out that Marilyn was Fred's biggest fan, and he didn't even know it.

SEVEN

Perry Mason Moments

The oddities of litigation often make fact much stranger than fiction, especially the deeper the discovery process proceeds and the more witnesses who take the stand. Many of Fred Levin's cases are no exception.

One of the more bizarre cases Fred handled involved Robert Llewellyn and the Yum Yum Tree.

Marilyn had an affinity for supporting the rights and causes of gay men, which led Fred to take a case with a twisted ending, to say the least. In the early 1970s, a man named Robert Llewellyn opened a nightclub in Pensacola called Robbie's Yum Yum Tree. There was a seating area for straight people so that they could watch pairs of men dance together. At the time, this provided entertainment for straight people, much like going to the fair to watch the freak show. Everyone would laugh at two men slow-dancing, kissing, and pawing each other.

"Although it is now considered to be in vogue, back then gays were more despised here in the Bible Belt than black people," Fred says. "I remember feeling very similar at the time to the way I felt when George Starke came to the University of Florida law school. I felt their pain, but really at the start, I did nothing about it. Marilyn insisted that I show my support."

One night at the club, Marilyn persuaded Fred to leave the straight area and go down and mix with her hairdresser, Andy, and his friends. Andy was a tall, thin cross-dresser who looked incredibly beautiful in drag. If Andy had not died of AIDS in the early 1990s, his friends believed that he would have had the potential to become as famous as the celebrity cross-dresser RuPaul.

At the end of each evening at the Yum Yum Tree, the gay patrons gathered on the dance floor and sang together. This night, Fred and Marilyn joined them. Fred had consumed numerous Crown Royal Manhattans, so he agreed. "Although I don't remember much of the evening, I very much remember looking up at the straight community laughing at everyone on the dance floor, not laughing in a good way, but in a disgusting way," Fred says.

In July 1974, Robbie's Yum Yum Tree was destroyed by fire. Investigators ruled that it was a case of arson. The insurance company refused to pay, claiming that Llewellyn either set the fire or had someone do it to collect the money. Llewellyn came to Fred and asked him to represent the club against the insurance company. Fred took the case and sued the insurance company in federal court.

At the trial, it was clear there was a bias against homosexuals. "I can remember having to go to the judge and have him instruct opposing counsel —and even ask the judge himself—not to refer to the male witnesses that I was putting on the witness stand as 'Miss,'" Fred says. The jury found for the insurance carrier and against Llewellyn. Fred appealed to the Fifth Circuit Court of Appeals, which then took up the case. The court heard the case in 1977, and more of the same antigay sentiment surfaced.

At the opening of the appeals trial, Fred introduced himself to the court and stated that his name was Fred Levin and that he was married and had four children. The chief judge raised his eyebrows and stated, "In other words, you are not one of them." The entire courtroom burst into laughter. This included all of the court personnel, as well as Fred's opposing counsel. The gay jokes and innuendos continued throughout the hearing.

But this time the result was not affected. The Fifth Circuit Court of Appeals not only reversed the jury verdict, but actually granted judgment in Llewellyn's favor, rather than sending the case back for retrial. You would think this would have been one of the happiest days of Llewellyn's life, considering the amount of insurance coverage involved. Instead, in a bizarre set of circumstances, Llewellyn had been sentenced to life in prison just two months earlier.

Between the date of the fire at the Yum Yum Tree and the Fifth Circuit ruling, Llewellyn had moved to Atlanta and opened another club that catered to gay men. He found his new Atlanta club competing with another gay club owned by Peter Winokur. To squeeze out his competition, Llewellyn allegedly hired a man named Robert Larry Schneider to burn down Winokur's club. After Schneider twice failed to burn down the club, and after Llewellyn refused to pay Schneider for the failed arson attempts, Schneider claimed that Llewellyn hired him to kill Winokur.

Court records show that on February 19, 1976, Winokur was out of town buying a car in Florida. Schneider and two accomplices arrived at Winokur's house to wait for him to return home. There, they encountered two teenage men who were friends with Winokur and also awaiting his return from Florida. Schneider and his accomplices tied up the friends. When Winokur arrived at his house that night, he, too, was tied up. Shortly thereafter, Winokur and his friends were taken out into the woods and killed by Schneider and one of the accomplices.

Not long after the incident, Schneider and the two accomplices were arrested. Schneider, who was reportedly "saved" by his local church, confessed to the crime and detailed Llewellyn's role in the killings. The two accomplices corroborated Schneider's story. After the arrests, Llewellyn offered to provide for Schneider's family if Schneider agreed to take responsibility for the murders and refuse to testify against him (according to Schneider's trial testimony). Llewellyn, Schneider said, told Schneider to turn the tables and testify that Winokur had hired him to burn down Llewellyn's club, and that Schneider had murdered him when Winokur refused to pay him. Schneider didn't go along with the cover-up.

Llewellyn was subsequently convicted on three counts of murder and sentenced to life for each count. "The entire situation certainly brings into question who actually set the Yum Yum Tree on fire," Fred says. If he were so inclined, Fred could actually pursue the answer, as Robert Llewellyn was paroled from prison on October 21, 2013.

The next memorable case was the one that caused Fred's confidence in the legal system to significantly erode. For the first thirty years he practiced law, Fred had absolute confidence in the system. However Pollyannaish it was, his attitude toward law enforcement and government officials was that they were inherently good and trying to do the right thing. But this began changing over time.

The tipping point was the George Lane case. Though Fred had tried the case in the late 1980s, the final chapter wasn't written until 1995—and it was a dark one. Based in Atlanta, Lane was one of the highest-volume apartment building managers in the country, with some 10,000 buildings under his control. He was indicted for bribery and asked Fred and Leo Thomas, the top criminal defense lawyer in the firm (and likely in the state), to defend him. Fred had not worked on a criminal case since the early 1960s, but he accepted the challenge—provided he received the largest criminal-case fee ever paid in the area, which was $400,000.

The guts of the case were that two bank officials from First Mutual, including the bank's president, had pleaded guilty to accepting bribes from developers, for which they received twelve years in prison. Part of their plea deal was to turn over the names of everyone who had bribed them. One of the names they gave was George Lane's. Consequently, the federal government indicted Lane on twenty-five different counts. As Fred delved into the case, he discovered that all the other loans involved in the bribes had gone bad, but Lane's loans were current, meaning there was little reason for him to bribe anyone.

The case went to trial. One of the key witnesses was the president of the bank. He took the stand. As he began to testify, Fred realized that the dates on the documents were different from the ones the bank president was citing. Either the prosecution's star witness was lying, or the bribery had never occurred.

"I tore him up on cross-examination, and Lane was acquitted on all twenty-five counts," Fred says. "The loss by the United States government was so embarrassing for the US attorney that I thought the assistant US attorney prosecuting the case was going to be fired, though he wasn't."

Cut to 1995. The president of the bank, whose sentence had been reduced to five years for helping the government, came to see Fred at his office. He explained that he wasn't as stupid as Fred made him appear to be on the stand. He told Fred that the assistant US attorney had made his secretary white out some dates and change records, so when he took the stand, all the dates were off. Fred was stunned. He could not believe that a federal prosecutor would do this.

"My whole life I had put so much faith in the system and in government, especially the federal government," Fred says. "Hearing that the government had been cheating on a case that far back and learning how corporations had systematically ignored the safety of their workers—often with the government's knowledge—eroded my confidence in the system."

One of the most bizarre cases Fred took happened in New Orleans. The setup for the case was so incredibly strange that if someone put it in a work of fiction, no one would believe it. The fact that it occurred in the voodoo capital of the United States naturally added to its oddity.

The backstory: Roger Ogden Sr., a wealthy philanthropist whose name was on many buildings, notably the Ogden Museum, was chairman of the Higher Education Board for the State of Louisiana. His son, Roger Jr., attended medical school at Harvard University, returned to New Orleans, married a local TV news anchor, and began his residency at Louisiana State University School of Medicine in New Orleans.

Another New Orleans resident, Carl Muckley, fell in love with and married a bartender named Michelle Iles after he had a couple of unsuccessful marriages. Carl, a retiree, attended the University of New Orleans (coincidentally one of the schools under Ogden's chairmanship) and became friends with several philosophy professors.

In 2002, Carl Muckley made out a will leaving $600,000 to his wife, Michelle Iles, and the rest of his estate—about $150,000 at the time—to the university. The following year, Muckley's mother died and left him about $5 million. Muckley realized that he was now worth almost $6 million and needed to change his will, or his wife would only receive $600,000 and the university would receive $5.4 million. He contacted a lawyer who drafted a will that would give $200,000 to the university system, $400,000 to relatives, and the balance of the estate, almost $5.4 million, to Iles.

One afternoon, Muckley and Iles got in their car and went to sign the will. They were driving westbound on Interstate 10. Roger Ogden Jr. was traveling eastbound. He had just left LSU Medical School and was en route to attend a seminar at LSU's medical school in Shreveport. The young doctor apparently fell asleep. His car crossed the median and struck Muckley and Iles' car. Muckley was killed; Iles was seriously injured. A beautiful woman, she was crippled and suffered not only brain damage, but also permanent double vision that required her to wear an eye patch.

"Her noneconomic losses would have been incredible," Fred says. "But the state said she should get only $500,000, because Ogden was a state employee on the job and state law limits noneconomic losses to $500,000 if the case involves a state employee on state business."

Here was the great irony. According to the will in force at the time of his death, the bulk of Muckley's estate—more than $5 million—would go to the same state university system that employed the man who caused the fatal crash. And Michelle would receive only $600,000.

Fred worked the case with his law partner Virginia Buchanan and Pat Kehoe of New Orleans. When the state offered to waive the jury trial, he objected. But Kehoe convinced Fred that a bench trial would be fine because the judge would be fair. Buchanan effectively presented the medical testimony and outlined the future medical costs. The total for Iles' medical care was estimated at $5 million, which the court awarded.

Fred's task was to focus on the economic losses. "Fortunately, the economist for the state was a plaintiff's dream from the minute he rolled up in his Porsche," Fred says. "He had been called into more than 5,000 personal injury and wrongful death cases in his career. He was dressed in a custom-tailored suit. He presented facts and figures that directly supported everything the defense had said, but then on cross-examination, he completely contradicted everything he said and made the opposite case. By the time he stepped down from the witness stand, his testimony was so ridiculous that his effectiveness as a defense economic expert was decimated. I really made a fool of him."

The judgment proved Fred right. The judge ordered the state to pay almost $30 million. (Incidentally, the state was allowed to keep the $5.4 million that was in the will before Carl Muckley could change it.) Fred and his team were able to show that Michelle Iles was due nearly $30 million due to past and future medical costs and from the huge loss of support that she would have received from the money she did not inherit—though eventually the appeals court reduced the verdict to about half the amount.

Another peculiar case Fred worked involved a lawsuit against the estate of Howard Hughes. The case started when Fred's law partner Lefferts

Mabie took a call one day from an attorney in Alabama who represented a young man and his sister. The two siblings claimed to be the adopted children of Hughes, easily one of the world's richest people in his heyday. Hughes had died a recluse in 1976 without leaving a will, and these two claimed to be his children and therefore entitled to a portion of his estate.

Their grounds for a share of the Hughes wealth centered on an Alabama law of "equitable adoption," which states that if a man left the impression that he was the child's father, then he was indeed the father. This opened the door for their claim, but the case was extremely complicated. For starters, Hughes had no will and, being a secretive man, left no records that could prove these were his adopted children.

"We had some evidence that Hughes would say to others that these were his children," Fred says. "If we proved it, they would have inherited the entire estate. In the end, rather than take a risk, the estate settled and gave the children 9 percent."

The Levin firm's legal fee was 1 percent. Even to this day, almost three decades later, Fred continues to receive small sums of money arising out of Hughes' ownerships.

"I used to enjoy walking through the Fashion Show Mall in Las Vegas joking that Howard and I shared ownership," Fred says. "Never in my craziest thoughts did I ever think one day I would be sharing in his estate."

Then there was one that Fred let get away, but he still tells the story. A few months before NFL great Johnny Unitas died, he came to see Fred about filing suit against the NFL because of a severe arm impairment caused by his professional football career. By then Unitas had been relegated to earning a living solely by signing autographs—ironic considering his nickname was "the Golden Arm."

"To watch him sign an autograph, he had to put the pencil or pen in the middle of his forefingers because his thumb was so damaged," Fred says. "It was obviously painful for him and painful for anyone who was watching. Here was an icon, one of the greatest football players of all times. I always admired him, and won some money betting on him. He now could barely sign his name."

Though Unitas told Fred that he had never received any compensation from the NFL or anyone else for his condition, Fred advised him not to pursue a lawsuit.

"I made a terrible mistake telling Johnny that I did not think that a lawsuit against the NFL would be of any benefit to him," Fred says. "He died a few months after this. As I look back at our conversation, it would have been an incredible amount of publicity had I filed the lawsuit back before any of these concussion suits. I also could have at least provided Johnny a sense of hope in his final months. To this day, I regret my advice to him."

During the conversation, Fred asked Unitas how much money he made during his top NFL days. Though Unitas was the league's MVP three times and is routinely listed as one of the greatest quarterbacks of all time, he had only earned $100,000 in his best year. Compare this to one of today's highest-paid quarterbacks, Joe Flacco, who plays in the same city that Unitas did and earns $20.1 million a year.

"Unitas and I talked about how painfully his arm, hand, and body ached, and I asked him about his thoughts as to whether it was worth it," Fred says.

As Unitas was leaving Fred's office, he turned and said to Fred that regardless of what the NFL had taken from him physically, there was one thing it could never take. He said that every time he entered Baltimore's football stadium, the announcer said, "Ladies and gentlemen, Mr. Johnny Unitas," and the entire stadium stood and cheered.

Unitas smiled. "They can't take that away from me," he said.

EIGHT

Wheeling and
Dealing Justice

All trial lawyers have war stories about their big cases, win or lose. One of Fred's biggest dollar wins came in the 1993 case of *Doc Hollingsworth v. Southeast Toyota*, which happened in Okaloosa County, Florida.

Southeast Toyota was owned by Jim Moran, a Chicago-based car dealer who was one of the first in the United States to realize the value of Toyotas. In 1968, he entered into an agreement with Toyota to import its cars into the port in Jacksonville and distribute them in Florida, Alabama, and North and South Carolina. His company would clean up the cars and then deliver them to the various dealers in those states. Toyota set a limited markup of $300 to $400 per car.

As consumers began to demand more fuel-efficient cars, Toyotas became hot commodities. Dealers were able to sell every unit they could get their hands on, and there were long waiting lists for the cars. To maximize profits, Moran started a financing company for both dealers and consumers. He also began putting different aftermarket additions such as pinstriping or rust protection onto the cars and charged for them.

Moran also devised a plan to incentivize dealers. The plan dictated that the more Toyotas a dealer sold in a given period, the more cars that dealer would earn from the next shipment from Japan. It was called "turn to earn"—you turn the cars, you earn more.

Southeast Toyota then began supplying additional cars to dealers who used its financing for the cars and their customers, and to those who would accept the most aftermarket additions. If a dealer took part in all the options Southeast Toyota offered, Moran would make $1,000 per car instead of $300. To make this work, Moran needed records that showed he was doing what he said he was doing, which was giving the cars to the dealer who turned them most quickly.

Moran came up with a false reporting scheme. It worked like this: The dealers who utilized all of Southeast Toyota's incentive programs would receive fifty cars, and those dealers would then report all of them sold in two days. Because they turned the cars, they earned more.

A Toyota dealer in Fort Walton Beach named Dr. Gerald "Doc" Hollingsworth refused to play Moran's game. Because of this, he was frozen out and received very few Toyotas. He hired Fred to sue Southeast Toyota. Fred turned the case over to his son-in-law Ross Goodman, the head of the commercial litigation department at the Levin firm. Goodman spent many of the next years devoting thousands of hours and hundreds of thousands of dollars to working up the case for trial. The first count of his multi-count case against Moran was for breach of contract, because Moran had a signed contract with each dealership that said Southeast Toyota would distribute cars based on the number sold. There was also a law known as Automobile Dealer's Day in Court. Due to the imbalance of power between either manufacturer and distributor or distributor and dealer, this law had been passed to allow the little guy to bring an action against the big guy. Goodman also asked for punitive damages, claiming that Moran had no intention of fulfilling the contract, which constituted fraud.

Hollingsworth's closest competitor was a wheeler-dealer in Pensacola named Ron Samuels. Goodman had the firm's investigators take aerial shots of the two dealerships. On one particular day, Hollingsworth's dealership had four Toyotas while Samuels' had two hundred. "It was clear to us that Southeast Toyota was starving Doc for cars, because he wouldn't use Moran's financing scheme and buy the aftermarket additions," Fred says.

During the discovery stage, the firm determined that Southeast Toyota had a terrible reputation. It had been sued by other dealers sixteen times and had received reams of bad publicity about bribes, document destruction, and coercion. In a 1992 South Carolina case, the company was ordered to pay $13.5 million in damages, in a trial in which Southeast Toyota's attorney was fined for contempt of court. The judge in that case said that Southeast Toyota had tried "to sabotage the trial before it began." He pointed to an unsolicited $10,000 donation that the company gave to a local school district where the jury pool lived.

Goodman discovered that in the South Carolina case, after the company was sued and realized the consequences of its schemes being found out, it bought a huge document shredder to destroy the incriminating files. The Levin firm investigators then tracked down one of the low-level employees involved in the shredding. The man gave a somewhat comical description of the process.

The employee said that the shredder, which cost $25,000, was placed in the airplane hangar where the company plane was parked. Over the course of two days, trucks went back and forth from the Southeast Toyota offices to collect boxes of documents. There were so many documents that the shredder kept clogging. "We were throwing whole banker boxes into it and the metal clasps would clog it up," the man explained. "To unclog it, we would walk into the shredder—that's how big it was—with a hammer and a screwdriver and unjam it."

As the case got closer to trial, Fred became actively involved in the discovery process (as he did with most of his cases) in preparation for serving as lead counsel during the actual trial. Fred chose to take the deposition of Jim Moran. Fred describes Moran as a wily character who tried to get into Fred's head during depositions. Though the two had never met, Moran seemed to know quite a bit about Fred and his family. "I was taking his deposition and he turned and asked, 'How's Marci doing?'" Fred recalls. "I said, 'She's doing well.' Then he asked, 'How are Brenton and Jackie?' Those were her children, my grandchildren. Then later he asked, 'Why do you drive a Mercedes when you could drive a Toyota?'"

But the kicker came when Moran told Fred he didn't have nearly as much money as Fred believed. Fred laughed. He told Moran that he had seen his 140-foot yacht, *Gallant Lady*, that day on the Intracoastal Waterway.

Moran laughed. "You think you can win this case?" he asked.

Fred said that he could.

"You win this case, and you, Ross, and Marci get a week on *Gallant Lady*," Moran said.

Fred laughed him off.

The only people less popular than plaintiff's lawyers are car dealers, but even they deserve their day in court.

One of the subplots that arose during the Southeast Toyota trial was that Fred and his colleagues had been trying to get hold of the financial records from Hollingsworth's closest competitor, Ron Samuels, whose dealership was in Pensacola. This would tell them how many cars Samuels was receiving. But Samuels' lawyer convinced the judge that the records contained too much proprietary information to turn them over to a competitor.

Then Fred and his team caught a break. In the middle of the trial, Southeast Toyota called a witness who started talking about Samuels' financials. The witness testified that Samuels was a model dealer and that was why he received so many cars. The witness said that his profits outstripped everyone else's because he was such a sophisticated businessman.

In a sidebar, or conference with the judge, Fred objected that Southeast Toyota couldn't have it both ways. Fred pointed out that the judge had given Samuels the benefit of not providing the records, so therefore they should not be able to discuss them in court. The judge agreed. Instead of dealing with Samuels and his lawyers, the judge ordered Southeast Toyota to produce the records.

The records arrived late one afternoon. Bobby Loehr and Bobby Blanchard, two partners in the law firm who were working the case with Fred and Goodman, spent most of the night poring over them to prepare to cross-examine the witness the following day.

There had been rumors for years that Ron Samuels was a crook and that he had been involved in the drug trade in South Florida before he moved to Pensacola and opened the car dealership. Loehr and Blanchard soon concluded those rumors might be true. They noticed something odd about the financial statements. There would be an entry for the number of Camrys sold in a particular month, say twenty. Then there would be an entry for sales of twenty Camrys for $400,000. After that was an entry for net profits, which was $380,000—meaning that Samuels was claiming he only paid $20,000 for 20 cars. "It appeared fairly obvious that he must be laundering money," Loehr says. "Once the figures were tallied, it came to more than $600,000 in a year."

Fred couldn't accuse Samuels of money laundering in open court, but he could use this information to his advantage. The other way to look at those numbers, if Samuels was not money laundering, was that it was only possible for Samuels to make $380,000 for twenty cars from a $400,000 gross profit if Samuels was being given the cars by Southeast Toyota.

The next day, when the head of Southeast Toyota's accounting department took the stand, Fred asked if Southeast Toyota was giving cars to Samuels in a last-ditch effort to drive Hollingsworth out of business because Hollingsworth was a whistleblower and he wouldn't buy after-market products. The woman didn't know what to say when Fred showed her the financial records obtained by Loehr and Blanchard.

Fred pointed out that the only obvious explanation was that not only was Southeast Toyota providing more cars to his client's closest competitor than he deserved, but they were also giving them to him for free. The Southeast Toyota accountant couldn't come up with any other explanation in court, leaving the jury to accept Fred's.

In an effort to show that Southeast Toyota was on the up-and-up, the company brought in several district managers to testify. Rather than the stereotypical hustler in a shiny suit with slicked-back hair, they were all clean cut.

Fred buttonholed one of them. He asked how much the man was earning. The guy said he was being paid $350,000 a year. Fred pointed out that was a sizeable amount for a district manager. How much, Fred asked, had the man earned in his previous job? The man answered he had been making an equivalent amount. Fred wondered where that was. When the man answered that he had worked at a Toyota dealership in Decatur, Georgia, a red flag went up.

Again, Fred called a sidebar. He asked the judge for the weekend so he could call the dealership in Decatur and verify the salary, because it seemed rather high for a car dealer in a city of just 17,000 people. The judge granted the request. And so on Saturday, Fred sent Blanchard and a court reporter to Decatur.

It turned out the guy had been making $42,000—and thus had perjured himself when he testified that he was earning $350,000. Fred put the man back on the stand on Monday, and the guy tried to wiggle out of it. But the difference was so vast, the jury didn't believe a word he said.

The most difficult part of the trial was the damages phase. Provided the jury agreed Southeast Toyota was guilty, it needed to assign actual and possibly even punitive damages to deter others from the same behavior. The actual damages presented something of a quagmire for both sides. Fred had to somehow prove that Doc Hollingsworth would have sold the cars had they been allocated to his dealership. Conversely, Southeast Toyota wanted to show that Hollingsworth wouldn't have sold most of the cars anyway, and therefore the damages were minimal.

As with other fields, there was a cottage industry of experts in the auto industry. These were econometricians, economists who used elaborate mathematical models to calculate damages and charged out-landish sums for their work. The Levin firm ended up spending close to $1 million to put together a damage model for the jury. The defense did the same.

The defense's main expert lived in Park City, Utah. He was handsome and well-spoken. Before trial, he had testified in his deposition that he had been a professor of economics at a prestigious East Coast university. He was now teaching at a small college in rural Utah. When Fred asked him why he had moved, the professor answered that his wife wanted to be closer to her mother, who was ill.

Fred sent his investigator to the East Coast university to check out the story. The investigators did some digging and found out that the man had been arrested for stealing computers and dismissed from the university faculty. Though the records were sealed, the investigators interviewed witnesses close to the situation who spilled the beans.

When the professor took the stand, Fred repeated his line of question-ing from the deposition, and the man gave the same responses. Fred then asked the jury to be sent out before he exposed the man so that the judge wouldn't declare a mistrial. The two sides argued for some time whether the stolen computers and the firing were admissible.

"The entire time, the professor sat in the witness chair, sweating and watching his career go down the drain," Loehr remembers. "The judge didn't allow it to come in, but the guy's confidence was shattered. He mumbled his way through the rest of his testimony."

The closing argument was the most theatrical part of the trial. Fred had pretty much boxed Southeast Toyota into a corner. He began by looping back to Jim Moran himself. In 1984, Moran had been in trouble with the IRS. He had been accused of tax fraud. To prevent authorities from arresting him, Moran sailed one of his yachts to the Bahamas and stayed there on the boat while his lawyers wrangled with the IRS. When the charges were eventually settled, Moran returned to the United States.

"We had asked him about the IRS case in deposition," Loehr recalls. "Moran said that it was a very odd thing. He said, 'I developed these cancers that sprung up all over my body and I went to the Bahamas to get medical care.'"

Fred was able to establish relevancy and bring the story in at trial. Though it was obvious that Moran had likely been evading taxes, Fred couldn't accuse him of that, so he came up with something better.

At the beginning of his closing argument, Fred placed the documents about the vehicle sales, which had been blown up onto foam boards, on an easel for the jury to see, but just out of view of the defense. In the upper right-hand corner, the documents had the VINs listed for the sold vehicles. Because the number of sold vehicles was fake, the lines where the VINs of the sold vehicles were supposed to be listed had the notation "999." Fred purposefully placed the foam boards upside down—so the numbers appeared as 666, the numerical representation of the Antichrist.

Fred then launched into a story. "Let's look at how we got here," he told the jury. "Jim Moran received life-altering news. He had cancers that popped up all over his body. He can't have but months to live. So he goes off on his yacht to live out his last few days in the Bahamas. And what happens? No one really knows what happened on that boat, but he was miraculously cured."

Fred gestured dramatically toward the 666, and then continued. "Jim Moran returned to the United States, and things started to line up in his favor. There was a fuel crisis that sent Toyota sales through the roof, and Jim Moran is the number one Toyota importer. People can't get enough Toyotas, and Jim Moran becomes a billionaire."

Again, Fred gestured at the satanic numerology. Then he flipped the board over and continued with the facts of the case.

Loehr couldn't believe his boss got away with the devil reference. "I was a young lawyer turning five shades of purple thinking we are all going to jail," he says.

Throughout the closing, Fred painted Moran in the worst possible light. At one point, he said: "Lucky Luciano controlled the unions and because of that he ran the harbors in New York during World War II. When there were rumors that German U-boats were coming in, he turned over his thugs to the military to help defend New York. Lucky Luciano was more of a patriot than Jim Moran."

Southeast Toyota's lawyer, Ray Bergan, was a hotshot from Washington, DC, who had once represented Teamster boss Jimmy Hoffa. Bergan was head of the civil litigation division for one of America's great law firms, Williams & Connolly. Fred recalled Bergan as being not only a terrific lawyer, but a true professional whose ethics were beyond reproach.

Bergan towered over the courtroom, standing 6 feet 5 inches and talking like a boisterous Irishman. But even Bergan apparently realized that his client ran a sketchy operation. At the beginning of his closing statement, Bergan stood up, lumbered toward the jury, and stood face to face with them. "Let me tell you something," he told the jury with authority. "I'm Raymond Bergan from Washington, DC, and I am proud to be here representing Southeast Toyota. I'll tell you why. Because everybody deserves a defense." It was, to say the least, not a ringing endorsement.

The jury came back after ten hours of deliberations with a $42 million verdict against Southeast Toyota—$25 million of which was punitive damages. There were five other similar cases pending against Moran, and Fred and Ross Goodman took them all on. They ended up settling all the cases, as well as reaching an agreement on the Hollingsworth case to avoid a lengthy appeal.

Six months after the trial, Moran's lawyer called Fred and asked when he would like to use the yacht. Fred was shocked. He had won an embarrassing punitive damage award and extracted a sizeable settlement from Southeast Toyota, and Moran was still going to let him use his yacht? For Moran, a promise was a promise. So Fred and several friends flew on Moran's corporate jet to the Bahamas and spent several days partying on *Gallant Lady*. Afterward Moran and Fred stayed in occasional contact,

The $42 million win against Southeast Toyota makes headlines.

with Moran inviting Fred as a guest on his yachts on several additional occasions, which Fred happily accepted. On one occasion, Fred dined with the president of Southeast Toyota, and the two shared stories of the trial.

Moran died in 2007, with a net worth listed at $2.4 billion by *Forbes*. At that time, he was distributing 20 percent of all Toyotas sold in the United States. His checkered reputation remained to the end. Bergan, the Washington lawyer, died of stomach cancer. Throughout his life, Bergan attended Mass on a daily basis. The president of Moran's car empire quipped, "I used to tell him it was because of the clients he had." For his part, after Bergan was diagnosed with stomach cancer, he shot back, "I told you your company was going to give me an ulcer, and that's what you've done."

But that was nothing compared to what happened to Ron Samuels, the apparent money-laundering dealer. In 1997, Samuels hired a hit man to kill his ex-wife, who was then living in South Florida with her new husband (whose father was a part-owner of the Minnesota Vikings). Samuels and his ex-wife were involved in a custody battle over their three young children. Samuels lost the battle, and was ordered to pay past and future child support. Samuels then hired the hit man, but the guy botched the job, instead leaving her paralyzed below the neck.

Samuels fled to Mexico. The FBI became aware of his whereabouts and notified the Mexican police. When the Mexican police went to arrest Samuels, he possessed six kilos of cocaine. The Mexican police placed him in jail and refused to extradite him to the United States. Samuels remained in jail in Mexico from 1998 to 2005, when he was sent to Florida to face charges of attempted murder. After a lengthy trial, Samuels was convicted and sentenced to life in prison.

Samuels' story became the subject of a *Dateline NBC* piece that aired in 2008. Unfortunately for Fred, his part in the twisted tale was not in the piece—causing him to miss out on the type of publicity that he loved.

From Barbecue to BLAB TV: Birth of an Entrepreneur

Success in the courtroom allowed Fred to pivot into other businesses. He wasn't afraid to try anything. He had an entrepreneurial mind, and inasmuch as his verdicts separated him from other lawyers, he hoped his fearlessness would distinguish him in business. However, he does admit that his favorite businesses centered on bolstering him as a personality.

"I've always been a closet entrepreneur," Fred says. "I love doing business, probably a trait I inherited from my father."

Fred's father started with a pawnshop in downtown Pensacola, and he went on to establish numerous businesses, including running the concessions at Pensacola Greyhound Track. Fred and his brothers all worked at the businesses from time to time. At the young age of eleven, Fred worked in his father's pawnshop. By the time he turned thirteen, Fred was actually in charge of loaning money when his father was not there.

"As remote as it may sound, this had a tremendous influence on my eventual success," he says. "After I had been working at my father's pawnshop for a few years, I could almost guarantee that when someone came into the store, before they said a word I would know a lot about their life. Reading people was a trait that served me well."

After Fred had made substantial money practicing law, he started looking for businesses to own. As much as he loved the law, Fred could never have been content with a single vocation. This led to him teaming up with relatives and friends, such as his old college roommate Fred Vigodsky and "Papa Don" Schroeder, who was a very successful disc jockey in Pensacola in the 1950s and 1960s, radio's heyday. Papa Don Schroeder was also a Grammy-winning music producer. During the 1960s and 1970s, he produced several records for rock 'n' roll acts, notably "Everlasting Love" by Carl Carlton and "I'm Your Puppet" by James & Bobby Purify, both of which peaked at Number 6 on the *Billboard* Hot 100 chart.

Things started small. Fred and his brother David, along with an accountant named Bill McAbee, bought a stake in Chick's Barbecue, a popular restaurant on the outskirts of Pensacola. The only thing they knew about barbecue was how to eat it, but they dove in. Things were going well when Fred Vigodsky called from South Carolina and said he was looking for a job.

"Fred set me up in more ways than one in 1964 when I wanted to leave my family's ladies' apparel business," Vigodsky recalls. "I called him and said I needed a job. Fred had just bought a share in Chick's Barbecue, and he said I could run the business."

Vigodsky arrived on a Friday night. Traffic in the area around the restaurant was backed up for blocks in all directions. That day, Papa Don was doing his radio broadcast from Chick's, and 1,000 people had shown up. Vigodsky couldn't believe his luck. The parking lot was full of kids listening to Papa Don. Inside, the cooks were slathering ribs as fast as the waitresses could serve them. He was sure he was being put in charge of the hottest restaurant in town.

"I thought to myself, 'My buddy Fred has come through and found a gold mine for me,'" Vigodsky says. "Only later did I realize that Friday was the busiest night, especially with Papa Don there, and Fred had picked a Friday night to show me the place." On Monday night, after Papa Don had returned to the studio, the restaurant was deserted.

But to his credit, Vigodsky didn't turn around and go home. He hung in and managed Chick's, which eventually turned into a moneymaker and was expanded. With Papa Don, the group delved into nightclubs, produced records and Christian music concerts, and started CNN Radio in Pensacola. They then added their coup de grace, a chain of women's dress stores called Sam's Style Shops.

Fred bought Sam's Style Shops in partnership with his brother David and Fred Vigodsky, who ran the company. They each put up $100 and borrowed the rest from the bank. Sam's turned out to be a bigger gold mine than Chick's first location. The original store was downtown, but they soon opened another store in the Cordova Mall in Pensacola. Business downtown jumped 20 percent, and the mall store was soon earning more than the first location.

Because business was booming, Sam's went into expansion mode. Stores were opened in malls in Clearwater, Florida; Mobile, Alabama; Macon, Georgia; and Memphis, Tennessee. Vigodsky then expanded the business into discount ladies' apparel. At their peak, they built up the company to fifty-three stores, from Dallas to Savannah to Fort Lauderdale, under three different names—Sam's, David Fredric's, and Brenda Allen.

"I must admit, I never pictured myself in the ladies' dress business, but in its heyday, it was very profitable," Fred says. "Interestingly, we were partners with a small buying group. We were far and away the largest operation in the group. There was a lot of talk about not only joining forces in buying, but also forming a company for retail operations." But they didn't. "Another terrible mistake on our part. Today, our former partner Elliot Jaffe's four small stores, known as the Dress Barn, is one of the largest women's retail apparel operations in the world. I sometimes wonder how I can miss so many moneymaking opportunities."

By far the most interesting, most complicated, and most controversial business Fred started was BLAB-TV, a local cable access channel. The idea for BLAB came to Fred in Las Vegas in 1984. After losing his limit at the craps table and then drinking too much, he retired to his room for the night. He was watching a TV show about talk radio, which was just taking off.

"This made me wonder what would happen if we had a local talk television station," he says. "What if lawyers went on the air and talked about the law and problems people have understanding the law? Aside from being interesting to the viewer, this made perfect sense to me as a marketing tool, because the firm was constantly searching for creative ways to make ourselves known at a time when there were fairly strict rules against advertising for lawyers, doctors, and other professionals."

Fred returned to Pensacola and presented the idea to his law partners. Most of them agreed the channel could be educational, and they all saw the upside for the firm. The timing was perfect. In 1984, the US Supreme Court ruled that cable companies, then in their infancy, were required to carry a certain amount of local broadcasting.

Fred called Larry Lewis, manager of the Cox Cable Company. Lewis needed more local shows to meet his mandate to provide topics of local interest. This enabled Fred to secure channel 6 on the dial, meaning that his channel was surrounded by ABC, NBC, and CBS. He also ran the idea by W. D. Childers, the state Senate president, who felt it would be good to have another medium for politicians to communicate their messages.

BLAB-TV was born. The station started in a small, nondescript building; now BLAB has modern offices and a state-of-the-art studio in downtown Pensacola. It revolutionized advertising in the area. BLAB was more affordable than most television, and the call-in format made it very interactive for anyone—attorneys, political candidates, gardeners, car buffs—who wanted to talk directly with the audience.

Vigodsky, who knew as much about TV as he did about barbecue, was put in charge. One of the first camera operators was a local high school

Roy Jones Jr., Sugar Ray Leonard, and Fred talk boxing on BLAB-TV.

student named Emmitt Smith, who later became the NFL's all-time leading rusher.

BLAB's top show was *Law Line*. The one-hour program, broadcast five nights a week during prime time, featured lawyers from Fred's firm dispensing free legal advice to callers. Fred hosted the most popular edition of *Law Line* on Wednesday night. The show developed a devoted following, both among people who liked Fred and among those who didn't. There was a fascination with Fred in the community—something like the feeling of seeing a Ferrari speed past and then hoping it crashes—and he capitalized on it. Critics called the station a running ad for the Levin firm, which, in many ways, it was.

For Fred, it was a pure marketing tool. "The legal business is all about marketing," he says. "Marketing is nothing more than convincing people of a position—whether it be convincing a jury that your side is right or convincing a TV viewer who has been wronged to call your firm."

BLAB underscored that Fred's personal marketing prowess was one of the reasons for the animosity toward him. People couldn't figure out how he was winning so many cases. Some wanted to believe he was cheating. Naturally, he encouraged them to spread that around. "I loved for my opponent to take a cheap shot at my client or me," he says. "I have always been a master at taking it and shoving it up their butt, which is pretty much what happened when I got myself in hot water over comments I made on BLAB."

Over the course of several shows in 1984, Fred criticized doctors' behavior and their ethics as part of his opposition to a proposed Florida constitutional amendment limiting awards in malpractice lawsuits. Doctors claimed that the lower awards would keep medical costs down, but Fred found that hypocritical at minimum, fraudulent at worst.

Fred colorfully pointed out that several doctors he knew had placed their assets in their wives' names. "The doctor sits back and laughs and says, 'I don't have anything. My $300,000 income per year is protected. My $4 million net worth, my Porsche and Mercedes, are in sweetie's name,'" Fred said on the air. He then said that he was waiting for those doctors to divorce so his brother David could handle the action on behalf of the wife and claim all of the assets.

Fred also pointed out that in his experience, doctors often ordered ten times the number of tests needed because they had ten times the equipment needed in the hospitals, and somebody had to pay for it. This easily hit home with viewers who had gone through medical issues. He also talked about the "conspiracy of silence" that kept doctors from testifying against one another. But the tipping point came when he said on the air that "some doctors have this God complex, think they are above the law, above lawyers for certain, and even above their patients."

As if to validate Fred's point, the constitutional amendment limiting malpractice awards was knocked down by the Florida Supreme Court— before it was even put to a vote in the legislature.

"My experiences with the medical profession had led me to become highly skeptical of its practices," Fred says. "My brother had died of leukemia at seventeen, and in a later case I handled, I discovered that one of the drugs he was taking, Chloromycetin, caused leukemia in certain situations. My wife's gastrointestinal illness, which doctors were declaring was mental, remained a mystery at the time, but I now know that was misdiagnosed, and it ended up causing her to self-medicate with excessive alcohol and drugs. The medical profession even failed to inform my brother Allen, my closest friend at the time, that he had a spot on his lungs that needed further diagnosis. Despite continuing to seek medical treatment regarding a chronic cough, and this being part of his doctor's records, the doctor never told him about the need for further diagnosis. By the time further testing was performed, one year later, it was too late. He died of lung cancer, even though he had not smoked in more than twenty years."

Fred certainly wasn't popular in medical circles. He had recently won a $10 million settlement in a case against a local hospital. In the case, the hospital transferred a one-year-old child from one room to another and failed to plug in her regulator for thirty-five minutes. Because she suffered from a rare disease that gradually paralyzed her muscles, she was irreparably harmed by the negligence. Like the *Thorshov* case, this one also involved a structured settlement. The $3.2 million settlement would be paid out over twenty years, bringing the total amount the victim received to $10 million.

The Escambia County Medical Society took exception to Fred's comments on BLAB. Actually, they went ballistic. The society asked a bureaucratic organization with the overwrought name of the Medical-Legal Interprofessional Relations Committee to hold a public hearing to determine if Fred had violated its code of conduct for doctors and lawyers. Their goal was to remove Fred from the local Bar Association.

"It was outlandish," Fred says. "For starters, I was the first person who had ever faced charges from the committee for exercising my right to free speech." The committee actually had no power to do anything beyond making a recommendation to the local Bar Association. "Even if they threw me out, it wouldn't have mattered to me because all the group did was meet every three months for drinks," he adds.

The hearing was like a kangaroo court. Fred's partner D. L. Middlebrooks, the former US district judge, defended him. Middlebrooks started by declaring that because no one would name Fred's accuser, he was inherently being denied due process. He also correctly stated that if the medical society was going to act in conjunction with the Bar Association to punish Fred, then they were violating antitrust laws, which amounted to a civil conspiracy.

At the hearing, Fred had plenty to say. He defended his First Amendment right to make the statements and mocked the process. "Now maybe the medical society tomorrow will be able to get all the people in the country together and pass an amendment that says you've got a right to speak and say whatever you want to, except about the medical society," Fred said.

The core issue was the proposed Florida constitutional amendment that would have limited malpractice awards. Fred maintained that doctors misled voters by telling them that the law would reduce medical costs even though they had no intention of lowering them. "That's a fraud, that's misleading," he told the hearing. "And it's not just me saying that . . . it's seven justices on the Florida Supreme Court that say that's a fraud and deceptive."

"The whole thing was a witch hunt and an example of doctors trashing a lawyer they didn't like," he says. "I also recounted one doctor making racist, sexist comments in a speech at a civic club. The doctor told the audience that plaintiff's lawyers attempted to seat juries who couldn't understand complex issues, notably blacks, Catholics, and divorced women."

Fred concluded the hearing by declaring: "I think the medical society needs to take a long hard look at itself. If anyone should be reprimanded tonight, it shouldn't be me."

In the end, the commission issued a lame report that meant nothing and went nowhere. But the result was that Fred Levin had again pissed off the Establishment, and they didn't forget it.

Years later, BLAB played an integral role in Joe Scarborough being elected to the US Congress. Scarborough, a lawyer in Pensacola at the time, began hosting a show on BLAB in the 1990s, but he didn't use it to promote his law practice or answer callers' questions about legal matters. He spent his time interviewing politicians and celebrities.

"I told him, 'You've got to do a law show if you're going to get law business,'" Fred recalls.

But Scarborough wasn't interested in attracting clients. He was building a base for his 1994 campaign. During the campaign, Scarborough ran his political shows at all hours of the day and night. He bought very little prime time, but instead focused on repeats. Fred thought Scarborough had no chance of being elected until his brother Stanley told him that he had polled the people in his poker game and found that four out of five planned to vote for Scarborough. They liked the platform he had presented on BLAB. Sure enough, Scarborough (who ran as a Republican) was elected to Florida's First Congressional District.

Scarborough entered Congress as part of the Republican Contract with America platform led by Newt Gingrich, and he quickly climbed in popularity and prestige among the conservative base. He was reelected with 72 percent of the vote in 1996, and ran unopposed in 1998 and 2000. He received a 95 percent lifetime rating from the American Conservative Union, and many insiders believed he was working toward a vice presidential nomination or the Florida governorship.

In 2001, however, Scarborough came to Fred and declared that he was going to give up his Congressional seat in the middle of his term. "I told him I thought he was making a big mistake, that he should at least finish his term," Fred says. "But Joe said it was a matter of money, and he asked to join our firm."

Scarborough publicly announced that he was resigning in order to spend more time with his children, but Fred always wondered if Scarborough had reached a point where he no longer could politically support the extreme conservative movement, given that Scarborough's true ideology

Fred comments as homegrown Pensacola congressman Joe Scarborough shakes hands with Governor Lawton Chiles.

seemed to Fred much more moderate or even liberal leaning. Fred points out that Scarborough had two pieces of artwork hanging on his wall in his office at the Levin firm. One was of Robert F. Kennedy and the other was of Martin Luther King Jr.

After Scarborough stepped down from Congress, the firm hired him. "Unfortunately, it proved that an ex-politician has absolutely zero power as a rainmaker for litigation," Fred says. "An ex-politician may be helpful to a law firm in lobbying and government work, but not for the type of litigation we do. It wasn't just Joe Scarborough. The same thing happened to Reubin Askew when he returned to practice after serving as governor of Florida."

Scarborough soon switched firms to Beggs & Lane, Fred's longtime rival. Not long afterward, he moved into television. He found huge success, and now hosts the MSNBC program *Morning Joe*, which consistently beats CNN in total viewers. "He's far better on TV than he was hustling up clients," Fred says. "I believe *Morning Joe* is the best morning show on television." In 2011, *Time* named Scarborough one of the 100 most influential people in the world.

Fred was quick to come up with ideas for businesses, and he had plenty of them. But he often didn't follow through.

"I would have been ideal working at one of the large ad agencies because I can sell," he says. "I can come up with an idea and sell it. BLAB was one of the first reality TV channels in the country. Imagine if I would have put together an experienced team and gone national with it. As great as I was at throwing out the idea and funding it, I always let somebody else run with the ball. Had I been better at follow-through, I could have been a billionaire."

Several ambitious ideas never got off the ground. One was a proposal to create a mixed martial arts sanctioning body, which would have been named the World Alliance of Mixed Martial Arts, or WAMMA for short. Mixed martial arts features competitors from various martial arts and Olympic sports, including karate, jiu-jitsu, tae kwon do, kickboxing, and judo. However, it had no unifying body, so there were hundreds of different champions spread around the world. A sanctioning body would recognize one champion, and for revenue purposes that belt could be sold to a sponsor (e.g., the Budweiser WAMMA Heavyweight Champion).

Fred recruited several of his heavyweight friends to be on the WAMMA board—Jack Kemp, former Buffalo Bills coach Kay Stephenson, and Terdema Ussery. He even asked his friend LeRoy Neiman to draw some illustrations for the presentations. "We wanted to be able to standardize the sport and enable the best fighters to face off against each other, giving it legitimacy and integrity," he says. "But in the end it was too complicated to bring all the sports together and agree."

Fred also came up with a "skilled" poker concept that would capitalize on public interest in poker, yet take the luck out of the game and increase the emphasis on skill. The idea was based on the concept of duplicate bridge, which heightens the element of competition. Again, he enlisted Neiman to paint a colorful logo.

"Here's an example of skilled poker," he says. "Start with four tables, thirty-two players. Each table is totally secure. Players can't hear or see the other tables, but we can carry the games on television and the Internet, where they would have a wide audience. Before the players sit down, an auditing firm comes up with twenty different orderings of a fifty-two-card deck, using a random number generator. The auditors then outfit each table with the twenty different decks. All thirty-two players start with the same amount of chips. The twist is that they don't compete with other players at their tables. Instead, they compete against the players who have the corresponding seat number at the other tables." But again, it was an idea that did not get off the ground.

There were other opportunities that came to fruition—just not with Fred attached to them. One notable idea was the insurance concept of "First to Die" and "Last to Die." Fred, who served as chairman of the board of both Orange State Life Insurance and Western Traveler's Life Insurance, suggested to the board of directors at Orange State the concept of First to Die and Last to Die. It was derived from his work as a plaintiff's lawyer in times when lawyers wanted to make a claim for a client's mental pain and suffering over a lifetime.

Here's how it worked. Let's say a couple's child has been killed, and the lawyers are looking to maximize the amount paid to them for pain and the one suffering. The actuarial table for the mother might be twenty-seven years and the one for the husband, twenty-four years. In attempting to collect for mental pain and suffering for as long as possible, the lawyer would combine the two actuaries, because the two combined are presumed to have a life expectancy greater than twenty-seven years. This is the same concept as life insurance. If two lives are being analyzed rather than one, there is a better chance that one of the them will live longer than his/her normal life expectancy. The man's estimate of twenty-four years to live is based on a thousand people, some of whom will live forty more years, some only a few additional years. So when you combine the mother and father in an actuarial table to compute pain and suffering, the table will show that the life expectancy is beyond twenty-seven years.

The idea Fred presented to Orange was that the company approach a well-to-do couple and sell them insurance on both of their lives jointly. The policy wouldn't pay out until the last of them died. The pitch was that this was a great marketing tool for them to take care of their heirs. It also allowed the company to sell them the same amount of life insurance for less money, say $2,200 a month instead of $3,000, because it was insuring the last of them to die. The policy makes perfect sense because it's more for less. The bottom line was that it would cost more to have a First to Die situation, but it would provide funds for the surviving spouse and children. The Last to Die for the couple would be substantially cheaper, and would be used to provide money for the heirs and for taxes and estate expenses.

"I outlined this idea to the board of directors," Fred says. "Problem was, they were better drinking buddies than life insurance executives. I couldn't convince them to take the chance, so I gave up on the idea. Ten years later, these were the hottest products in the life insurance business and both concepts are now multibillion-dollar programs. I just didn't follow through by taking it to another life insurance company. Put that together with me not pressing the structured settlement idea, and there's another billion dollars out the window."

Even if Fred wasn't great at following through, he was loath to accept failure. He was very hands-off in business and preferred to let others handle the details. But his ego being what it was, he always figured that if something went wrong, he could somehow fix it.

When Sam's Style Shop ran into financial trouble, Fred was able to navigate the bankruptcy laws and turn a total loser into a financial gain. The problem started when Sam's expanded from three stores to fifty-three in eight years. During the expansion, the shops began to take on lower-quality merchandise. The trouble came when interest rates spiked from 6 to 18 percent, causing the entire profit to be consumed by interest payments on the inventory. Sam's went into bankruptcy, paid off the creditors, and sold the stores, thus avoiding liquidation and near-total loss.

Fred also refused to let Chick's Barbecue go under. Again, expansion crippled the business. The owners tore down the original building and put up a bigger one. They figured that if they could pack a building that was 3,000 square feet, they could fit even more people into a building that was 10,000 square feet. "Apparently, barbecue places aren't supposed to be so big," Fred says.

Diminishing returns set in. Where they once packed 3,000 square feet, they were only filling 2,000 square feet in the bigger space. Fred searched for buyers who were interested in owning a restaurant for the sheer ego of it. He eventually came across two doctors who wanted the restaurants almost as much as Fred and his partners wanted to get rid of them. "We sold the restaurants to the doctors and breathed a sigh of relief, concluding that those doctors may have saved more bad businesses than lives," he says.

When Fred's bar business ran aground because of the popularity of nightclubs, he found a buyer for them named "Big Daddy," who ran a chain of bars named, you guessed it, Big Daddy's. His company held 137 liquor licenses in Florida. Big Daddy was worried about proposed legislation that would limit individuals in Florida to holding no more than three liquor licenses. He said he would fly to Pensacola in his private plane and talk to Fred about the deal. At the time, Reubin Askew was governor, and Big Daddy had read that Fred had some influence in the state house.

After Fred and his partners wined and dined Big Daddy for two days, they all met at Fred's house to discuss the deal. Big Daddy listed his terms. He was offering the group three times what they could otherwise get for the bars. Then came the caveat. He would make the deal only if someone killed the legislation to limit the number of liquor licenses.

Fred said nothing, but Vigodsky jumped to his feet, pointed at Fred, and declared, "The boy can do it!"

Big Daddy returned to Miami and sent a formal contract for the purchase, based on the proviso that the legislation be killed. "I wasn't about to call Reubin about bar licenses," Fred says. "It turned out I didn't have to. A few days after we received the contract, the legislation was withdrawn. Three days later, Big Daddy's check arrived. I don't think he ever realized that I had nothing to do with the legislation dying. It was dumb luck, but I wasn't about to tell him otherwise."

CHAPTER

TEN

In the Center of the Ring

R oy Jones Jr. was the hottest boxing prospect in the world. A Pensacola
native, he made an international name for himself at the 1988 Seoul
Olympics. In the most controversial gold medal bout in Olympic history,
Jones had clearly beaten the South Korean Park Si-Hun, landing eighty-
six punches to Park's thirty-two. However, Park was given a 3–2 decision.
It was later revealed that the three judges who voted against Jones had
taken graft from the South Korean officials. Though this resulted in their
suspension, Jones was never awarded the gold medal he deserved. The
boxing world was itching to see what Jones could do as a professional.

One afternoon in January 1989, a man whom Fred Levin had never
met walked into his office. He introduced himself as Roy Jones Sr., and
asked Fred if he would manage his son, who was turning professional.
Fred knew nothing about boxing, but immediately agreed. He brought in
his brother Stanley to help. In partnership with the Joneses, they formed
a company called Square Ring to promote Roy Jr.'s fights.

Representing Roy Jones Jr. was a move that would heighten Fred's
profile in the press considerably and vault him onto the national stage.
Because many of the fights were in casinos, Fred immediately became

a VIP. And because the fights were televised by HBO, Fred found a new outlet to promote himself.

Fred was hired seven months after Jones was robbed of the Olympic gold medal. Jones had been in the news because he and his father had rejected signing with Sugar Ray Leonard and his partner, Mike Trainer, despite the fact that Leonard had visited Jones in Pensacola before the Olympics. Don King also wanted to handle Jones. Bob Arum was the only major promoter not interested, calling the Jones team "ingrates" for misleading Leonard and Trainer.

Though the choice of Fred was an unorthodox one, Roy Jones Sr. felt it was best to keep his son independent of boxing's inner-circle promoters. "He wasn't in the business, and he wasn't a boxing lawyer, so I figured I would get a better shake and a fairer deal with Fred than with some," Roy Sr. says.

After hiring Fred to be his son's lawyer, Roy Jones Sr. brought in Harold Smith, who had tenuous ties to Muhammad Ali. Smith also happened to be a convicted felon. Under the name Ross Fields, Smith had served five years in prison for embezzlement. Smith had just been paroled when he was hired to help promote Jones, and this added to the circus-like atmosphere.

"We did our research and Harold Smith didn't have any problems with boxing," Roy Sr. says. "His problem was with banking. There was no question in my mind who was representing Roy. It was Fred all the way. We really brought Smith in more or less like a tutor for Fred."

Jones' first professional fight took place in Pensacola in May 1989. The media came out in force. A weigh-in was staged on the USS *Lexington*, which was docked in Pensacola Harbor. Boxing greats Ken Norton, Larry Holmes, and Alexis Arguello attended. The actual weigh-in, however, was on the night of the fight.

The fight was a huge success for Jones. The referee stopped the bout in the second round and awarded Jones a technical knockout. Coming off the resounding victory, Fred wanted to move Jones into the national spotlight. Fred booked his next fight for Atlantic City, to be televised on NBC. The whole situation was chronicled by *Sports Illustrated*, which covered the fight and wrote a feature on Jones going pro and his management team, complete with a picture of Fred Levin.

To many, it looked odd for a plaintiff's lawyer to be immersed in the life of the next great American boxer. To Fred, it was yet another way to

In the center of the ring: "The most fun I ever had," Fred says.

keep things in his life interesting. If it also promoted his name and law practice, that was a bonus.

Fred worked to move Jones into the big time. However, Jones' father wanted to ensure his son kept winning fights, so he insisted that he fight subpar opponents. Twelve of Jones' first thirteen fights were in Pensacola or the Panhandle against lesser opponents. "My reason of keeping him fighting around [Pensacola] was not to establish the record but to build a good home base," Roy Sr. says. "If he was not from somewhere, he would have no idea where he was going."

Eventually, Jones had a falling out with his father over personal matters that resulted in him actually moving in with Stanley for two years. Jones' father attributes the situation to part of the growing process for his son. "He always was in charge of his own life," Roy Sr. says. "When Roy was a kid, I stood over him and watched him, but when he got to be an adult, you got to stand back and watch him."

With Jones' father out of the picture, Fred began looking to expand the boxer's horizons. He regularly booked fights for Jones in Atlantic City, Las Vegas, and New York, and Jones kept winning them. Fred also worked out a deal with Nike to help market Jones. At the time, Nike had a division called Nike Sports Management that was run by Terdema Ussery. The division had a group of top athletes that it endorsed and worked with on overall career strategy, including NBA players Scottie Pippen and Alonzo Mourning, NFL stars Deion Sanders and Bo Jackson, and Olympic down-hill skier Picabo Street. Though the group would not take a boxer, Fred and Ussery worked out an arrangement to bring Jones into the Nike family.

"Fred was the voice of reason, and he was someone I grew to respect from a business perspective, but also to like a lot," Ussery says. "He was a guy who had Roy's best interest at heart, and he didn't talk the normal BS talk. We could have really good, intelligent conversations, and he got it. He was willing to stand up to his client. Normally these guys don't want

Terdema Ussery, Fred, and Morris Dees enjoying time together at Fred's home.

to tell their clients the truth. They sell them a bunch of snake oil and then try to figure out afterward how to get out of it."

Fred was anything but typical in the way he approached his work with Jones, and that eventually ruffled the feathers of the boxing world. Jones wanted to remain independent of the sport's big promoters, Don King and Bob Arum, who were none too pleased. As retribution, Fred says, they refused to give Jones title fights.

Don King ruled boxing with an iron fist. King wanted to manage Jones. He called Fred and asked to meet with him, so Fred and Martin flew to Las Vegas. In the meeting, King said he had reconsidered. He told Fred

Fred and the boxing world's make-or-break promoter, Don King, at a press conference in 1998.

and Martin that he no longer wanted to manage Roy. Then he pointed at Martin and declared, "I want this young man as my lawyer."

Fred laughs at the recollection. "Don had recognized the relationship between Martin and me, and how Martin had so much influence," Fred says. "Martin and I walked out of the meeting and Martin turned to me and said, 'Daddy, he's a smart guy. We have to do business with him.'

"Don King was the best negotiator I have ever encountered," Fred continues. "He was not formally educated, but he was very smart. He often recited the Bible and quoted great philosophers in conversation. If his name was on a fight as the promoter, it added 15 percent to the gate. That said, he had a reputation among many in boxing for screwing his fighters and not allowing fighters he didn't represent to have opportunities at lucrative fights. To me, however, he was nothing other than very straightforward and wise. We both are much older now, but still share a good friendship that I always will enjoy."

As Fred worked with Jones, he began to realize how disorganized professional boxing had become, with different organizations proclaiming different boxers as champions. The competing categories resulted in multiple champions in the same weight category, which made the sport impossible to follow for even the most devoted fan. Fred wanted to bring more integrity and clarity to the sport. He had seen how some boxers were manipulated by their managers, and how unscrupulous promoters tried to stack the rankings to benefit their fighters.

Jones' situation was especially bizarre. During the 1990s, he was considered by many in the sport the best pound-for-pound fighter, yet only one of the four boxing federations listed him as champion. The other three didn't list him at all, because they were controlled by promoters who could largely dictate the rankings to favor their fighters.

Senator John McCain had noticed this injustice and called Fred to testify before the Senate Committee on Commerce, Science, and Transportation. McCain then drafted legislation that would change these practices, but it never took. "I was also unable to convince enough people to back my idea of unifying all the boxing organizations or creating a new organization that would do a better, more honest job than the existing system," Fred says.

However, when Fred threatened to sue the Powers That Be in boxing for withholding opportunities from Jones, Jones was given the title fight he deserved. In an International Boxing Federation Super Middleweight title bout, Jones fought James Toney at the MGM Grand in Las Vegas in 1994, and won a unanimous decision.

By 1995, Jones had captured the World Boxing Council Super Middleweight title and the IBF Middleweight and Super Middleweight titles. He had run up a record of 27–0 (on his way to 34–0 before he lost a fight on a disqualification). For Fred's part in positioning and managing Roy, he was given the Rocky Marciano Award as boxing manager of the year in 1994. The following year he was named manager of the year by the Boxing Writers Association of America.

"One of the most pleasant situations that arose as a result of my managing Roy Jones was meeting the great artist LeRoy Neiman," Fred says. "I asked him to do a painting of Roy, and he agreed. LeRoy and I became very, very good friends. I now own thirteen of his works, five of which he gave my wife and me. His original of the Three Tenors hangs in the entry of my house."

It was new territory for this personal injury trial lawyer.

Through his boxing ties, Fred became friends with the greatest boxer of all time, Muhammad Ali. In February 1997, Fred hosted an event in Pensacola for Ali's nationwide healing campaign. Ali arrived the day before the event and stayed at Fred's house along with Governor Lawton Chiles and his wife. That evening, Fred hosted a cocktail party fundraiser and an exclusive dinner.

Before the event, Ali was signing autographs. During the session, an African American man named Herman who worked for Fred came into the room. Herman couldn't believe he was actually in Ali's presence. He stood riveted in place, gawking at Ali.

Ali, who still retained his mischievous sense of humor, then turned around and asked Herman, "Did you call me a nigger?"

Herman stood erect. "No sir!" he said.

That evening, Fred's brother David arrived with a friend. They were directed to the cocktail party on the first level. When David asked where his brother and Ali were, security informed him that they were upstairs eating dinner. David bolted past them and entered the dining room.

Like Herman, when David spotted Ali, he stopped in his tracks and stared at him. Fred saw David standing wide-eyed, looking at Ali. Realizing

"Who's the Greatest?": With Marilyn looking on, Fred trades punches with Muhammad Ali at a cocktail party held at the Levins' home.

Ali's humor, Fred loudly said to Ali, "Muhammad, this is my older brother David. He's the one who called you a nigger."

David turned ashen. "Are you crazy? I did not say that!" he exclaimed. "I never use that word."

Ali broke up laughing.

Some 7,600 high school students were bused to the event at the Pensacola Civic Center. The day was not without controversy. There were protestors outside the arena declaring that the event was designed to convert Christians to Islam. Christian conservatives railed that the event ran afoul of the school's speaker policy that discouraged religious topics.

Fred served as master of ceremonies. When Fred mentioned Ali's book *Healing*, which focuses on healing racial and religious bigotry, there was a smattering of boos. In the book, Ali, a Muslim, talks about his mother, a Baptist. She believed that Jesus Christ was the son of God, while he does not. "If you want to read it, read it," Fred told the crowd. "If you don't want to read it, you don't have to."

Roy Jones Jr. and Governor Chiles both spoke in glowing terms about Ali's work. Though slowed by Parkinson's, Ali shadowboxed on the stage. When a girl asked if he could beat current heavyweight champion Mike Tyson, Ali stomped on the stage, prompting cheers from the crowd.

A week later, Governor Chiles wrote Fred a letter and said, "The ceremony in [Ali's] honor will be one of the most memorable days of my life."

Fred became well known in boxing circles as a straight shooter. He was approached to manage Ghana's Ike Quartey, who was the Michael Jordan of Ghana. Fred accepted and built him from a fighter averaging $50,000 per fight to one who earned $5 million for fighting Oscar de la Hoya in February 1999.

Through representing Quartey, Fred met the members of Ghana's royal family. They were grateful for his work on Quartey's behalf and impressed with his record in helping blacks and other minorities. For his contributions, they recommended that Fred be named a chief in Ghana.

On January 22, 1999, Ghana's government held a beautiful ceremony at the United Nations in New York. The entire Levin family turned out for the event—despite the fact that Fred had missed nearly all their events.

"At first, I had no idea how significant the honor was," he says. "I thought it was like being named an honorary colonel in the Florida Highway Patrol. I was amazed at the importance they placed on it."

Fred was decked out in a chief's official robe. Ghana's ambassador told the press, "The honor is only conferred on individuals who have demonstrated they care for humanity." Fred was given the Ghanaian name "Nana Ofori Agyeman." Under Ghanaian law, if a person does not bow and hold their hands together upon meeting Fred, they owe him a slaughtered cow or goat.

"To me—aside from all the meat I would likely be receiving—the biggest part of the honor was that I was one of the first three Americans to receive the distinction," Fred says. "The other two were Shirley Temple Black, the actress and former US ambassador to Ghana, and Barbara Jordan, the first Southern black female elected to the House of Representatives. The tribal title is something a chief can hand down to his male heirs, so when I die, my son Martin will inherit it, and he can in turn pass it on to his son."

One for the books: Marilyn (on Fred's right) beams as her husband is named a chief of Ghana.

At the same event, US Representative William Jefferson presented Fred with a letter from the US Congress, which read in part:

We of the Congressional Black Caucus wish to join with the distinguished world citizens and other leaders in congratulating you on your designation as a Ghanaian Chief. But more specifically, we wish to honor your lifelong contributions to bettering the lives of the people of Ghana and the people of America. Long before we became aware of your outstanding contributions in Africa, we knew of your work as a lawyer fighting on the side of underprivileged people in America. We thank you for that rich legacy. We are proud that the world community is now beginning to recognize your valuable service to it as well.

Some of Fred's famous friends attended. LeRoy Neiman commemorated the event by painting a tribal-type picture of Fred. Seth Abraham, the head of HBO Sports, joked with Fred about the irony of a white Southern Jew from Pensacola whose father was a pawnbroker becoming a chief of an African country. Don King called Fred and summed it up best: "Only in America!"

Fred's time working with Roy Jones Jr. was often like something out of a Martin Scorsese movie. One morning Fred received a phone call from a man who said that he had photos of Fred and Roy Jones Jr. doing cocaine with young girls and demanded $10,000 for the photos. Fred knew the entire story was a fabrication, so he brushed him off.

"I told that guy I'd had a rough day and didn't have time for this shit," Fred says.

A few hours later, the man called back, and they had the same exchange. Fred went for lunch, and when he returned, the guy had left word with Fred's secretary that he was going to expose the photos.

Fred figured the guy was crazy, so he called the police. The police came to Fred's office and planned to trace the call if the man called again. Sure enough, he did. Fred held him on the line for forty-five minutes, making the arrangements to pay him off. The two agreed that Fred would bring $10,000 in a gym bag to a phone booth in a strip mall. The man would place the pictures in some nearby bushes. Fred hung up, but the trace hadn't worked because the firm had so many phone lines tied to its main number.

The police told Fred to go through with the exchange so they could catch the blackmailer. Fred withdrew $10,000 in twenty-dollar bills from the bank and put the money in a gym bag. The police gave him a bullet-proof vest to wear. To snare the guy, the police surrounded the area with plainclothes officers.

Fred drove to the strip mall and put the cash in the phone booth as directed. As he walked to the bushes, the man came running around the corner and grabbed the bag of money. He was immediately arrested.

Fred went to the police station with the officers and the perpetrator. The police called his father, who vowed to get his son some help. Fred had no interest in pressing charges. He only wanted the young man to receive treatment. Yet Fred wasn't about to let such a great hoax end.

He called the chief of police, a friend of his. He told the chief the story, only he changed a few details. "Your guys told me to put this money in the bag and put it in a booth," he said. "Then this kid came running in and took off. You all couldn't catch him. Now he's got the $10,000, the photos of Roy and me with the cocaine and the girls, and I've got the newspaper calling me for comment." There was complete silence on the phone. When the chief arrived at Fred's office, Fred let him in on the joke.

After one of Jones' fights in Atlantic City, a guy came up to Fred and introduced himself. He was Lenny Dykstra, the great New York Mets baseball player. Dykstra told Fred that Roger King, who had started the television syndication company King World with his brother, wanted to meet and talk about promoting Roy. The next morning, King's plane flew Fred and Dykstra to Palm Beach, where they stayed at Roger's palatial home on the Intracoastal.

"It was sheer insanity," Fred says. "After his personal chef served us enough stone crabs to sink a fishing boat, Roger and Lenny began seriously partying, but I demurred, using some lame excuse."

After King and Dykstra shot several games of nine-ball for $5,000 a game, they made arrangements to meet in New Orleans at the King World board meeting. Partying aside, having a TV syndication company promote a boxer was a revolutionary—and potentially lucrative—idea.

Fred returned to Pensacola and filled Jones in on the meeting. Jones, by this time, had hooked up with a guy that Fred called Hollywood. The guy was working on putting Jones in the music business—on Roy's dime. Jones explained that Hollywood would be coming along to meet with Roger King. Fred invited his friend Terdema Ussery, who had signed Jones to the Nike endorsement deal.

Team Jones drove to New Orleans from Pensacola, a mere three-hour drive. The night before the meeting, Jones told Fred that he wanted Hollywood to do the talking in the meeting. "I didn't like the idea, but that's how we played it," Fred says.

The following day they met with King during a break in the King World board meeting. If the deal was put together, King planned to announce it to the board. The meeting started. Hollywood stood up. "Let me tell you something," he lectured Roger King. "Roy Jones is the biggest name in boxing today, and we are willing to enter into a long-term fight contract with you where you do the promoting and you pay him $75 million a fight."

King stood up. "You people are crazy," he said. He grabbed his crotch. "You want to know who has the biggest dick in this room. You want to know." King reached into his pockets and pulled out a wad of cash, and threw it on the table. He then unbuttoned his pants. "The person with the most money has the biggest dick. Now get out of my office."

That was the last Fred ever saw of Roger King.

Fred's boxing ties placed him on the elite list among casino owners. Fred met Donald Trump at a Jones fight. When a mutual friend introduced them, Trump acknowledged that he knew who Fred was. "He kicked our ass at the table last night," Trump said. Fred had won $50,000, not a small sum but certainly not a killing. Clearly, Trump kept count of his money.

Nevertheless, Fred was surprised when he received an invitation to Trump's birthday party in Atlantic City. Why not? he reasoned. When he called to accept the invitation, he was told to bring as many people as he could. He invited enough friends to fill two tables and headed to Atlantic City to party with The Donald.

The party was predictably over the top and somewhat surreal. "As you walked in, there was a re-creation of Fifth Avenue in ice carvings," Fred recalls. "My wife was with me. All she wanted to eat was caviar. They brought her a container of caviar that must have cost the casino $5,000. But as I looked around, I realized there were more people in the band than there were guests. It turned out that they had to bring in his employees at the last minute to be extras at the party to fill the room."

After everyone was seated, Trump stood up and spoke. "He said, 'Last night, I had a birthday party in New York at Trump Tower,'" Fred recounts. "'It was wonderful. The mayor was there. Tomorrow night, I'm having another birthday party in Las Vegas. But you are the lucky people, because I want you to know this is my real birthday.'" Fred laughs. "I don't think he realized one third of the room were his employees in rented tuxedos."

As Jones won fight after fight and became a big draw in the boxing world, Fred received a call from Las Vegas casino operator Steve Wynn's marketing manager. Wynn wanted to promote a Jones fight in Vegas and asked to meet with Fred.

Wynn had owned the Golden Nugget, where Fred had a history. On a previous trip, Fred had won a nice haul late one night at the tables with his brother Allen. When Fred reached his suite, he had a phone call from the cashier's office saying that they had overpaid him by $5,000. Fred was drunk, so he told them he would come by in the morning to sort things out.

After breakfast, Fred and Allen went to the manager's office. The manager played a video of the payout, but it was inconclusive. All it showed was two drunks cashing their chips and skipping off for more drinks.

"The manager said he was certain that the cashier had overpaid me," Fred says. "I asked, 'What would've happened if you'd underpaid me?' He said, 'We would have found you and paid you.' I then asked him if this had ever happened before. He said that it hadn't but if I didn't return the money, he would have to fire everyone working the cage that night. I decided to return the money on the condition that he never tell anyone what an idiot I was for giving money back to a casino."

That evening, Fred and Allen were eating in the hotel's restaurant. Seated to their left were Joe DiMaggio and his party. The president of the Golden Nugget came up to Fred's table and thanked him for saving the cage workers' jobs. He told Fred he was like family and to call if he ever needed anything.

Fred took him up on his offer when Martin was planning a trip to Las Vegas. "I called my 'family' at the Golden Nugget to get Martin a room," Fred says. "They said, 'If he's not a high roller, we don't give rooms away.' So much for family in Vegas."

With that in the back of his mind, Fred flew to Vegas to meet with Steve Wynn about Roy Jones fighting at the Mirage, another Wynn hotel. The meeting went well, but nothing came of it.

Not everyone knew who Roy was, however, despite his rapid rise in boxing. One night, Fred, Allen, Martin, and a close friend named Cliff Mowe were in Biloxi shooting dice. They started hitting it big, and all four began increasing their alcohol consumption. There was a limit of $10,000 per bet at the table, and Allen eventually began busting the limit per bet, but no one with the casino said anything until after he won the hand. They then tried to not pay him for the amount over $10,000.

There was a large crowd of people standing around watching. Martin, who was highly intoxicated, started arguing with the pit boss, insisting that the casino pay Allen the full amount. The pit boss began ushering the group back to security, and demanded to know who Martin was. Allen quickly responded that Martin was his lawyer. At that point, Martin exclaimed: "I want you to know that if you do not pay my uncle the full amount, then Roy Jones will never fight in this casino again."

Jones had fought several times, including defending his championship belt, in the coliseum the casino had on the property. However, the pit boss evidently didn't know this, because he turned to Martin and responded: "I can assure you, young man, that if anyone starts a fight in this casino we will throw them out."

As drunk as Martin was, he quickly changed his approach and demanded to have all surveillance tapes above the table preserved for evidentiary purposes for the lawsuit he was about to file. The casino then agreed to pay half of the excess winnings, and the group went to celebrate over chili dogs.

By 2003, Fred says, it became too hard to control Jones in the face of all the people that Jones had around him trying to help him get into the music business. Fred says Jones also became erratic. He was supposed to be a presenter at the ESPY Awards, but he didn't show up. Fred booked him a $100,000 ad with Tommy Hilfiger, but he didn't show up for the photo shoot. The Hilfiger shoot was rescheduled, but Jones again missed it. A *TV Guide* cover never came to pass because Jones wouldn't schedule it. But the kicker was when Jones stood up Time Warner chairman Gerald Levin (no relation to Fred) for a dinner meeting.

For his part, Jones says he was focused on boxing and training. "They may say [I was irresponsible] but they don't know what I was going through, trying to make weight, training without eating," Jones says. "It wasn't all what it seemed to be. They don't know what I was going through trying to get ready for those fights where people were trying to knock my head off."

Fred's last fight with Roy was the pinnacle of both of their boxing careers. Fred arranged for Roy to fight John Ruiz on March 1, 2003, in Las Vegas for the heavyweight championship of the world. Ruiz had recently defeated Evander Holyfield for the championship. Jones officially weighed in at 193 pounds to Ruiz's 226 pounds. Incredibly, Jones ended up winning a unanimous decision, becoming the first former middleweight title holder to win a heavyweight title in 106 years, the last being Bob Fitzsimmons in

1896. Jones also became the first fighter in history to start his career as a junior middleweight and become a heavyweight champion.

Though Fred was sad that the run with Jones ended after the Ruiz fight, he reflects on the time he worked with the talented boxer as the most fun he ever had in business. During the run, Jones lost only one fight and that came on a controversial disqualification. In the rematch, Jones knocked the opponent out in the first round.

"Even with the craziness, I loved working with Roy," Fred says. "I was certainly not hard to miss at Roy's fights. I sat ringside, and after every fight, I was the first guy in the ring to congratulate him. Anyone watching Roy's fights on TV couldn't miss me."

Jack Kemp summed it up best when he quipped, "The most dangerous place in the ring of a Roy Jones fight is after the fight if anyone tries to get between Fred Levin and the TV camera."

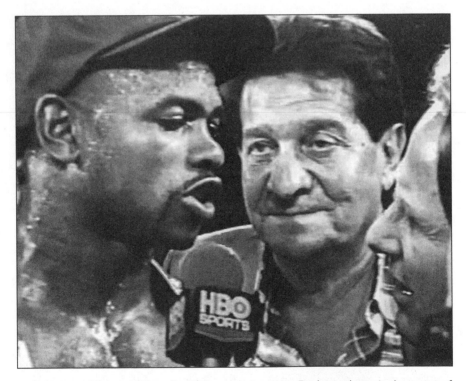

In the center of the ring: When the HBO cameras were on, Fred was always in the center of the shot.

Photo courtesy of Tom Casino

The best "pound for pound" boxer ever, Roy Jones Jr with his managers, the Levin brothers.

Fred's picture regularly appeared in magazines that profiled Jones, notably *Sports Illustrated*. During the time he represented Jones, Fred estimates that Jones earned more than $50 million. After Fred and his brother Stanley were reimbursed their $1.5 million investment in developing Roy's career, they were paid just $100,000 each per fight, a virtual pittance compared to what most boxing managers take.

Fred has no complaints. "It was the most fun I ever had, and I got $100 million of publicity out of it," Fred says. "I love Roy. We still are friends. One of the funniest times of my life occurred with Roy. We were in New York City in Manhattan. We had a limo driver. It was Roy and me. For some reason, Roy started joking around and he put me in a headlock, and had me up against the hood of the limo. I began yelling, 'Help! Help! The nigger is trying to kill me.' Not one person stopped or tried to help. They kept walking. Roy and I couldn't stop laughing when we got in the limo."

Representing Roy Jones Jr. turned out to be good for business. People who needed a lawyer would call the law firm and declare they wanted Fred Levin as their lawyer because he represented Jones. In one case that Martin and Fred took on in West Palm Beach, they reached a $5.9 million settlement for a man who was put in a wheelchair when a construction vehicle driven by a partially blind man smoking marijuana hit the platform he was working on.

"It's funny what draws clients to a firm," Fred says. "Boxing didn't make much money for us, but the association with Roy Jones Jr. was fantastic. It brought us a lot of lucrative cases. People kept saying, 'If anybody can manage Roy Jones so well, I want him to be my lawyer.' So while former US congressman Joe Scarborough couldn't draw a fly, Roy Jones was a magnet for business."

Fred and his friend, Pensacola native Emmitt Smith, the NFL's all-time leading rusher.

In 2002, the year before he parted with Jones, *Worth* magazine acclaimed Fred as the richest man in Pensacola, the 100th largest city in the country. He was also named the most influential person in the Panhandle. In a poll taken by a survey company, more people in Escambia and Santa Rosa counties in Florida (with a combined population of more than 500,000) knew the name Fred Levin than knew the governor's name.

Even more outstanding was his facial recognition in the town. When Fred walked down the street, people constantly would come up to him or yell out, "Hey, Fred"—never "Mr. Levin." People felt like they knew him, and he enjoyed the attention and interacting with everyone. The black community in particular adored him because they could tell that he genuinely loved their company.

"He makes people feel comfortable with who they are and with what he is doing for them," explains Emmitt Smith, the former Dallas Cowboys star who grew up in Pensacola and became friends with Fred. "I think that has a lot to do with him. Fred and his family have been well known in that community for various things. Knowing the good he has done is one reason why African Americans support him."

CHAPTER

ELEVEN

A Good Old-Fashioned Southern Mystery

Fred Levin loved getting under the skin of the corporate lawyers. These were the buttoned-down WASPs who had refused to hire his brother David in the 1950s. Decades later, their bitterness toward plaintiff's lawyers had increased as the successful plaintiff's lawyers became extremely wealthy. But Fred wasn't content to stay in his place and let them handle the lucrative corporate work. In 1983, Fred moved in on their territory—a move that ended up with him being investigated for murder in a bizarre case that captured the attention of the national press.

The situation began routinely enough. A friend of Fred's, Ed Addison, was promoted from president of Gulf Power, which supplied the Pensacola area, to president of Gulf's owner, Southern Company. The largest utility company in the country at the time, Southern Company owned power companies in Alabama, Florida, Georgia, and Mississippi.

Fred had gotten to know Addison well over the years. Their relationship had started in the 1970s when Chick's Barbecue opened a steakhouse. Addison was then a marketing executive for Gulf Power. He convinced Fred Vigodsky to install all-electric appliances in the kitchen, a big change as most restaurants relied on natural gas. The restaurant encountered problems because the soy in the steak marinade kept dripping into the electric burners, so Gulf Power was often on site servicing the units.

When Addison became president of Gulf Power, the company was regularly losing civil lawsuits. Addison decided the most effective way to combat this was to hire the best plaintiff's lawyer he could find to take on the other plaintiff's lawyers. Addison went to his board and proposed that Fred be hired as outside counsel to handle litigation. The board resisted, saying they absolutely did not want a plaintiff's attorney, and insisted the company stay with Bert Lane's firm, Beggs & Lane.

But when Addison took the reins of Gulf Power's parent company, he sent word that Fred was to be hired. Fred became the only plaintiff's lawyer in the country representing a major power company. He promptly won an appeal for Gulf Power on a difficult case. Soon, Fred was being paid bonuses of $100,000 for winning other cases, on top of a $500,000 annual retainer.

During this time, Fred also became close friends with Jake Horton, who was a senior vice president for Gulf Power, in charge of government relations. Horton had been with the company for more than thirty years. He had also grown up with W. D. Childers, Fred's close friend who became president of the Florida Senate. When the legislature was in session, Horton and Fred often visited Tallahassee and stayed with Childers in his apartment.

It was pretty heady for a trial lawyer, typically the nemesis of large corporations, to be the lead litigator for Gulf Power. Fred was picked up in limousines and flown around in the company's corporate jets. This was during the time that Fred was using his elaborate penthouse, Triton, to entertain politicians and other bigwigs and to raise money for charities. At the power company's request, Fred hosted parties for senators, governors, and presidential candidates.

Entering Triton, guests knew they were at a Fred Levin party. To say the place was over the top does not begin to describe it. Named for the legendary shell, considered to be the finest in the world, Triton was 5,300 square feet and had a 1,300-square-foot terrace overlooking the Gulf of Mexico. The place looked like somewhere Liberace might have lived. The living room walls were covered in Korean silk, while those in the "Party Room" were black acrylic, and the Italian glass chandeliers throughout were as gaudy as they were shiny. The marble floors ranged in color from peach to white to gray to black, depending on the room. The guest suite had stainless steel floors and silver-sheen fabric on the walls.

Fred, Kim, Bob Hope, and Marilyn at Triton Penthouse.

Bob Hope once requested to stay there, despite the fact he didn't know Fred. He was coming to the Panhandle with his wife to do a USO show at Eglin Air Force Base. Fred was more than willing to accommodate a major celebrity. Fred staffed the place with a chef, housekeepers, and butlers. Though Fred was so busy that week he only managed to get to the penthouse for dinner with the Hopes, for him the publicity was well worth it.

Trouble broke up the party at Gulf Power in August 1988. US Attorney Robert Barr Jr. out of Atlanta convened a grand jury to investigate several allegations against Gulf Power's parent company, Southern Company. The first was for tax evasion. An informant had turned over taped conversations to investigators that allegedly revealed the company kept bogus accounting records for spare parts that it never used, thus saving it some $25 million in federal taxes.

The IRS' criminal division was simultaneously investigating the murder of a couple named Robert and Kathryn McRae in Graceville, Florida.

Robert McRae had been on Gulf Power's board of directors, and the investigators were trying to determine if the killings were somehow related to Gulf Power. During the investigation, they had discovered allegations of irregularities in campaign contributions from Gulf Power. The IRS investigators were looking into claims that the company pressured employees to make contributions, and that the company funneled its own contributions through third parties, such as subcontractors and people like Fred. In other words, the IRS was questioning whether Gulf Power was overpaying Fred Levin in exchange for his making large campaign contributions that benefited them.

The stakes in the investigation were raised when one contractor supposedly agreed to come forward and testify that he had received cash from Jake Horton to make political contributions. Mysteriously, the day before the contractor was scheduled to testify before the grand jury, he skipped town and never returned.

"There were all kinds of shenanigans going on," Fred says. "People were getting political contributions. Gulf Power was getting rate increases. I was having parties for the utility commission. And the IRS started looking into the wining and dining of the utility commission and the political contributions, and also the murder of the McRaes."

Things reached a boiling point at Gulf Power in April 1989. On a Friday, the audit committee of Gulf Power's board of directors voted to fire Jake Horton over the IRS investigation and the alleged overpayments to contractors for political contributions. The following Monday, April 10, Jake was notified of the vote and told that would be the board's recommendation to Addison. He immediately drove to Fred's office to talk to him.

Horton was upset. He had devoted his life to Gulf Power, and he felt that he was being treated unfairly.

"He told me, 'They're going to fire me. I'm going to go up to Atlanta and discuss this with Ed Addison,'" Fred recalls.

Horton then walked across Fred's office to the guest phone and called for a corporate plane to take him to Atlanta. The company sent one from Mississippi. Fred says he and Horton made plans to meet back at his office as soon as Horton returned from Atlanta.

"As he was leaving, he said two things to me," Fred recalls. "The first was, 'If something happens to me, make sure Frances [his wife] is well taken care of.' I told him that was crazy talk. Then he mentioned the McRaes, saying, 'They're wanting to find out why they were killed.'"

Hours later, the corporate plane carrying Jake Horton crashed near Ferry Pass, Florida. Horton, the pilot, and the copilot all died.

After hearing the news of the crash that evening, W. D. Childers and Fred went to Horton's house to offer condolences to his wife. While they were there, Childers went into the bathroom. On the sink were Horton's Auburn University ring and his watch.

"W. D. said Jake would never leave without those items, especially his cherished ring, unless he knew he wasn't coming back," Fred says.

Fred says he later learned that Horton had returned home and picked up a bag that might have contained the material that allegedly caused the explosion that led to the crash. Horton had run into Frank Patti, Horton's neighbor, who operated a large fish distributorship. Patti told Fred that Horton was smiling and saying everything was going fabulous. "To me, it appeared he became delusional and made up his mind to kill himself," Fred says.

Fred believes that Horton committed suicide because he was being made the scapegoat in the IRS investigation. "The day after the plane crash, I went to Gulf Power to tell them that they shouldn't make Jake a scapegoat," Fred says. "They told me the IRS investigators had been there and that I wasn't allowed to enter Jake's office. It was clear that they believed I was somehow involved in the mess."

He also believes that Horton being passed over for promotion may have affected him, too. When Addison was president of Gulf Power, Horton had done a lot to talk up Addison's name. When Addison became president of Southern Company, Horton had hoped to become president of Gulf Power, but someone else was chosen.

Though Fred's firm was earning more than $500,000 a year from Gulf Power, Fred immediately severed ties with the company because he believed they were assassinating Horton's character.

"I was sure Jake had done nothing financially inappropriate," Fred says. "His life had been devoted to Gulf Power. I felt that the company had abandoned him in the grand jury investigation and was now denigrating him by releasing information about the investigation after the crash to get itself off the hook in the IRS investigation."

Fred served as a pallbearer at Jake's funeral. There, he told Horton's brother that he thought Jake had committed suicide. That didn't go over well, and even though Fred was an avid supporter, he became persona non grata with the family.

Because the crash was so horrific, federal investigators could not pinpoint its cause. This led to theories piling up across the Panhandle about who killed Jake Horton and why. Added to the plane crash were the stories of tax evasion, the McRaes' death, and the IRS political-payoff investigation. A good old-fashioned Southern mystery was under way.

The story became one of national intrigue. Reporters from the *New York Times*, the *Wall Street Journal*, the *Miami Herald*, *Newsweek*, and *Forbes* descended on Pensacola to cover it.

There were plenty of odd twists. Shortly after Horton's death, dead yellow canaries with their necks snapped started showing up on the doorsteps of Fred's office and house. "To me, this was a warning that I shouldn't 'sing' to authorities about my final conversations with Jake," Fred says. "I don't know who did it, but it was clearly somebody who wanted the situation to appear to be Mafia connected."

All types of theories started springing up as to what occurred. One theory was that Horton had been murdered because he was going to Atlanta to spill the beans to the US attorney general on what he knew about Gulf Power breaking the law. Supposedly, Horton was going to reveal that Southern Company had been charging its own customers for coal from its own mines. This theory was put forward in the conspiracy theory book *Vultures' Picnic* by Greg Palast, but there was never any evidence to back it up.

For his part, Fred wanted to put his conversations with Jake out in the open so whoever was threatening him would leave him alone. At the time, he declared: "The public has a right to know, just as I have the right to survive." Fred asked Gulf Power to absolve him of attorney–client privilege so he could talk about the final conversation he had with Horton. The company decided to allow him to talk only to the grand jury that was investigating the plane crash, not to the press or public.

Fred eventually testified before the grand jury in Atlanta for two days and told them about his last conversation with Horton. Fred continued to insist that he be allowed to divulge the conversation with Horton to the public to get himself out of the crosshairs, but the company refused. "As if the previous threats weren't enough, someone called my office the first day I testified and threatened to kill me," Fred recalls.

Fred's next problem was Charlie Johnson, the Escambia County sheriff. Sheriff Johnson had been elected in 1988 and began his term in January 1989. Based on the information of two informants, Jimmy Birge and Bobby Kay, Sheriff Johnson pursued Fred in an almost comical way, but one that caused many in the community to believe that Fred had Mafia ties.

"Birge and Kay turned out to be world-class bullshitters," Fred recalls. "Birge had been an informant for the sheriff's department for years. As I look back now, Kay was either an informant or very close to the police. Both of them developed a relationship with me because of the University of Florida. It was less my being naïve than my trying to help out young Gators."

Fred says that Birge was a low-level drug dealer, though Fred didn't realize that until much later. From time to time, Birge would call Fred and talk about his great love of the Florida Gators. Birge also had an extensive collection of memorabilia, including autographs by Babe Ruth and Lou Gehrig—all of which turned out to be fake. But Fred tolerated him because Birge was full of tales that he had supposedly overheard in the underworld, which Fred found humorous.

One of the stories that Birge told Fred concerned Fred Vigodsky. One evening, while Vigodsky and his wife, Brenda, were asleep, someone broke into their house and robbed them. They had always suspected a neighbor. Birge came to Fred and said that if Fred paid him $1,000, he would turn over the name of the person who did it. Fred paid the grand. Birge told him that Fred Vigodsky's son Craig was the perpetrator, because he had needed money to buy drugs. "That turned out to be a total lie," Fred says.

The press delights in reporting the threat to Fred's life if he testified in the Gulf Power trial.

Then there was Bobby Kay, who had appeared on Fred's doorstep some years before Jake Horton's death. He said that he had found nematodes (parasites) in the lawn. Kay was supposedly a University of Florida alumnus, and told Fred that he would exterminate them for free.

One morning in 1983, Fred found Kay sleeping in his garage. Kay told Fred that his mother had kicked him out of the house and he didn't have any place to stay. Fred's kids were grown and gone by then and he had an extra bedroom, so he offered it to Kay, which was not uncommon for Fred. Over a thirty-year period, he'd had numerous troubled young people live in his house, many of them friends of his children. A few years after Kay had started staying there, Fred returned home one Wednesday night from doing his BLAB-TV show and found the door wide open. Kay was gone. On his patio, Fred found several dead yellow canaries with their necks broken.

The following Sunday, Fred was having his weekly fried-mullet breakfast with his father and brothers when Kay strolled into the house. "I started making fun of him, joking about how he was going to protect me, but instead he vanished for three days and left the front door open as soon as a few small birds showed up dead," Fred says. "We were all laughing, but Bobby grew very angry and stormed out. He never returned. Instead, I was informed he had called Jake Horton's wife and told her that W. D. Childers and I had Jake killed."

Kay then allegedly went to Sheriff Johnson and told him that Fred was Mafia—in charge of drugs, boxing, the power company, and local businesses, according to information Fred says he came upon later. Kay supposedly also told the sheriff that he had listened in on conversations between W. D. Childers and Fred in which the two men discussed "getting rid of Jake." This occurred during the time that Gulf Power was being investigated by the Criminal Investigation Division of the IRS.

"I have always suspected that Kay told Sheriff Johnson that I had Jake Horton killed," Fred says.

As for Birge, after he was convicted of a number of different crimes, he became an informant. He would create incredible situations, such as talking people into committing a crime but informing the sheriff's department that the crime was about to be committed, and they would make the arrest. One of the funny situations occurred when Fred gave Birge a check for $100 for questionable memorabilia. On the memo line of the check, Birge had written in "cocane" (an obvious misspelling for the correct term, "cocaine"). Birge photocopied the check and gave it to the sheriff's department. Even the sheriff wasn't stupid enough to buy into that story.

However, the sheriff still took Birge's word on other occasions when it came to Fred. Birge ended up getting arrested in Montgomery, Alabama. He called Sheriff Johnson and told him that he was ready to reveal everything he knew about Fred Levin. Birge told Sheriff Johnson that Fred had given him $2 million in cash from the Mafia operations and had him bury the money in Destin, Florida.

Incredibly, the sheriff bought the story. He sent money to bail Birge out and brought him back to Pensacola. Sheriff Johnson then put Birge up in a motel in Destin, and for two days, Birge led sheriff deputies around the beaches in Destin, pointing out where he thought the money was buried. As the deputies were digging up parts of the beach, the *Pensacola News Journal* got wind of the boondoggle. Though the paper never published the story, it became an embarrassment to the sheriff.

"Of course, they never found anything, but the sheriff always believed I had done it," Fred says.

Based on Birge and Kay's information, Sheriff Johnson made a large poster that looked like a Mafia "org" chart and hung it in his office. There was a picture of Fred at the top with lines drawn to several well-known people in Pensacola. One line was drawn to Vince Whibbs, a member of Gulf Power's board of directors. Another line was drawn to Roy Jones Sr., the leader of boxing in Pensacola along with his son. A third line was drawn to Horton's neighbor Frank Patti, a shipbuilder who ran an extremely large seafood distribution business and who the sheriff thought was involved with bringing drugs into the city. A fourth line was drawn to Fred McFaul, the head of the FBI in Pensacola. A fifth line was drawn to Dean Baird, Fred's good friend and a bookie. A sixth line was drawn to Ted Ciano, a highly successful car dealer who was rumored to have Mafia connections.

Things came to a head when Bobby Kay called Fred one afternoon. He said he needed to talk. Fred told him to come to the office, but Kay said he didn't want to talk there. He asked Fred to meet him outside, in Plaza Ferdinand. Fred walked over to the plaza to meet with Kay.

"I saw an old van parked near the plaza, but I initially didn't think anything of it. Then Bobby started acting very strange, even for Bobby,"

Fred recalls. "'Mr. Fred, you can tell me what happened with Uncle Jake and Uncle W. D.,' he said. 'Remember, you told me that y'all had to get rid of Mr. Jake?'"

Fred stopped him. "What in the hell are you talking about?" he said to Kay. Fred figured he was crazy and left him standing there in his strange world.

Months later, Fred got a call from Frank Patti. Patti said he had seen a transcript of a conversation Fred had with Kay, who apparently was wearing a wire.

One afternoon, two sheriff's deputies came to see Fred. "They said they had learned that I had ordered a hit on Sheriff Johnson, but that they wanted me to kill them instead and spare the great sheriff," Fred says. "I gave them the brush-off and decided I needed to contact the FBI. I began to think that they were trying to set me up, and were going to kill me in the process.

"I wanted word to get back to the sheriff that this game was over," he says. "The next day, three FBI agents arrived at my office—not to protect me, but to question if McFaul had any role in the Jake Horton situation. I couldn't believe it. Everyone was giving credence to these absolutely crazy theories."

The mystery of Jake Horton's death was never definitively solved. In June 1989, after two months of investigating the crash, the National Transportation Safety Board announced that it was unable to determine the cause. This only added to the public's frustration and kept the rumor mill spinning.

As the *New York Times* reported: "Pensacola has suffered. The city has been split between those who support the utility and those who do not,

Stranger than fiction . . .

with the division sometimes angry. Everyone has a different theory about what is going on in the company that so dominates this town."

"This matter is beginning to tear this community apart," the *Pensacola News Journal* said in an editorial. "It can't go on much longer. It must be resolved."

As for the pressure being put on Fred, it eventually turned out that some rogue IRS agents were convinced that Fred was paying off Childers for political favors. The investigators figured that Horton's death could be somehow related, so they were trying to set a trap for Fred. A *Miami Herald* writer summed it up best when he wrote that the entire affair was like something out of a John Grisham novel.

"Sheriff Johnson was not the brightest police officer and between Jimmy Birge and Bobby Kay, the sheriff began to believe that there was Mafia in Pensacola and that I was the don," Fred says. "But one can imagine why so many people believed that I had something to do with the killing of Jake Horton. In fact, the owner of a popular local seafood restaurant told me that the sheriff actually told him that I had killed Jake Horton."

There has never been a definitive resolution as to what happened on the Gulf Power plane that took the life of Horton and the two pilots. No one knows for certain whether it was a mechanical issue, pilot error, a suicide, or a homicide. To this day, there are people who remain convinced that Fred Levin was somehow responsible, as was made clear to me by a complete stranger the first day I was in Pensacola and he heard I was writing a book on Fred.

CHAPTER
TWELVE

Prosecuting
Fred Levin

By 1989, there was perhaps more of Fred Levin than some people cared for—partly due to his success, partly due to the controversy that followed him around, and partly due to his flagrant self-promotion.

Fred had won ten jury verdicts in excess of $1 million, one for $5 million, and two in excess of $10 million. By his count, Fred had lost only one trial. He owned a string of local businesses. He served as special counsel to the president of the Florida Senate. He was representing the local hero, boxer Roy Jones Jr. He was appearing on BLAB-TV and being written about in the local paper for the controversial opinions he expressed on the air. And he represented Gulf Power, the largest utility company on the Panhandle.

Florida Trend magazine wrote in a cover story: "Levin is a renegade among renegades." He was pictured on the cover, standing in the firm's offices. Next to him was a crystal chandelier dangling from a twenty-foot ceiling against rose-colored walls.

The animosity toward Fred Levin was growing among the country club set in the Florida Bar Association. It seemed that at each turn of

© Florida Trend

Not your average magazine background for a cover shot of a lawyer.

Fred's notoriety, the Bar—whether justified, almost so, or not at all—came after him.

"Dad loved the limelight," Martin says. "He loved being the center of attention. That's good and bad. The good is that you become famous or infamous, and people either love you or hate you. There's not much in between."

The Florida Bar first went after Fred in June 1989, the most chaotic time in Fred's life. It was six weeks after Jake Horton had died and a month after Roy Jones Jr. had made his professional debut. Fred was up to his eyeballs in investigations and title fight preparations. The Bar filed charges against Fred for admitting on BLAB-TV—in 1987—that he had bet on football with a local bookie and saying that he saw nothing wrong with gambling as a recreational activity. "Really, the Bar was just out to get me," he says.

The story had begun in 1986 when Fred's friend and bookie, developer F. A. "Dean" Baird Jr., was arrested and charged with running a $7 million, eighty-person gambling ring. Baird says that when he was indicted, law enforcement officials were pressuring him to tell the grand jury that Fred was the kingpin behind the operation, which wasn't true. "They tried to get me to testify that Fred was running the business," Baird says. "All I had done was run a gambling business, and they wanted me to say that we were paying off politicians. That was ridiculous, but they wanted to get Fred. At one point, they said to me, 'We want you to give us anything that will put Fred Levin in jail.'"

Baird refused. He was eventually tried on state gambling charges. In his trial, one of his clients turned state's evidence. Baird was convicted and sentenced to seven years in prison.

"Dean was his own worst enemy," Fred says. "I always treated people nicely, no matter where they were socially, but Dean was country club. Dean was, and still is, a good friend. However, he always mistreated people lower than him. His attitude was his downfall. He was making good money and he would flaunt it, and the cops and the prosecutors and the judge were out to get him."

During the trial, it was revealed that ten lawyers, of whom Fred was one, bet on football games with Baird. All ten were called before the Bar's grievance committee because gambling is a misdemeanor in Florida. Nine of the lawyers admitted wrongdoing and their cases were promptly dropped.

Fred stubbornly refused to admit wrongdoing. Instead, he took to the airwaves. He went on BLAB and mocked the cops for overkill. He declared that he saw nothing wrong with gambling because everyone bets on everything—golf, football, the Oscars. Gambling on dog and horse races and jai alai was legal in Florida. The state also ran the biggest numbers game in the world—the Florida Lottery. And the governor of Florida talked publicly about betting a crate of oranges against the governor of Georgia's crate of peaches on a college football game. The grievance committee suggested a private reprimand, but Fred refused and opted for a trial.

The Florida Bar convened a public hearing before retired circuit court judge Fred Turner. Turner was best known as the trial lawyer for the defendant Clarence Earl Gideon in the retrial of the landmark US Supreme

Court case *Gideon v. Wainwright*. In that case, the Supreme Court found that indigents were entitled to counsel, which led to the establishment of public defenders. The story behind this is well chronicled in the book *Gideon's Trumpet*, by Anthony Lewis.

Fred was charged with placing bets from $500 to $2,000 on football games with Baird. He was also charged with admitting on BLAB that he bet on games and asserting there was nothing wrong with gambling even though it was against the law—all of which Fred freely admitted that he had done.

"The Bar wanted to stage my public execution," Fred says. "But I had no trouble putting my character on trial. I felt that the Bar should be going after crooked attorneys who stole their clients' money, not a guy who wagered his own money on a few football games."

The hearing had the exact opposite effect than the Bar expected: It turned out to be a testimonial for Fred Levin.

Fred testified first, admitting what he had done. As he didn't play golf at the country club or sail, he explained that gambling was his recreation. Speaking of country clubs, he pointed out they were no doubt full of elitists who gambled on golf every weekend. He said that he thought the gambling laws were arcane, not unlike the laws that were on the books when he first became a lawyer that made it illegal for a black person to drink from the courthouse water fountain.

At one point, Fred was asked if he felt lawyers should be held to a higher standard. "Lawyers," he told the packed hearing room, "are no better than anyone else, and I resent all these lily-white elitists hanging around country clubs who think they are."

When Fred concluded his spirited testimony, even Judge Turner appeared to be on his side. The judge quipped that he would swap ages with Fred and give him $10,000 to boot. The entire courtroom applauded.

Then came fourteen witnesses whose words, as the *St. Petersburg Times* put it, "were ringing through the court in praise of Pensacola's Fredric the Great." The head of the Florida United Way testified that Fred was the organization's largest contributor. The president of Florida State University talked about Fred's contributions to education. Roy Jones Sr. said that there was no person in the boxing world more ethical than Fred—which, in retrospect, probably didn't say much. Escambia County

State Bar may act against Levin

By Ginny Graybiel
News Journal

The Florida Bar plans to file a complaint, probably within the next month, against Pensacola attorney Fred Levin because of his public admissions that he has gambled, two sources said Thursday.

The complaint arises from Levin's comments on a cable television station after the 1987 arrest and conviction of his friend, Pensacola Beach developer F.A.

bet in Florida and saw nothing wrong with it. Under Florida law, gambling is a misdemeanor offense.

The Florida Bar complaint will allege that Levin violated Florida Bar rules for attorney conduct, the sources said. Susan Bloemen-

prevented him from commenting on whether he's even aware of a Bar investigation.

"I admit that I have bet on football games," he said. "If the Bar is investigating me for that, I'd suggest their time would be better spent investigating lawyers who steal from their clients. I would think the general public would be much more concerned about that than whether I take my money, and I don't hurt anyone,

Bar Association," he said on the program. "You'll see in the coming weeks what I mean by that."

He then suggested the Bar should perform public services rather than spend "a lot of time doing a lot of things that they ought to keep their nose out of."

Levin was one of at least 10 Pensacola lawyers on whom gambling complaints were filed with the local Bar grievance committee, according to the sources who

Levin faces disciplinary hearing

By Michael Burke
News Journal

The Florida Bar today will begin its attempt to prove Pensacola attorney Fred Levin violated ethical rules by betting on football games then insisting he saw nothing wrong with it.

Levin, who was listed by Forbes magazine as one of the nation's highest paid trial lawyers in 1988, said he believes today's disciplinary hearing marks the first time a bar organization has charged a lawyer with gambling

cuit Judge W. Fred Turner of Panama City. Levin will be represented by Gulf Breeze attorney Alan Rosenbloum.

After hearing testimony and evidence, Turner will report his findings and recommendations to the Florida Supreme Court. The Supreme Court has final authority to determine guilt and impose discipline on lawyers, which can range from a reprimand to disbarment.

The Bar's charges arose from a 1987 state investigation into an illegal football gambling

Although gambling is a misdemeanor offense under Florida law, the state did not file criminal charges against Levin and other bettors.

But Levin said he was "singled out" by a Bar grievance committee that voted 10-0 to bring a formal complaint against him for violating lawyers' rules of conduct.

In July, the Bar said Levin violated disciplinary rules which say that a lawyer shall not act contrary to honesty, justice or good morals,

Hearing becomes testimonial for Levin

By Ginny Graybiel
News Journal

Florida Bar charges that Pensacola attorney Fred Levin violated ethical rules by betting on football games are "outrageous," his lawyer told a judge on Tuesday.

"We are going to tell you about a man who is charitable, who is compassionate ... who may be one of the best lawyers in the country," attorney Alan Rosenbloum said. "... The Florida Bar should be giving this man a medal."

Rosenbloum's comments came during a hearing at the Escambia County

cuit Judge W. Fred Turner of Panama City to take evidence in the two-day hearing scheduled to end at mid-day today. Turner will recommend what, if any, discipline the court should impose.

Florida Bar attorney David McGunegle of Orlando said the Bar is seeking a public reprimand, but the Supreme Court can impose punishment up to disbarment or suspension.

Levin testified Tuesday that he has not bet on football games since 1986, when Pensacola businessman Dean Baird, his friend and former business partner, was arrested on charges that

The Florida State Bar brings Fred up on charges—and he turns the tables.

Commissioner Willie Junior detailed all the free legal advice Fred had given to poor community groups.

The high point came when state senator W. D. Childers testified. The president of the Florida Senate praised Fred's work with the legislature and said that he was a man of principle. Childers cited the fact that Fred had resigned as Gulf Power's attorney when he felt they were morally wrong. Childers then admitted that legislators have regular poker games and often bet on football. That was the kicker for most observers.

But Fred says that any chance that Judge Turner was going to rule in his favor soon disappeared. The *Pensacola News Journal* ran a story that Turner had served a year in federal prison for failing to file tax returns in

1955, and that he had been reprimanded in 1982 for judicial misconduct. Under immense pressure not to appear soft, Turner recommended a reprimand, which the Bar gladly accepted.

Fred appealed to the Florida Supreme Court, but the court upheld the reprimand—not surprising, as there was no denying that he had broken the letter of the law. But that didn't shut him up. "I told the press that all this showed was that I didn't have the constitutional right to state that I saw nothing wrong with gambling," Fred says. "In my mind, the charges equated lawyers betting on football with those using illegal drugs, as both were misdemeanors under Florida law."

The Florida Bar went after Fred again in 1996. These charges came as he was basking in the spotlight brought on by representing Roy Jones Jr. and by changing the law so Big Tobacco could be sued. Fred had also continued to win major verdicts at trial: one for $42 million against Southeast Toyota for price fixing; one for $3.76 million for a railroad accident; and another for $7.88 million against Baptist Hospital on behalf of a client named Keith Rawson, who had been put in a wheelchair after a scuba accident due to the hospital mishandling his treatment. For Fred's legal track record, in 1994 he received the Perry Nichols Award. The award was named after the lawyer who had pioneered plaintiff's law in Florida, and is given to attorneys whose perseverance, commitment, and unmatched dedication to the civil justice system are at the forefront of their lives.

The 1996 charges stemmed from a 1993 case against Sacred Heart Hospital. Fred's client had been hit by a pulpwood truck that had swerved to avoid colliding with a Sacred Heart bus that had made an illegal turn. In his opening argument, Fred told the jury, "The best way to determine how substantial the case is, is for you to look at the extent the lawyers in this case are going to try to convince you with what we consider to be ridiculous testimony." In his closing argument, Fred told the jury that if they felt "the defense witnesses were trying to sell you a bill of goods, then I think you should be very harsh with them."

The jury awarded damages against Sacred Heart to Fred's client, who had sustained severe pelvic injuries, in the amount of $4.5 million. The judge upheld the verdict in the Sacred Heart case, and it went to the appellate court, which reversed the verdict. It ruled that Fred should not

have described the defense case as "ridiculous," which it said was preju-
dicial to the jury because Fred was stating a personal opinion regarding
the facts of the case.

That ruling came down the day before Fred presented his closing argument in the Keith Rawson scuba case against Baptist Hospital. Though
he had talked to Martin that day, Martin didn't mention the ruling so as
not to distract Fred from his closing. That unfortunately only ended up
making things worse for Fred.

In the Rawson case, Fred's client was scuba diving in the Gulf of
Mexico when he came down with the bends. Rawson was admitted to
Baptist Hospital. The doctors then sent him to a hyperbaric chamber in
Panama City—103 miles away—rather than the local Naval Air Station
chamber that was 4 miles away. They also transported him by helicopter,
which is to be avoided when possible with a bends patient. The delay in
treatment, coupled with the flight, left him a paraplegic.

Unaware of the appellate court ruling in the Sacred Heart case, in the
Rawson closing Fred characterized the Baptist doctors' decision to transport a man in dire circumstances two hours away as "the most ridiculous
decision that anybody has ever made." Fred then called their defenses
"unbelievable" and "insulting." Though Fred won a $7.88 million jury ver-
dict, the defense attorney, Nixon Daniel, knew about the appellate court
ruling and succeeded in having the verdict against Baptist Hospital thrown
out on the same grounds.

Based on the rulings by the appeals courts in those cases, the Florida
Bar filed two charges of misconduct against Fred. The Bar charges were
for violation of the ethics rule that stated a lawyer shall not "allude to any
matter that that lawyer does not reasonably believe is relevant or that will
not be supported by admissible evidence" or "assert personal knowledge
of facts in issue."

"This likely made Dad the first person in the history of jurisprudence
to have charges brought over statements that were not even objected to
at trial," Martin says. "I attribute the whole thing to the animosity that
was building. People were jealous over Dad's success and they despised
his flamboyance."

"I felt like the boxer who says, 'I not only had to fight my opponent, I
also had to fight the referee,'" Fred says. "I had used the word 'ridiculous'

so many times over the years that I wondered publicly if I would face a thousand-year suspension. I doubted I would live long enough to survive such a punishment."

And of course, he couldn't resist publicly calling the charges against him "ridiculous." Knowing when to retreat was not a specialty of Fred's.

The consequences, however, were potentially serious because the previous "gambling" charge had been upheld and resulted in a public reprimand. Now Fred faced the possibility that he could have his license to practice law suspended.

The hearing itself was treated like a sporting event. The *Pensacola News Journal* ran a "Want to Go?" graphic normally reserved for a concert or sailboat race that detailed the "Who, What, When." The hearing was standing room only.

Martin represented Fred. He argued that sanctions against Fred were extreme, if not bizarre. At the two trials in question, defense counsel had not objected to what Fred had said, nor had the judges said anything. The fact was that the statements he made were tame in comparison to some in the history of Florida jurisprudence, Martin said. He also pointed out that the charges were the first ever brought in any jurisdiction based on statements a lawyer made in arguments to a jury. And, not to put too fine a point on it, he added that Fred was being selectively prosecuted because he had made negative statements about the Bar in the past.

The evidence Martin cited was clear. In seventeen previous cases where the Florida appeals courts ruled that an attorney had violated the ethics rule on interjecting personal statements into a trial, the Bar did not bring charges in fifteen of those cases. In one case, the Bar was uncertain whom it charged, and in the other case, the charges were not related to closing arguments. But none of those seventeen lawyers was Fred Levin.

As at the previous disciplinary hearing, Fred booked a parade of notable witnesses to appear on his behalf and to argue that he had not violated ethics rules. In his corner were Morris Dees, founder of the Southern Poverty Law Center; Philadelphia attorney Larry Fox, who chaired the American Bar Association's ethics committee; Florida State University President Sandy D'Alemberte, a former president of the American Bar Association; and highly regarded attorney J. B. Spence.

Their collective opinion was that Fred was zealously advocating for his clients and that sanctioning a lawyer for this would have a chilling effect on the legal process. The rule Fred was accused of violating was put in place to prevent lawyers from offering testimony to the jury and had nothing to do with strongly conveying a point based on admissible evidence.

Larry Fox testified that rhetorical flourishes were within ethical rules. J. B. Spence, known as the dean of closing arguments, said that a lawyer "cannot come in like a little timid schoolboy and try to persuade a jury." Sandy D'Alemberte clarified that the rules are "not intended to stifle advocacy." Morris Dees had gone through the transcripts of both trials. He read passages where the defense lawyers had made numerous personal observations, and pointed out that they were not being sanctioned. Dees concluded that the Bar was misconstruing its own rules by saying that under the Bar's interpretation of its rules, "everybody in the O. J. case would be disbarred by now, even that Akita dog."

The Bar called no witnesses. Their lawyer, David Ristoff, briefly cross-examined Fred's witnesses, all of whom said there were no ethical violations on his part. All of Fred's witnesses also criticized the entire process. The judge ruled in Fred's favor, concluding that he did not violate ethics rules. "In the end, the whole thing was ridiculous," Fred says.

As for the matter of the two cases that had been overturned because of the comments, the Sacred Heart case was eventually settled for an amount close to the verdict. The Rawson case, however, dragged out for five years.

In the retrial of the Rawson case, one of the potential jurors was a retired Navy captain. One of the attorneys working with Fred, Ed Holt, said the captain was an acquaintance and should make a great juror. "I certainly thought so," Fred recalls. "Every time I spoke, he took notes."

Surprisingly, the jury came back with a ruling for the defense. Fred later learned that the captain had told the other jurors that he knew for a fact that the Naval Air Station's hyperbaric chamber wasn't appropriate for Fred's client. The juror also supposedly said, "I just can't wait to see Fred Levin's face when we come back with a verdict for the defense."

Judge Kim Skievaski ordered a third trial. The judge ruled that he had made a mistake in the second trial by allowing the late addition of a defense expert witness. In the third trial, Fred won a $31 million verdict, the largest medical malpractice judgment in Escambia County to date.

"I told Ed Holt, 'Next time you see the Navy captain, tell him he could have avoided all this by giving us a $1 million or $2 million verdict,'" Fred says. "I also thanked the First District Court of Appeals for reversing the

$7.88 million verdict over my calling the defense ridiculous and giving me a chance to win the near-ridiculous amount of $31 million."

Fred's third brush with the Florida Bar was a doozy. It came in 2003 and led to an appellate court judge accusing him of a conspiracy involving another appellate court judge, former Florida Senate president W. D. Childers, and Governor Lawton Chiles.

The complicated case—which would take a PowerPoint to fully explain—began when Fred agreed to represent his old friend Childers against charges of violating the Sunshine Law, which held that governmental business should be conducted in the open with full honesty.

After Childers was term-limited in the Florida State Senate, he returned to Pensacola and was elected a commissioner of Escambia County in 2000. Though they were still in contact, by this time Childers and Fred weren't seeing as much of each other as they once had.

The case began when Childers and three other county commissioners were charged with violating the Sunshine Law. One of the commissioners, Willie Junior, turned state's evidence on Childers in hopes of a reduction in sentencing. Junior claimed that Childers had bribed him with a $100,000 loan as part of a deal for the county to buy a vacant soccer field, from which Childers would profit.

The Sunshine Law violation was a misdemeanor for a government official. However, after that trial, Childers would be tried for the more serious felony charge of bribery, which could land him in prison for several years. "W. D. called me about the misdemeanor case and I volunteered to represent him for free," Fred says. "I fully expected to represent him later on the more serious bribery charges as well."

Childers faced five counts in the Sunshine Law case. At the trial, he was found guilty of one charge. Fred says he later learned that one juror forced this because he was adamant that they find Childers guilty of something. The judge sentenced Childers to sixty days in jail for the conviction and refused to stay the sentence while Childers appealed.

Fred was shocked at the judge's unusual ruling not to allow Childers to remain free pending the appeal. This was a misdemeanor case, and the judge knew that by not allowing Childers to remain free pending the appeal he was ensuring that Childers would serve the entire sentence before the appeal would be resolved. The Friday that the ruling came down, Mark Proctor, the firm's president who was in charge of its public face, went to Fred's office and said that he was leaving for the weekend. He asked Fred not to blast people in the press over the conviction. He told Fred, "Just say, 'No comment.'" Fred said he would do just that—but it didn't quite turn out that way.

As usual, Fred couldn't hold his tongue. When a local TV station interviewed him, Fred called Willie Junior a "rat fink." He then told the *Pensacola News Journal*, "If Willie Junior was on the *Titanic*, he would dress like a woman and jump on the first lifeboat." Fred called the judge's ruling not to free Childers while he appealed "unconscionable." He also assailed the judge. "I have never been so embarrassed or ashamed of the legal profession," he told the paper. "I believe the inmates have taken over the asylum." Asked what exactly he meant, Fred replied, "That means the nuts are in charge."

So much for no comment.

A firestorm erupted. Fred was blasted by a local county attorney for making disparaging remarks about Junior. Fred backtracked slightly. He called his comments on Willie Junior a "joke" and said they were meant to be "humorous." He also admitted they were in "poor taste." One of Junior's lawyers sent Fred a toy rat wearing a dress. Though the lawyer said Junior did not see the comments as humorous, the Bar Association chose not to pursue a claim against Fred.

However, Fred's comments about the judge's ruling were another matter. These led to an ethics complaint being filed against Fred with the Florida Bar Association—the third in his career. Predictably, Fred came out swinging.

Fred railed that he had the right to free speech and continued to advocate for Childers. "Never in history has someone spent a day in jail for breaking the Sunshine Law," he told the *Pensacola News Journal*. "I thought it was wrong and I said so. I am very upset that I am being denied my right to say what I think."

Months later, the Florida Bar's grievance committee ruled there was no cause to pursue a full investigation into the matter. The Bar sent Fred a castigating "letter of advice" as to how to act in the future. The letter said: "While your conduct in this instance does not warrant formal discipline, the committee believes that it was not consistent with the high standards of our profession. The committee hopes that this letter will make you more aware of your obligation to uphold these professional standards, and that you will adjust your conduct accordingly." Of course, it was not likely Fred would follow that advice.

The fallout led to a fissure in Fred's lifelong relationship with Childers and more trouble for Fred. For their part, Childers and his family were upset at the single-count conviction, so they hired a different lawyer for the bribery trial. "This was a turning point in our relationship," Fred says. "His daughter was a lawyer in West Palm Beach. She and the family were real upset, thinking that I had screwed up the case."

In the bribery trial, it came out that Junior had previously stated that Childers had loaned Junior the $100,000 before the soccer field deal in question, but that he later changed his testimony to say that the $100,000 loan was because Childers needed Junior's vote on many issues, not just the soccer field. However, the court would not let Childers' lawyer point out that the reason Junior changed his testimony was that prosecutors had threatened to pull his immunity deal if he did not testify in a certain way.

Childers was convicted of bribery. Though Fred was on the sidelines as the Childers case worked its way through appellate courts, his name was about to be dragged back into the mix. Childers appealed his conviction to the Florida District Court of Appeals. One of the judges on the panel was Charles Kahn, a former partner at the Levin firm. Judge Kahn recused himself from all cases involving the Levin firm, but because Fred was not Childers' lawyer in the bribery case, he did not recuse himself from the Childers case.

The three-judge District Court of Appeals panel (led by Kahn) voted to send the case back for a new trial on the grounds that the circumstances surrounding the changes in Junior's testimony had not been admitted. But then, days before the decision was released for publication, one of the appellate judges asked for a rare en banc hearing, despite the fact that none of the lawyers had requested it. This meant that the full panel of fourteen appellate judges had to review the case. In the en banc hearing, the full panel reversed the panel of three and affirmed the conviction. In the opinion, Kahn wrote a strong dissent that the full panel was completely mistaken. He said that the law was clear that this was an evidentiary question that had never been before the court, and that the case should be retried.

Judge Michael Allen, one of the judges who voted to affirm Childers' conviction, responded with a blistering criticism of Kahn. Judge Allen also outlined what he saw as a potential conspiracy among Judge Kahn, Fred Levin, W. D. Childers, and Governor Chiles. Judge Allen pinned this on the fact that Kahn had been a former partner at the Levin firm and was the first judge Governor Chiles had appointed. He wrote: "And more suspicious members of the public would have assumed that Judge Kahn had simply returned past favors provided to him by Mr. Levin and Mr. Childers, thus allowing them, once again, to 'snooker the bastards.'"

Fred had gone through his share of run-ins with the Florida Bar and the courts, but he was slack-jawed that an appellate court judge was accusing him of being part of a conspiracy with the governor. Oddly, the facts not only did not support any of the allegations, they actually refuted them.

Judge Kahn had been appointed by Governor Chiles years before Fred enlisted Childers to change the law that allowed Big Tobacco to be sued and Childers went to Chiles with the plan. Fred was also not even part of the case, as Childers had retained a new lawyer after he was convicted of the one Sunshine Law violation. Further, accusations that Kahn had been paying back his old law partner were way off base because he recused himself from all cases involving the Levin firm.

Fred wasn't going to let this go. On Fred's behalf, Martin filed charges against Judge Allen—a twist that put Fred on the offense rather than the defense when it came to conduct. "It was absolutely crazy what he had said," Fred says.

The Florida Supreme Court reviewed the facts and found that Judge Allen had violated the Judicial Code of Conduct. He was cited for unethical conduct in the writing of his opinion on the Childers case. The court issued a televised reprimand of Judge Allen.

In the reprimand, the Supreme Court said that Judge Allen had "abandoned the requisite dignity" in writing his opinion. It said, in part: "Judge Allen failed to mention in his opinion that Judge Kahn was appointed to the district court in 1991, well before Childers, Fred Levin, and Governor Chiles were involved in the tobacco litigation. Judge Allen also did not mention that the Levin law firm did not represent Childers in his case. Judge Allen instead merely assumed that because Fred Levin, Childers, and Governor Chiles had professional relations and Judge Kahn had worked with Fred Levin before 1991, that Judge Kahn may have paid Levin back for past favors with his vote in Childers." The reprimand led to Judge Allen resigning from the bench.

But this was not the end of the case for Fred.

By now, Childers had appealed his conviction to the Florida Supreme Court, the same court that had sanctioned Judge Allen. Nevertheless, the Florida Supreme Court affirmed the conviction. The case then went to the US Circuit Court of Appeals, which reversed the conviction and sent the case back to the trial court in Pensacola based on the testimony issue. That appellate court then went into an en banc hearing on the case, where the court affirmed the conviction. As all these judicial machinations were taking place, Childers served four years in prison and was released. He continued to appeal because overturning the conviction would mean that he would receive his state pension and also have his legal bills paid by the state and clear his name, but a federal appeals court ruled against him in November 2013.

The strangest turn of events came when Willie Junior went missing the day before he was scheduled to be sentenced for his violation of the bribery law under his plea agreement. A month later, on December 9, 2004, Junior's decomposed body was discovered underneath the home of a former employee of his. There were empty Heineken bottles and a pill vial nearby. He had $60.76 in his pockets.

Authorities later announced that an autopsy found no signs of foul play. It was determined that Junior died from ingested antifreeze. His death was ruled a suicide. However, there were no shortage of conspiracy theorists in Pensacola that doubted the official cause of death. To this day, some remain convinced that Fred Levin was somehow involved.

"So that's the way things go," Proctor says. "Has there been from time to time a problem because of Fred? Sure. Has it brought the firm in ill repute? No. Have we all benefited personally and professionally because he is Fred Levin? Yes. Have we had to deal with people saying, why is he doing this or that? The answer: He does what he believes in even if it causes himself problems. That's just part of being Fred Levin."

CHAPTER

THIRTEEN

Up in Smoke

F red Levin was in his usual spot at 5 P.M.—at the bar, sipping a Crown
Royal, smoking a Benson & Hedges menthol. This particular gin joint
was in a hotel in Whistler, the Canadian ski town, where he was attending
an August 1993 meeting of the Inner Circle of Advocates. A lawyer from
South Carolina named Ron Motley pulled up a stool to join him. Motley
gestured toward the cigarette. "You've gotta stop that or they're going to
kill you," he told Fred.

It turned out that Motley wanted to talk tobacco, though not about
Fred's use of it. Motley was leading a concerted effort with lawyers in
several states to sue all of the major American tobacco companies. He
was preparing the first case in Mississippi, where he was working with
Attorney General Mike Moore and a crusading local lawyer named Dick
Scruggs. Their tactic was to file suit against the major tobacco companies
to recover all the Medicaid expenses that the state had spent on behalf of
smokers. They were planning to use antitrust and consumer fraud laws as
the basis for the suit, and they had asked the judge to remove the assump-
tion of risk factor associated with smoking. They had similar actions ready
to go forward in Minnesota and West Virginia, and Motley wanted Fred
to take the lead in bringing Florida into the fold.

"I thought he was out of his mind and told him, 'No way,'" Fred recalls. "Big Tobacco had never paid a nickel in court." And that was even if they could get the cases to court without the multibillion-dollar companies spending them to death—a big if.

But after Fred returned to Pensacola, he began to think about what Motley was attempting and wondered if it was possible. There was no entity more powerful than Big Tobacco, and taking them down would be legendary. Fred loved playing the angles. Was there an angle that no one had thought of?

First Fred consulted Harold Lewis, a friend who had served as general counsel for the Agency for Health Care Administration in Florida. Lewis told him that smoking-related illnesses were responsible for rapidly rising Medicaid costs that totaled in the billions of dollars. Fred then talked to Senator W. D. Childers about how unfair it was that the state couldn't recover money it had spent on tobacco-related illness. Childers agreed. But other than throw the long ball and sue, there didn't seem to be much that could be done.

One day, Fred was leafing through some law books and happened to turn to the Florida Medicaid Recovery Act, the state's third-party Medicaid liability statute. The light fantastic hit him. He realized that if he could change just a few words, it would be possible for the state to file a class action suit against Big Tobacco.

Fred then figured out that he could use statistics about smokers from the Centers for Disease Control and Prevention, rather than call in experts. Nationally, these were huge numbers: Tobacco use accounted for some 440,000 deaths per year and a staggering $157 billion in annual health-related economic losses. The evidentiary admission of these numbers was critical, because at that time each case had to be filed individually, followed by testimony from a doctor, whom the tobacco companies could counter with their own experts. Another small change in the current law would hold each company liable based on their market share, meaning that if a company had a 40 percent share of the cigarette market, then it would have to pay 40 percent of any damages.

With Martin and Bobby Loehr, Fred rewrote the Medicaid Recovery Act so that it could be used against Big Tobacco to recover Medicaid costs spent on smokers. However, to skirt due process and equal protection issues—and so Big Tobacco wouldn't notice they were being targeted—they wrote the law so that it was generic and could be used against any industry.

Fred called Childers and told him the idea. The Senate president fully backed the plan and set a meeting with Governor Lawton Chiles. Over breakfast, Fred explained the plan to the governor.

"He loved it," Fred recalls. "He said, 'Those bastards hooked me on their cigarettes when I was a kid.' He calculated that billions of dollars could be recovered for our state and other state governments from Big Tobacco to pay for the medical costs of people harmed by cigarettes."

Fred was excited. He wanted to hold a news conference, but Chiles was smart enough to know that would kill the whole thing. "Don't open your mouth. Don't even show your face," Chiles warned Fred. "Big Tobacco is too powerful. I can't even raise the cigarette tax by five cents a pack."

Chiles sent Fred and Childers to meet with Bob Butterworth, the attorney general. Butterworth was completely in favor of the idea, but he was highly skeptical that the bill would pass. Besides, he cautioned, the attorney general's office didn't have the personnel or the money to fight Big Tobacco in court even if the legislation did pass. "I told him to leave both issues to us," Fred says.

Clearly, a stealth strategy was needed to push the amendment through the legislature without anyone detecting its true purpose. Childers waited until the last day of the spring 1994 legislative session, always the most chaotic time. He was presiding over the Senate, and he presented the matter as a routine issue in the waning hours. The bill, called the Third Party Liability Recovery Act, was just four pages. It was slipped into a larger bill that transferred the responsibility for Medicaid fraud from the auditor general to the attorney general. None of the bill's sponsors mentioned Big Tobacco. The bill passed the senate unanimously, without debate, and the house followed suit on a voice vote.

Applying those four pages to Big Tobacco on the issues of subrogation, comparative negligence, and causation meant that tobacco companies could no longer use as a primary defense that smokers assumed the risk when they took up smoking—because the state never agreed to assume that risk. Second, and perhaps most importantly, it meant that the state did not need to prove that each Medicaid patient's illness was caused by smoking; rather, the state could use statistics to show that cigarettes caused a certain percentage of all illnesses. Last, it meant that any potential award would be based on a company's market share, which rendered irrelevant the brand that each of the Medicaid recipients smoked.

"When Big Tobacco found out what had been done, all hell broke loose," Fred says. "Initially, critics began hollering about politics and lawyer profits and overlooked the fact that this legislation would save thousands upon thousands of lives."

John French, a lobbyist for Philip Morris USA, railed, "This is probably the single biggest issue to ever have been run through in the dead of the night." John Shebel, president of the pro-business organization Associated Industries of Florida, told the *Orlando Sun-Sentinel*, "This is probably one of the worst laws ever passed by any Legislature." And Walker Merryman, vice president of the Tobacco Institute, said, "It's certainly creative, and it demonstrates how a government will try to impose a significant financial burden on one portion of the economy."

The focus was on the fact that the law Childers had changed could enrich his friend's law firm. The new bill was dubbed "the Fred Levin Relief Act." Predictably, tobacco company lobbyists were screaming that no other state had ever done anything so brazen. They vowed a fight to the death to have the law overturned.

Gannett News Service summed up the situation: "What they engineered was a first-of-its-kind bill making it much easier for the state to recoup money it spends for treating cancer patients and others with smoking-related diseases . . . It's created such an uproar in Tallahassee that tobacco companies have pledged millions of dollars to fight the bill either by getting it vetoed or using the upcoming special session on health care to change or eliminate it."

The Mississippi contingent of Ron Motley, Dick Scruggs, and Attorney General Mike Moore was also none too pleased. They wanted to take the national lead in the fight against Big Tobacco and felt Fred had stolen some of their thunder. Scruggs accused Fred of appropriating his idea to collect on Medicaid spending. "I said, 'Goddamn, this is smart,'" Scruggs told the *American Bar Association Journal*. "'How did they ever get away with it? They stole our idea, took it back to Florida, and did it better than we did.'"

But one thing was clear. Big Tobacco was being taken to the brink. "I could say, I think without exaggerating, that the financial life of the tobacco industry is riding on [the veto of the bill]," said John Banzhaf, executive director of Action on Smoking and Health.

It was time for the state to lawyer up. Governor Chiles instructed Fred to put together a team of lawyers to represent the state in what was sure to be a very long and expensive court battle.

"Because I got word that the lobbyists had their knives out for me, I knew that I could not be one of the lawyers," Fred says. "Neither I nor my firm could be part of the case because I had been involved in developing the law. That would give them ammunition to spin the story as Fred Levin changed the law to benefit himself. Worse, the whole thing could have been portrayed as Governor Chiles, who I met in the 1970s through Reubin Askew and struck up a friendship with, giving me a political payoff. So it was decided that I wouldn't be on the list; I would make the list."

There's a little bit of spin in Fred's take, according to Martin Levin. The fact is that his own law firm did not want the firm to be involved in the litigation because of the required manpower and costs.

"Dad's memory on that is not quite accurate," Martin says. "We were going to keep the whole thing, but we couldn't. We were deep into breast implants and HIV and neither one of them was working and we told Dad no way we had the resources, personnel or financial, to do it. That's when Dad went to get others for us to keep an interest."

Fred began calling lawyers all over the state. Very few were willing to accept. The estimated costs were $1 million per firm, with no cap and no guarantee of ever recouping those expenses. There was also a further downside. Because the lawyers represented the state, they could be sued for malpractice if they lost a multibillion-dollar case. This likely wasn't an issue with Governor Chiles in office, but should the case carry over, his successor might not see things the same way.

After a month of hitting the phones and lobbying lawyers at the Inner Circle of Advocates meeting in Manalapan, Florida, Fred signed up eleven firms with deep enough pockets to take the risk, including those of Bob Montgomery, Steve Yerrid, Shelley Schlesinger, Wayne Hogan, and W. C. Gentry. Fred dubbed the group the Dream Team.

"I had a personal stake because of my parents and their smoking addictions," Yerrid recalls. "I thought it would be a unique challenge. I love people who have never been beaten telling me they can't be beaten."

Pensacola attorney Bob Kerrigan was one of the last people Fred called. Kerrigan was a local plaintiff's attorney with a small firm, but he and his partner had made large sums of money in trial law and business investments. Martin told Fred that Kerrigan was a great lawyer and a friend, and would do an excellent job.

"I was the last one called," Kerrigan confirms. "I later found that out. They made it seem like I was on the first list. Then I talked to lawyer after lawyer who turned Fred down. I finally asked Fred and he said, 'We did ask a few other people—eighty or ninety.' Doing it just for image was enough for me. When I heard those names involved, to me it was an honor to be associated with them. I figured, hell, it will probably crash and burn, but it will be pretty cool."

State of Florida v. American Tobacco was filed on February 21, 1995. The suit sought to reimburse the state for $1.43 *billion* in Medicaid costs for past damages—a figure that could climb much higher because of other counts in the complaint, including future tobacco-related Medicaid costs and racketeering. In addition to Medicaid recovery, the case sought to stop the tobacco companies from selling their products to minors. In short, the suit stood to become a centerpiece for public health reform in the state, as well as an example for every other state. It also stood to generate attorney fees in excess of $350 million.

Meanwhile, Big Tobacco was hard at work filing court motions that declared the law unconstitutional and also twisting arms to have the law repealed. Using their incredible political muscle, they actually convinced the Florida State Senate—including the bill's champion, W. D. Childers—to repeal the bill. But Governor Chiles held his ground and vetoed the repeal. The bill went back to the Senate, and Big Tobacco pushed for a two-thirds vote to override the veto. They thought they had the votes, but on the day of the vote, a state senator whose uncle had died of lung cancer declared she could not live with herself if she voted for the repeal. She switched her vote, causing the repeal to lose by a single vote. The court case stayed alive.

But this was a gut-wrenching time for the lawyers. Steve Yerrid would call Fred at 3 A.M. and ask if he was awake. Groggy, Fred would reply that he had been sleeping soundly and ask why Yerrid was waking him up. Yerrid said that he was worrying about the case, and felt that Fred should be as well. Yerrid would complain to Fred: "I've already gone through a prince's ransom in costs and I've got people threatening me and following me, and you brought it all on. It's like we're retreating from Leningrad, and we are eating the horses and running out of horse meat."

"Well," Fred said, "we're gonna buy Leningrad when we win this."

Though the Levin firm had essentially stepped aside in the Florida case against Big Tobacco in 1994 as the other lawyers mounted the court battle, by 1997 circumstances had changed. It started to appear as if Big Tobacco would actually settle, provided, of course, the law held up. This led to the beginning of a scramble for millions of dollars in legal fees.

Nationally, the tide had started to turn against Big Tobacco. One of the key events occurred a year after the Florida case was filed. Jeffrey Wigand, a former vice president of research and development for the tobacco company Brown & Williamson, blew the whistle on the company. In an interview with Mike Wallace on *60 Minutes*, Wigand declared that despite the company's public denials, it intentionally altered the blend of tobacco in cigarettes to ensure increased levels of nicotine, the substance responsible for making cigarettes addictive. Essentially, Wigand told Wallace, the cigarette was simply a nicotine delivery system designed to keep people hooked.

The Levin firm began to stake out its position for Fred's role in the case. Martin and other law partners looked closely at what the firm would receive. According to Martin, the original deal with the Motley firm and the Scruggs firm was for the Levin firm to receive 25 percent of the Florida fee and 5 percent of national fee. The firm expected a similar arrangement with the other lawyers on the Dream Team, but it soon became clear that several of the lawyers involved didn't want to pay Fred Levin anything. These lawyers maintained that they would love to pay the Levin firm, but the rule was that it had to have clients in the case, which technically it didn't. As with Fred's pattern in other businesses, he had never followed through on getting a signed agreement with the Dream Team or the governor.

Martin and Mike Papantonio, the firm's senior partner, met with Ron Motley's partner, Joe Rice, to solidify the fee arrangement. "When Joe

Rice started being cagey, that's when Dad got involved," Martin says. "Dad and Mike began negotiating with Joe Rice, and I became involved from the legal standpoint to find a way to make sure we were protected on a fee. That's when we started to realize the ethical issue with not having something in writing."

In August 1997, the Florida case was set to go to trial. The only hurdle was one final test of the constitutionality of the bill. The Florida courts had affirmed its constitutionality, as had the US Court of Appeals. Big Tobacco appealed to the US Supreme Court, but the high court refused to hear the case, thus affirming the lower court's decision that the bill Fred wrote and his buddy W. D. Childers pushed through was constitutional. Rather than risk being on the hook for all the Medicaid expenses during the statute of limitations, Big Tobacco decided to settle. Governor Chiles and his lawyer stepped in to handle the final details.

On August 25, 1997, a settlement was reached for a minimum sum of $13.2 billion, at the time the largest settlement in the history of American civil litigation, and an absolutely staggering sum for companies that

Fred and Dream Team (close friends Bob Montgomery, Shelley Schlesinger, and Bob Kerrigan).

previously had refused to pay a nickel. In addition to reimbursing the state for Medicaid expenses, money was also earmarked for advertising and health education classes to help smokers quit, and to convince young people not to start. All of this was a complete and total reversal of how Big Tobacco had marketed and defended its products.

It was now time for lawyers to be paid. "As part of the fee process, we ended up becoming heavily involved with the state and all parties in the legal paperwork dealing with the resolution," Martin recalls. "This, along with the legal services we had provided prior to the time of the appointment of the Dream Team, allowed us to be listed as one of the counsel and entitled us to a portion of the fee."

Fred asked Childers to intervene and take the firm's fee request to Governor Chiles. "W. D. was extremely helpful, going to Governor Lawton Chiles and helping to convince him to allow us to receive the money," Fred says. "The governor agreed that we should share in the fee, but wouldn't allow any money to be paid to his top two legal advisers who had helped with the case. On December 11, 1998, the arbitration panel assigned the task of determining the fee released its decision, awarding the Florida attorneys $3.4 billion in fees to be paid by the tobacco companies. The next day, Lawton died of a fatal heart attack.

Though some of the Dream Team resisted paying Fred or the Levin firm, others, like Bob Kerrigan, felt it was fair. "The governor approved, it was a referral fee, and I never gave it a second thought," Kerrigan says. "I called Fred repeatedly about strategy. I didn't tell the other people that. I would ask, will this work, will that work? He stayed actively involved from my side, which was working up damages."

Out of the $3.4 billion fee awarded by the arbitration panel, Fred personally received 1.5 percent ($51 million). The Levin firm ended up with another 8 percent, or roughly $275 million, to be paid out over twenty-five years—roughly half of which goes to Fred. "I promised Lawton I would use it to better the state," Fred says.

The Florida case was the first time that all of the tobacco companies had paid any money resulting from smoking-related health issues. By the time the Florida settlement was reached, twenty-nine states had filed on similar grounds. Partly because the Florida law stood and the case was settled, Big Tobacco saw the writing on the wall: They and the plaintiff's lawyers forged a Master Settlement Agreement in November 1998. Big Tobacco agreed to pay the states $206 billion over twenty-five years—a landmark victory against a powerful force that nobody thought would ever capitulate.

"The tobacco litigation was controversial and continues to be, but history is on the side that these suits were both legitimate and necessary and very important to the financial compensation to the states," explains Richard Matasar, a dean at New York Law School until 2011. "History in this regard has been kinder to the plaintiff's bar than at the time it might have been."

For Fred's role in developing the law and putting the legal team together, he received a lot of publicity—both good and bad, which was all the same to him. Plenty of articles criticized him for not being one of the lawyers on the case but wanting a share of the lawyer fees for changing the law and putting together the team.

"When he put together the Dream Team and sued the state, I didn't like the Dream Team and didn't like the result," Florida attorney and former University of Florida president Marshall Criser says. "That was a bunch of rich trial lawyers that I thought took advantage of the situation. In fact, the case was settled not by the plaintiff's lawyers, but the governor, Lawton Chiles, and his lawyer." However, Criser concedes there was no denying the Dream Team took a large financial risk taking on Big Tobacco to reap a huge reward.

The *American Bar Association Journal*'s chronicle of the case and Fred seeking his fee was headlined "For Rigging a Statute, Lawyer Wants a Slice." Never mind that if the law hadn't been changed there would have been no case, or that those lawyers would not have been on the case had Fred not brought them in. "To me, all that came with the territory," Fred says.

On the flip side, Fred was the first of six lawyers who appeared in a *George* magazine photo spread titled "Puff Daddies," spotlighting the lawyers who had a hand in bringing Big Tobacco to its knees across the United States. In a two-page-wide photo, he was pictured as only he could be—standing on the putting green of his house wearing a tuxedo and sunglasses, sipping a cocktail, and holding a cigarette. To amp things up, he was also pictured on the contents page standing shirtless in a boxing pose next to Roy Jones Jr.

"I'm not sure whose nose I was rubbing it in, Big Tobacco or my enemies at the Florida Bar," he says. "But it sure was fun."

Probably the most attention Fred received was when he went on ABC's *20/20* to discuss the tobacco litigation. While correspondent John Stossel was interviewing him, Fred lit up a cigarette. "It was the least I could do after costing the tobacco industry billions of dollars," Fred says.

The lawyers working on the case were horrified. "Fred thought that was great," Steve Yerrid says. "That image was a killer for everyone on the Dream Team. It wasn't the impression we were trying to make. By that time, Big Tobacco was having us followed and videotaped, and we were all a little paranoid, but there Fred was flaunting it."

Eventually, Fred dealt with his own addiction to cigarettes—up to three packs a day at some points—which he had been hooked on for decades. The turning point came when he received a call on a Friday from his doctor. Fred had just undergone a routine physical. His doctor explained that he wanted to schedule an MRI the following week because the chest X-ray showed "just a little abnormality."

Fred was in a panic. He called a doctor friend to ask what this meant. The friend dismissed his concern, saying the odds were three to one that the MRI would show nothing. "I realized this meant there was a one in four chance that I had lung cancer," Fred says. "I became crazy with worry. I made a promise to myself that if I were free and clear, I would quit smoking cold turkey."

Fred was too nervous to wait until Monday for the MRI. He called a friend who arranged for a local doctor to open her imaging center that weekend. Fortunately, the test showed there was nothing of concern, but Fred kept his promise. That Monday, he gave away his last carton of cigarettes.

"One thing helped me kick it," he says. "I realized that I smoked the most when I drank. My drink at the time was whiskey. I switched to red wine, which is healthier, and it also reduced the association with smoking that booze triggered."

As the smoke cleared, so to speak, it became evident that the passing of the Florida statute that Fred Levin wrote was the engine that drove the train for the national tobacco settlement. Professor Richard Daynard of Northeastern University called the Florida law "the most significant piece of health care legislation ever passed in the US." That one law is credited with saving 100,000 lives every year in this country alone by convincing people to quit or avoid smoking. And one of those lives is probably Fred Levin's.

CHAPTER
FOURTEEN

Fred Levin's Presidential "Wall of Fame"

P eople who seek the spotlight angle to meet and be photographed with celebrities, athletes, and politicians. Fred has his "Wall of Fame" of 8 × 10s in his house. There are photos of him with President Bill Clinton, Don King, Bono, Elie Wiesel, Bob Hope, Emmitt Smith, and Mikhail Gorbachev. Through his interests and connections, Fred became friends with five men who were serious candidates for president of the United States. Three of them—Reubin Askew, Jack Kemp, and Bob Graham—were close friends. His friendships with the other two, John Edwards and Gary Hart, arose more out of circumstance.

Reubin Askew was a founding partner in Levin & Askew in 1958 with Fred's brother David. Askew and David met in the Boy Scouts and became lifelong friends. Throughout Fred's teenage years and during his time in law school, Askew was a constant presence in the family's life.

Askew's parents had divorced when he was young, and he liked the closeness of the Levin family. Though he didn't consider Fred's father a stand-in for his own father, Askew did call him "Pop."

Fred with three global leaders: former president Bill Clinton, former congressman Jack Kemp, and former Soviet Union president Mikhail Gorbachev.

"I loved Fred like a brother," Askew says. "Our families bonded. I became very close to them."

Fred recalls Askew always being around his family's house. As Fred grew up, Askew took it on himself to try to put Fred's wild side in line. "Reubin was like a big brother," Fred says. "He constantly lectured me on my smoking, drinking, and gambling. We were very different in many ways, but we thought the same politically and socially."

Askew recalls, "When Fred really started developing professionally, I could see that he was going to be a superstar. But he drank too much and gambled too much. I probably talked to him harder about those things than his own father or his brothers. He was an extremely bright, successful lawyer. I worried that these things were going to overshadow the accomplishments."

As a lawyer at the firm, Askew was popular in the community, and he soon turned to politics. In 1958, he was elected to the Florida House of Representatives. His political trajectory continued in 1962 when he was elected to the Florida State Senate. In those days, he was allowed to continue practicing law at the firm while he served in the state legislature. A significant turn of events came when Askew ran for governor in 1970—and won. When he was inaugurated, he resigned from the firm.

As governor, Askew undertook a reformist agenda. He was known as the first of the "New South" governors, along with Jimmy Carter of Georgia and Dale Bumpers of Arkansas. He dared to tax businesses, and he preserved land from development, something that powerful developers hated. He also made sweeping improvements in government ethics. He tossed out three cabinet members and three Florida Supreme Court justices due to ethical lapses, and he appointed the first African American Florida Supreme Court justice. He made "Government in the Sunshine" a cornerstone of his administration.

"Integrity could have been his middle name," Fred says. "Long before most politicians, Reubin voluntarily made his tax returns public. He said he wanted people to see where the money was coming from."

Fred recalls Askew delivering a powerful speech at the University of Florida on the need to bus children to integrate public schools. Afterward, Fred told him that he had destroyed any chance of being reelected. But Askew wasn't bothered. "Somebody has to show the strength to do the right thing and bring this country together," Askew said to him.

"Reubin didn't play it safe," Fred says. "My brother David, who worked in his gubernatorial administration, said people were amazed that Reubin changed the culture, which had been so corrupt. Reubin made sure that 'merit, not money' decided the issues."

During the 1972 presidential campaign, Askew was offered the vice presidential spot on the national ticket with nominee George McGovern, but turned it down. In 1974, he rose to the top of the list as the Democrats searched for a candidate for the 1976 presidential election. The election would play out in the wake of the Watergate scandal and President Gerald Ford's pardoning of Richard Nixon, so the Democrats knew they had a very good chance of recapturing the White House.

Askew was in Fred's office when Robert Strauss, the chairman of the Democratic National Committee, called and asked him to run for president. Strauss believed that a Democrat would win in 1976, and he was certain it would be a Southerner because the New South was an increasingly important part of the political map. Lady Bird Johnson, the widow of President Lyndon B. Johnson, was also on the phone call, lending her full support.

After Strauss laid out his case for Askew to run, Askew demurred. He told Fred that he didn't believe he was yet ready to be president. He also felt he needed to keep his commitment to serve as governor. Sure enough, a Southerner was elected president in 1976—Jimmy Carter, the governor of Georgia.

Askew entered the Democratic presidential race for the nomination in 1984. Though he visited all fifty states, his candidacy never gained any traction. As forward-thinking as he was on civil rights, Askew held conservative views that were at odds with liberal Democrats, such as being pro-life and opposing the nuclear freeze.

"There's no telling how things would have turned out if Reubin had run in '76 and been elected president," Fred says. "Reubin was an effective governor, and he wasn't afraid to take criticism if he knew what he was fighting for was just. That meant a lot back home because Reubin was more liberal than the typical Pensacolian."

Askew was later named one of the top governors of the twentieth century by Harvard scholars, as well as Florida State University's Alumnus of the Century. After he finished his second term as governor, he served as trade ambassador in the Carter administration. To this day, his portrait hangs in the lobby of the Levin law firm.

Through Reubin Askew, Fred was introduced to the next shining star in the Democratic Party, Senator Gary Hart, the man that the party faithful hoped would take back the White House in 1988. Hart was looking for moneymen, and with Askew's endorsement, Fred was willing to help. Fred hosted a lavish fundraiser for Hart at his Triton penthouse in Destin in 1987.

Hart called Fred a few weeks later and invited him to the Kentucky Derby. Hart explained that one of his biggest supporters was an owner of a favorite. Fred immediately accepted—despite the fact that the Derby was on the day of his daughter Marci's law school graduation.

Fred with Democratic presidential hopeful Gary Hart at Penthouse Triton.

Fred took Dean Baird with him to Churchill Downs. As the guests of the owner of the Derby favorite and friends of Gary Hart, Fred and Baird were treated like royalty. They were picked up at the airport and escorted through traffic by the Kentucky Highway Patrol. Their first stop was the stable of the iconic horse Secretariat.

"It was the most gorgeous horse you have ever seen in your life," Fred recalls. "A group of us were all standing around the horse. There were ten people, two ladies, two highway patrolmen, Dean and I and others. The horse got an erection. Dean said, 'One of those ladies must have the rag on.' I almost fell over."

At the Derby, Fred and Baird sat with Hart, and the candidate and the trial lawyer hit it off. Fred told Hart that he was off to Atlantic City to gamble for a few days. "I think because of Reubin and all the talk about gambling that Gary thought I had more money than I did," Fred says.

A couple of weeks later, Hart called Fred and invited him to Fort Lauderdale to go on a friend's boat for the weekend, but Fred had a work commitment. It turned out to be the infamous boat trip aboard *Monkey Business* where the married Hart was photographed cavorting with the vivacious blonde Donna Rice.

"When my favorite magazine, the *National Enquirer*, arrived with a picture of Gary Hart and Donna Rice on the cover, I pictured myself on the boat playing the drums and how that would have looked," Fred said.

Being a supporter of Reubin Askew and Gary Hart, and a liberal, Jewish Democrat to boot, Fred barely listened when his friend Kay Stephenson asked him to back Republican Jack Kemp for president after Hart dropped out of the 1988 race. Stephenson was close friends with Kemp. The two men had been roommates when they played for the Buffalo Bills, and Stephenson later coached the team when Kemp represented Buffalo in the House of Representatives. Stephenson had also coached Kemp's son in the Canadian Football League. No matter—Fred wasn't even interested in meeting him.

Kemp's 1988 presidential campaign didn't get far, as Vice President George H. W. Bush quickly locked up the nomination and eventually won the election, but Bush appointed Kemp his secretary of Housing and Urban Development. Kemp had another chance on a national ticket when Senator Bob Dole chose him as his running mate in 1996, but the Dole/Kemp ticket was steamrolled by Clinton/Gore, who won reelection.

After the 1996 loss, Kemp moved on from politics. He began serving on boards of large corporations, such as Toyota and Oracle, and start-ups, such as the Cinderella-story, business-to-business Internet startup Proxicom.

In 1999, Stephenson introduced Fred to SmartCop, a software business launched to help public safety agencies share information and react better to emergencies and day-to-day activities. Stephenson hoped to expand the company, and he asked Fred to invest and help recruit a strong board of directors to fuel the national expansion. Fred agreed, believing that it was both a promising business idea and an important nationwide law enforcement tool.

Fred recruited Terdema Ussery, who had become president of the Dallas Mavericks, and Robert Kennedy Jr., a law partner at the Levin firm. Stephenson suggested bringing on Kemp, who was interested. Kemp was speaking in Sarasota and then traveling to Biloxi for the wedding of Senator Trent Lott's daughter. Fred sent his plane to pick up Kemp and bring him to Pensacola, and then arranged for a limo to transport him to Biloxi.

Fred Levin and Jack Kemp hit it off from the minute they met. After spending the day together discussing SmartCop, the two men became friends until Kemp's death in 2009.

"Jack was a fighter and Fred's a fighter so there was a common respect there," Stephenson says. "They developed a very close friendship. There was lot of common ground between Jack and Fred. Fred is a most caring, kind person. Jack had a tremendous amount of empathy for those that were in need. That bond also extended to a lot of common interests as well."

Jimmy Kemp, Jack's son, says Fred's broad interests made him a natural friend for his father. He recalls there was a lot of ribbing between the two men over their ideological differences. "He got a kick out of Fred," Jimmy Kemp says. "Dad loved needling Fred about his being a trial attorney and a Democrat, and Fred always gave back just as good as he took. They had a very jocular relationship."

He says the fact that Fred attracted controversy was of no consequence to his father. "Dad liked people who were interesting and who had flaws because all of us have flaws," Jimmy Kemp continues. "He felt you couldn't trust people who were afraid of their flaws and had to appear perfect all the time. Dad never worried about guilt by association, so to speak. If somebody wanted to judge him by someone he was hanging out with, then that was their problem. He wasn't going to let that stop him from being friends with them."

Jack Kemp loved boxing, and Fred invited him to several of Roy Jones Jr.'s fights. Kemp returned the VIP sports invitation by taking Fred to the Super Bowl. "Jack and I partied together, and we had conversations that I will never discuss and the content of those conversations will die with me," Fred says.

Political connections: Fred and his friend Jack Kemp with Colin Powell.

Jack also invited Fred to the reunion of his Buffalo Bills championship team. Other than immediate family members of the team, Fred, Ussery, and Stephenson were the only three nonplayers invited.

"What I came to realize is that Jack Kemp would have been a great president and that party labels don't matter much," Fred says. "Character matters more."

Fred speaks equally highly of his friend Bob Graham, who ran for president in the 2004 election. Graham served as governor of Florida from 1979 to 1987. He was elected to the US Senate in 1987 and served three terms. He was best known for his work on the Senate Intelligence Committee, which he chaired during and after the 9/11 attacks.

Graham announced his bid for the Democratic presidential nomination in December 2002. Unfortunately, the following month he underwent open heart surgery, which dampened his campaign. Fred raised a sizeable amount for Graham's presidential bid. He had a major fundraiser planned for his house in Gulf Breeze, but the night before the party, Graham announced he was withdrawing from the race. Nevertheless, Fred held the party as planned.

"We have always maintained a close relationship," Fred says. "He was a fraternity brother at the University of Florida with my law partner Clay Mitchell, and he was a dear, dear friend of my partner Mark Proctor's family. Every time he would come to Gainesville, he would stay with Mark's parents."

After John Kerry had secured the 2004 Democratic nomination, many political pundits believed that Kerry would put Graham on the ticket because he was so popular in Florida, which could be the decisive state. However, Kerry instead chose another friend of Fred's, trial lawyer John Edwards.

About ten years after Fred was inducted into the Inner Circle of Advocates, the elite trial lawyers' association, John Edwards was elected a member. Fred found common ground with Edwards. Most of the members were big-city lawyers, such as Johnnie Cochran, but Fred and Edwards were both smaller-town lawyers who hit the big time in personal injury law. They met in 1990 when Edwards and his wife, Elizabeth, had drinks with Marilyn and Fred. "We hit it off immediately," Fred says.

Edwards told Fred that he was seriously considering running for Senate. Fred suggested that he do what Joe Scarborough had done in Pensacola. A virtual unknown in political circles, Scarborough had gone on BLAB-TV to become known and ended up winning a congressional seat over five challengers. Edwards liked the idea of building his profile through cable access.

"Lo and behold, the next time Edwards came to an Inner Circle meeting it was as Senator Edwards," Fred says.

Edwards—whom Fred calls by his given name, Johnny—pushed his way up through the political hierarchy. After serving four years in the Senate, he decided to run for president, a move that resulted in him winding up on the Democratic ticket with John Kerry. During that time, Edwards came to Pensacola for a fundraiser and stayed at Fred's house.

"What I remember most is that Johnny's status seemed to be going to his head—that and all the women loved him," Fred says.

After the Kerry/Edwards ticket lost the 2004 election, Edwards and Fred kept in touch—or rather Edwards kept in touch with Fred. Edwards' political ambitions were only buoyed by the 2004 loss. He entered the race for the Democratic nomination in the following presidential election cycle. Very quickly, the race turned into a three-person contest among Edwards and fellow senators Barack Obama and Hillary Clinton.

Edwards returned to Pensacola for fundraisers on two occasions. Fred was more than willing to round up donors for someone he knew who could possibly become president. However, Fred says that Edwards saw himself on a different plane altogether.

"Johnny became bigger than life in his own mind," Fred says. "When he came into my office the last few times, he tried to be like old times. I could tell it was, 'I'm here because you can raise me money. But you are beneath me. You're just a trial lawyer, and I'm going to be president of the United States.' It was as if he had forgotten where he came from. That is one of the things that is most important to me. I try to never forget my past and those who helped me get to this point. Still today most of my closest friends are from high school and college."

Of course, Edwards didn't become president. Far from it. At some point, he lost all touch with reality. He convinced an aide to take responsibility for his fathering a child out of wedlock with a campaign worker. Though he repeatedly lied about the situation publicly, he was eventually forced to take responsibility because of a *National Enquirer* article. Worse, this all occurred while his popular wife, Elizabeth, was undergoing chemotherapy.

Fred doesn't believe that Edwards' moral failings damaged the image of trial lawyers because ultimately people saw him for what he was: an overly opportunistic politician who forgot his own tagline—that he was the son of a millworker who had worked his way up from hardscrabble origins.

"His cover-up was the craziest thing anybody had ever heard and served as an example of hubris run amok," Fred says. "He was a great trial lawyer, but there was no way he could sell that story to anyone."

CHAPTER

FIFTEEN

Lady Justice Removes Her Blindfold

O ver the course of the 1990s, trial lawyers became viewed as shysters, pariahs, and bloodsuckers on society. In popularity, their ranking plummeted below used-car salesmen—perennially last on such a list. Many trial lawyer associations actually went so far as to remove "trial lawyer" from their organization's name, including the Academy of Florida Trial Lawyers becoming the Florida Justice Association.

One of the flashpoints for the change in public attitudes toward trial lawyers came in 1994 with what was known as the "Hot Coffee Case." A woman who suffered third-degree burns from McDonald's coffee that spilled in her lap sued the restaurant chain. She was awarded $160,000 in medical expenses and $2.7 million in punitive damages. ABC News called the case "the poster child of excessive lawsuits," and late-night comedians ridiculed the verdict.

The facts show that this was an overreaction. McDonald's franchisees were mandated by the parent company to keep their coffee at between 180 and 190 degrees, a temperature that the evidence showed could produce a third-degree burn in two to seven seconds. The reason McDonald's made its coffee so hot—145 degrees being the desired drinking temperature—was to make the coffee stay hotter longer, thus allowing them to sell more coffee. The judge reduced the punitive award to $480,000. Both parties appealed, and the case was eventually settled out of court. Though HBO later aired a documentary that showed the verdict was reasonable, the damage to public perception had been done.

The Levin law firm found itself adapting to a rapidly changing landscape, but it was a challenge that Fred embraced. Numerous forces were conspiring against the single-event cases that were Fred's bailiwick, and the large number of personal injury cases that were the firm's bread and butter began shrinking. This was due to a concerted effort by the US Chamber of Commerce (a mom-and-pop-sounding organization actually funded by Big Business), the insurance industry, and the medical profession, all backed by the politicians who relied on campaign funding from those organizations. The result denigrated the rights of injured victims and painted the trial lawyer as a pariah, blaming him for almost all societal ills.

The laws restricting victim's rights tightened considerably in many states. The lobbyists from those powerful organizations targeted the legislators to pass laws favoring Big Business. If the state representatives did not comply, then those organizations would withdraw their support and fund an opponent who would support their agenda. Damages and attorney fees were capped in many states, and laws were passed making it much more difficult to prove liability against wrongdoers, especially enough liability to warrant damages. The US Supreme Court also stepped in with rulings that made it more difficult to collect damages.

The standards for admitting expert testimony were also radically altered with the *Daubert* ruling. In *Daubert v. Merrell Dow Pharmaceuticals*, the Supreme Court ruled that the standard for admitting experts to testify in federal courts required a series of tests to be met before an expert could testify. This replaced the long-held *Frye* standard, which allowed an expert's opinion to be admitted based on what was generally accepted in the scientific community.

Though many states continued to follow the *Frye* standard, all federal courts shifted to the *Daubert* standard. This allowed judges to unilaterally *"Daubert* out" witnesses, thus declaring there was not enough scientific evidence for an action to be brought. Trial lawyers felt that this circumvented the entire premise of the jury system, because rather than allowing the jury to decide the credibility of the case and the witnesses, judges would be litigating from the bench.

Big Business compounded this situation by mounting political campaigns to remove unfavorable judges. As a result, the appeals courts turned dramatically in favor of the corporations. This meant that even if a large verdict were awarded at trial, it would likely be overturned on appeal. One by one, appeals courts in Alabama, Louisiana, Mississippi, and Texas all aligned against the common man and with Big Business. In fact, it reached the point in Texas where an astounding 96 percent of personal injury verdicts were being overturned on appeal. No matter what your point of view, there was clearly no way that such a high percentage of cases were improperly tried. It was a matter of judicial activism.

There was also a palpable shift in the attitude of juries. "When I started practicing law, juries were typically inclined to be on the plaintiff's side because they were the little guy, too," Fred says. "They put themselves in the place of the wronged party and wanted to believe that the case against the large corporation was legitimate. All I had to do was prove my case. But over the course of a decade, things changed."

When Fred stood in front of a jury, he says they felt as though he was one of them, not part of the Establishment. But as trial lawyers started winning bigger and bigger verdicts, and the Chamber of Commerce, the insurance industry, and the medical community started airing TV commercials railing that the trial lawyers were out for themselves, juror attitudes changed.

Because Fred had become so well known, the bar was even higher for him. There was a feeling every time he entered a courtroom, particularly in Escambia County, of juries saying to themselves: "That's Fred Levin. I'm not going to let him trick me." These suspicions were confirmed in the second trial on the Rawson scuba accident case when one juror declared that he wanted to see the shock on Fred's face when he lost.

There were endless TV ads claiming that lawsuits were driving up costs in the medical profession. Some ads said that hospitals could not afford to staff the ER because of trial lawyers suing them. Other ads claimed that because of trial lawyers always suing, cities might be forced to shut down the fire department, and that because of excessive lawsuits, public playgrounds might have to be closed. The ads were incredibly effective, and they slowly but surely moved the juries away from the trial lawyers. So instead of seeing themselves in the shoes of the plaintiff, the jury members began thinking, "I'm too smart to let that happen to me."

All of this propaganda against trial lawyers went a long way toward convincing jurors to support defendants. They would often make the case about the plaintiff's money-grubbing lawyer, rather than about the plaintiff's injury claim. The backlash among jurors against all plaintiffs made them less likely to find for the plaintiff, let alone award damages.

"Though people stopped seeing the trial lawyer as the protector of the little guy, the fact became that the trial lawyer was—and is even more so today—the only thing standing between corporate America and the consumer," explains Fred's partner Mark Proctor. "Certainly, the government isn't an effective defender. Even if the government does get involved with the FDA or Consumer Product Safety Commission, it's often too little, too late. And big corporations certainly don't police themselves."

One of the great ironies was that the deterioration of the single-event case was also partly due to its success. Plaintiff's lawyers had been instrumental in bringing about safety changes everywhere from the auto industry to Big Pharma. Looking back at the single-event cases, such as many of those Fred had won, companies were getting hit with so many repetitive, high-dollar verdicts that it became more cost effective to make the changes.

Take the Ford Pinto. When the fires due to the Pinto's faulty gas line were first reported, Ford was warned, yet did nothing. Then it lost a benchmark lawsuit and was hit with a punitive damage award meant to strip all of the profits made on the car. Though the award was radically reduced, Ford began settling other cases. As the number of cases mounted, the automaker finally just rebuilt the car—because doing so was cheaper than litigating and paying out settlements, or risking a huge punitive award that might stick.

Air bags are a prime example of the shift in car companies' actions. Lee Iacocca, the famed chairman of Chrysler, originally fought against air bags. He testified before Congress that mandating automobile manufacturers to install air bags in every vehicle would cripple them financially. But after verdicts began to pile up against the car companies for making unsafe vehicles, the math changed their thinking.

"Let's say you have a single-event case where someone is injured because their car didn't have an air bag," Martin Levin explains. "While that person may not be dead, they may be mentally impaired or paralyzed, and the amount of damages could be so huge that the car maker could spend $1 million trying that case and then be hit with punitive damages. Eventually, these companies were getting hit with so many verdicts that it became cheaper to install air bags and three-point harness seat belts than to continue being thrashed in the courts."

In the late 1980s, the Levin firm was regularly handling trucking cases. These involved major trucking companies running rigs with defective brakes, drivers smoking dope on the road, and every imaginable safety violation in between. The firm won several major lawsuits against irresponsible trucking companies. But by the late 1990s, these cases dried up almost completely. After being hit with so many large verdicts, the trucking companies initiated major changes in safety to prevent those accidents. They doubled their efforts to test the brakes on all commercial vehicles, and they began drug-testing their drivers. The result was a precipitous drop in accidents—and lawsuits, accordingly.

By doing their job, trial lawyers were destroying their own business. With people wearing seat belts in their air-bag-equipped cars, they were less likely to be seriously injured. Accidents still happened, but more and more people were walking away from them. As the world became safer because of what the trial lawyers did, the single-event case slowly but surely became a shrinking business.

To capitalize on its reputation and maintain its flow of cases, in 1993 the Levin firm started advertising locally. "This caused great turmoil within the firm," Fred recalls. "My brother David, who had started the firm, was vehemently opposed, as were some of the other older, more conservative lawyers. They thought it made us look like ambulance chasers, the worst of the plaintiff lawyer's breed."

After a lengthy internal debate, the firm reached an agreement to undertake certain limited TV advertising as long as it was classy. It also made what Fred considers to be the greatest legal ad ever. The ad featured Fred sitting on the edge of his desk, talking to the camera.

> *Over thirty-one years ago, I started practicing law in this firm with Reubin Askew. At that time, I never imagined that Reubin would become governor of Florida, that we would have two former judges in*

the firm, that we would have twenty-four attorneys, a medical doctor, and a seven-person investigation department. A lot has changed in thirty-one years, but one thing hasn't. When you call for me, I return your telephone call.

The impact was tremendous. "It said that you still have an ally, a friend, and a lawyer in Fred Levin," Fred says. "The University of West Florida marketing school called it the best legal ad they had ever seen."

The ad certainly made its mark. Many years later, long after the ad had stopped running, one of Fred's partners, Troy Rafferty, was trying a case. He was in the process of selecting a jury. As a matter of course, Rafferty told the potential jurors that two of his partners, Fred Levin and Mike Papantonio, were rather well known. Would this affect any jurors? A lady in the back of the courtroom raised her hand. "This is against Fred Levin," she said. "On September 1, 2005, I called his office, and he never returned my call." In actuality, she had called for Fred's brother Stanley.

"The ad stemmed from hearing so many people say they couldn't get a return call from a doctor or a lawyer," Fred says. "As a result of this, I never leave the office without returning my calls."

Sometimes talking to everyone can be a dicey proposition. People in a mental institution will call and tell Fred's secretary they must talk to him. He'll take the call. The woman will be all wound up and say, "Fred, the doctors have put a transistor in me and they can hear all my thoughts." He'll respond, "Well, we have to do something about that." Calmer, she'll say, "Yes, Fred, we do." He'll then say, "You tell your doctor that you talked to me, and you tell him to call me." She'll thank him and hang up feeling much better about her situation. "Most lawyers won't take calls from people they don't know, let alone from patients in a mental institution," Fred says. "For me, it's part of the business."

Despite the changes occurring in the profession, Fred and the firm were still able to win several big cases and use the existing laws in their favor. One case that took several years to bring to a close involved negligence on the part of behemoth retailer Walmart. The case, which Martin led, stemmed from the 1991 shooting of a man during an auto parts store robbery. Two young men, one eighteen, one seventeen, shot and killed the client's husband. They had purchased the ammunition at Walmart despite the fact that federal law prevents the sale of pistol ammunition to people under twenty-one. The widow sued Walmart, claiming the store was partly responsible for the killing of her husband. It was the first case of its kind in Florida and the only one in the nation to that date dealing with the purchase of ammunition.

When the case was first brought in 1992, a circuit court judge dismissed it. The judge agreed with Walmart's lawyer that the store could not foresee the teenagers would use the bullets to murder someone; therefore it did not bear any responsibility. In 1994, the District Court of Appeals reinstated the case. The court cited the Gun Control Act of 1968, which Congress had passed to prevent people deemed to be dangerous from obtaining firearms or ammunition. Walmart appealed the ruling to the Florida Supreme Court.

In a landmark 1995 ruling, the Florida Supreme Court held that Walmart could in fact be held liable. It was the first-ever case where the court ruled that a seller may be liable for an illegal sale of ammunition. During this time, the two gunmen were convicted of murder in criminal court. One was sentenced to death, and the other received life in prison.

The Walmart case was tried in circuit court. The jury found that Walmart was 35 percent responsible for the killing and the gunmen and their three accomplices were 65 percent responsible. The jury said that the family was entitled to $2.1 million in damages, which the Florida Supreme Court eventually held Walmart was fully responsible for paying.

The victory provided some justice for the widow, but also was a takedown of Walmart. Throughout the process, Walmart's lawyers pushed back with all their might. "In all my years, I have never dealt with a more callous company," Martin said at the time. "Not only did they deny everything, they attacked and belittled my client."

This was a classic example of a plaintiff's lawyer using deep pockets to institute a positive change. Holding stores that sold ammunition and weapons to minors accountable was a small step toward curbing juvenile crime. It drew the beginnings of a line in the battle to keep guns and ammunition out of the wrong hands. "The case resulted in better training procedures for all large corporations selling firearms and ammunition throughout the country," Martin says.

But the changing tide against trial lawyers and personal injury lawsuits also empowered the insurance companies. Many insurers began to push back against large—and in some cases, any—settlements. In a 1999 case in Alabama, Fred represented the estate of a seventy-five-year-old doctor who had been killed by a drunk driver, who had also died in the accident. Several Alabama attorneys had refused to take the case, saying it was not worth enough money to justify the time and costs because the drunk driver had already received the ultimate punishment: death. The insurance company for the drunk driver eventually offered the estate $400,000, despite the fact that there was $11 million of coverage available. Fred took the case to trial.

The law in Alabama required that the jurors punish a defendant as a deterrent to others, which is unlike the damage law of any other state. Fred zeroed in on this point at trial. While questioning potential jurors, Fred stressed that the case was one of deterrence. The drunk driver had a blood alcohol level three times the legal limit, as well as several drugs in his system, including cocaine. Fred told the prospective jurors that they needed to send a message to everyone in the state that such behavior was unacceptable.

At trial, Fred won $7.5 million for the doctor's estate, an award that could not be contested because of an agreement set in advance called a "high-low," which established the range of the award in the event damages were awarded.

"One of the potential jurors argued with me about all the lawsuits in the country and said that he was sick of everyone wanting a handout," Fred recalls. "I pushed back with the law and the facts and made him out to look like a nut. Though he wasn't seated, before the trial even began I had made my point to those who were seated."

By 2000, trial lawyers had become Public Enemy Number One. *Time* ran a lengthy feature story in July of that year headlined "Are Lawyers Running America?" There was a picture in the magazine of Fred wearing a red blazer and sunglasses and leaning on his vintage Rolls-Royce. The article used as the flashpoint the fees being paid out from all the tobacco settlements—some $10 billion in all—and it delved into several attention-grabbing class action cases. "We're the last bastion," Fred declared in the article. "We're the last fighters available for the little guy."

Forty-five states had enacted civil justice reforms that restricted large punitive damage awards. Senate Republicans had put forth the Litigation

Fairness Act, which was meant to curtail the types of lawsuits that could be brought against corporations. Then, in his 2000 presidential campaign, George W. Bush portrayed trial lawyers as evil—not surprising since his campaign was funded by Big Business, which was often on the defense in personal injury lawsuits. He promised to be "a president tough enough to take on the trial bar." Bush vowed to institute national reforms on lawsuits similar to those he had enacted as governor of Texas in the mid-1990s, and he followed through after he was elected.

The Bush administration also moved to limit medical malpractice awards. Rising insurance rates and health costs were blamed on trial lawyers, rather than on insurance companies and mismanagement in the medical community. Companies began saturating the airwaves with ads against trial lawyers.

"When people hear the president of the United States demonize trial lawyers as he did over his entire presidency, there is inevitably going to be a change in attitudes," Fred says.

The judges that Bush and other Republican leaders appointed were uniformly pro-business, anti–personal rights, anti–trial lawyer. "Far too many appeals court judges were politicians rather than lawyers who appreciate the beauty and consistency of the law," Fred says. "This is the result of Bush and his 'brain,' Karl Rove, who made a big point of taking over the appeals courts and allowing judges to put their conservative political leanings into their rulings.

"To me, it was sad that Bush and Rove and the Republicans were able to do this to the court system, but it is what the US Chamber of Commerce and the insurance companies wanted," Fred continues. "The only advocate for the consumer remained the trial bar, but the fact is that we don't have the money to stand up to the Chamber and these groups that are the agents of Big Business."

Florida was also joining the anti–trial lawyer bandwagon. "The Chamber raised money to oppose retention of two Florida Supreme Court justices," Fred says. "They have also successfully painted the trial lawyer as a dastardly guy who convinces juries to do things that are ridiculous. This has made trying cases and seeing them successfully through the appeals process to get justice for people very, very difficult."

Yet even as the tide was changing throughout the 1990s, Fred continued to win cases. By 1999, he had won thirty jury verdicts in excess of

$1 million over his career, including one for $25 million and another for $50 million, and had settled more than seventy-five other cases in excess of $1 million. Still, it was clear that a shift in his firm's focus would be necessary if it was going to thrive—or even survive. Single-event personal injury cases were drying up. The future, it appeared, lay in the emergence of a new breed of cases that had begun to take shape over the 1990s known as mass torts.

CHAPTER

SIXTEEN

Mass Torts: One Case, One Thousand Clients

Mass tort cases are civil actions that involve misconduct by a single wrongdoer that causes harm to many people, but not enough harm to any single person to justify bringing single-event cases. These differ from class actions, where all plaintiffs are treated the same. In a mass tort, each plaintiff may have a different level of injury and still be part of the action.

The costs of pursuing a mass tort action generally exceed the recovery any single case can attain. Thus, the cases have to be bundled in large groups with the liability being established as a whole, followed by individual damages being assessed. It is not uncommon in mass tort cases for lawyers to spend millions of dollars establishing liability in order for thousands of clients to individually receive tens of thousands of dollars to millions of dollars, and everything in between.

Fred Levin had little interest in getting involved in mass torts himself. He was an old-school lawyer who met his clients and tried cases in front of juries. Mass tort lawyers would never meet their clients, and settling the cases was far more financially viable than trying them. But he had also built his firm to take chances.

The Levin firm's mass torts adventure began in the late 1980s, when Mike Papantonio (then a young partner in the law firm, known to one and all as "Pap") took over some asbestos litigation from Dick Warfield, a senior partner in the firm. One Friday afternoon, Papantonio received a call from Warfield's office. Warfield was supposed to be in trial on Monday, but he was calling to tell Papantonio he couldn't handle the litigation.

"I went to Dick's office and there were file boxes everywhere," Papantonio recalls. "It was a complete mess. I took the files home over the weekend and discovered that Dick had not done anything to prepare these cases for trial. Worse, the statute of limitations was running out on many of them."

Papantonio got the Monday case continued, and then put the asbestos cases back together and took control of the process. Though he lost the first several cases, Papantonio was thinking big picture and long term. He contacted Ron Motley, the lawyer who eventually would spearhead the national tobacco litigation. Motley was one of the few attorneys in the country who was handling asbestos from multiple client standpoints. Papantonio, Motley, and a few others then began to team up for purposes of combining talent and assets to fight the asbestos industry.

At that point, the litigation started to change, and Papantonio and Motley began securing million-dollar verdicts. Papantonio decided it was time to expand the operation and contacted his college roommate, John Morgan, who was developing a successful personal injury law practice in Orlando. Morgan was a master promoter, particularly when it came to television advertising.

Morgan and Papantonio began a television campaign in Florida to round up as many asbestos cases as they could. Papantonio's vision was that he could leverage the volume of cases in order to get timely and proper recovery for his clients.

"Many lawyers in the firm had concerns about Pap expanding us into multiclient litigation," says Martin Levin. "Pap quickly went from a few hundred asbestos clients, to thousands, and began pushing the firm toward other nascent cases such as breast implant and hemophiliac AIDS cases. Very few lawyers could understand this, and most of the firm thought Pap was nuts. But Pap envisioned the future of mass torts and would not be deterred."

The expenses of developing a mass torts department rapidly began to balloon, and the firm's partners had to invest a significant sum of their money and personally guarantee the loans being made to the law firm from various banks. In the same way that a plaintiff's lawyer was at risk for the costs of putting on a personal injury case, the firm had to front the expenses for mass tort cases. The difference was that mass tort cases by their nature were much bigger, far more expensive, and on their face more complicated to bring. The risk of each project became enormous, and a source of much contention within the firm.

In the early 1990s, when Papantonio was attempting to create a mass torts department, the Levin firm was a full-service law firm. It handled criminal law, family law, wills and trusts, corporate documents, and of course, personal injury. Papantonio was on the fourth floor of the Levin firm's high-rise building creating what appeared to be a secretive yet expensive fiefdom, while Fred was on the ninth floor continuing as the high-profile and ostentatious rainmaker handling single-event cases.

By this time, Martin had become the acting managing partner at the firm, and he was caught in the middle of a developing internal struggle. Personal injury single-event cases were responsible for close to 80 percent of the firm's entire revenue. Mass torts was not paying its way at that point due to the high staff and expenditures needed to develop the cases, and the fact that cases were not yet getting resolved.

Fred also didn't perceive mass torts as real lawyering. "I don't see the practice of law as representing 1,000 clients that you don't know with the basic purpose—in the vast majority of cases—being to reach a settlement," he says. "To me, this was a business more than the practice of law. I've always believed there was the need to represent a person who you had some relationship with, not a group of names on a list."

On the other hand, Fred was troubled by the immense number of people harmed by the grotesque conduct of corporations, and the fact that these individuals were going uncompensated for their injuries. "The outrage I felt seeing what some of these corporations had done over a period of decades mirrored what I had experienced in some of my cases," Fred says.

While Fred didn't like the immense costs involved in the litigation, and didn't really agree with it being lawyering, he decided to support Martin on the bet that Papantonio's vision of the future of mass torts would pay off. Fred's position was that he had built the firm to have the wherewithal to take chances. The older lawyers couldn't understand his support of mass torts; to them, it was a boondoggle that they were convinced would bankrupt the firm. "I didn't know if it would or not, but my family and I were well taken care of, so I was willing to take the risk," Fred says.

Many of the other lawyers in the firm, especially the non–personal injury lawyers, were not as complacent, and in fact were openly antagonistic. Their anger escalated when Martin recommended that the focus of the firm needed to change. Martin did not believe the law firm could continue as a full-service firm, and he felt that all non–personal injury attorneys needed to switch to personal injury law, except for his uncle David, who had founded the firm; his uncle Stanley, who had been with the firm since the 1960s; and Leo Thomas, who was an accomplished criminal defense attorney.

Animosity against Martin began to appear, but there was nothing that could be done, as Fred supported him. Fred was also the rainmaker keeping the firm profitable. For his part, Martin was becoming one of the higher wage earners based on a string of million-dollar jury verdicts and settlements.

By the mid-1990s, the firm had reached its boiling point. Martin did not believe it could continue in its present structure. He went to Fred and convinced him that the firm needed to be split in two. There would be Levin-Papantonio (for mass torts), and Levin-Middlebrooks (for single-event cases). Fred would be part of both, but everyone else had to choose sides. Fred agreed. A special meeting was called at the eighth-floor dining room.

The room had been specifically designed with an extraordinarily large round table in the center so that all of the lawyers could sit and see one another. Martin called the meeting to order and announced the plan. He began going around the table, asking everyone which firm they wished to be a part of. He explained that different books would be kept, so that no one in either firm would be responsible for the liability or debt of the other.

Lawyers began announcing their intentions, and things were proceeding just as Martin had hoped. The vote came to Bobby Blanchard, a partner in the law firm. Blanchard was the son of M. C. Blanchard, one of the most respected judges to come out of Pensacola. The Escambia County courthouse is named after Judge Blanchard. He once wrote a reference about Fred to the Florida Bar in which he stated that Fred was the best lawyer in Escambia County and likely the state of Florida.

Bobby Blanchard was silent. He didn't know what to say. The emotional toll it was taking on him was obvious. Blanchard finally commented he would go with the personal injury firm.

The vote finally reached Fred, who announced: "This is not the right thing to do. We have been a firm for forty years, and we should remain a firm. We simply need to work it out."

Martin was floored. His father had reneged. Later, when Martin asked Fred privately why he did it, Fred said he couldn't divide the firm after seeing Blanchard's reaction.

The firm would stick together, but everyone surmised that Martin never would have brought this up for vote without Fred having first agreed. Thus, they knew everything was close to blowing up. Martin was tasked to come up with a solution. After he met with every lawyer individually, it was decided that all lawyers would have to start paying their own way. Specifically, at the end of the year, the costs of all staff a lawyer hired would be set off against their revenue to determine the actual net revenue the lawyer created for the firm. Each lawyer's net revenue would be compared for purposes of determining his or her annual income. The goal of this new compensation system was to significantly lower the incentive for an individual department (such as mass torts) to hire numerous employees in the hope of recovering future income.

The system seemed to appease most of the lawyers. Those who wanted to participate in mass torts (specifically Papantonio, Martin, Fred, and Larry Morris) began paying for TV ads on mass torts out of their own pockets, and they also began taking a huge hit against their annual revenue to pay for the mounting costs of mass torts. Fred's son-in-law Ross Goodman and Jim Green soon joined and headed up the hemophiliac HIV litigation.

Fred remained skeptical of mass torts, especially as the costs were mounting without any real returns, other than for asbestos. He continued to support the division simply because he wanted to defer to Martin's judgment on this, and wished to see the injured recover. After all, Fred foresaw turning the firm over to his son one day.

By 1999, the mass torts department was building an extensive caseload and national reputation, but was not extremely profitable. Asbestos was doing well, but the firm barely broke even on breast implants, hemophiliac HIV litigation, and *qui tam*. Pursuing mass torts cases, however, had become accepted (or better to say, tolerated) among those lawyers remaining in the firm, which by now did not look nearly the same as it had a decade earlier when it was named Levin, Middlebrooks, Mabie, Thomas, Mayes & Mitchell. To reflect the new hierarchy, the firm now was known as Levin, Papantonio, Thomas, Mitchell, Echsner & Proctor, or Levin-Papantonio for short.

In 1999 and then again in 2001, there were dramatic changes at the Levin-Papantonio firm. In 1999, the firm gained immense national exposure when Fred appeared in numerous magazines and television programs being credited with the tobacco litigation. It became well known that the Levin firm was to receive close to $300 million for its efforts. Then, just two years later, the firm once again made national news in the legal community when the firm received in excess of $100 million in attorney's fees for its part in the litigation over the diet drug Fen-Phen, which caused an elevated risk of cardiac arrest.

With mass torts' success making national news, suddenly every lawyer wanted to be in mass torts, and many thought they could effortlessly enter the field. From their perception, all the Levin-Papantonio firm (and specifically Pap himself) was doing was advertising for cases, and then settling them en masse because of the pressure on defendants of large potential liability. Lawyers all over the country began popping up on television advertising for mass torts cases. Toll-free numbers like 1-800-BAD-DRUG were used in television ads to solicit cases. Many, if not most, of these lawyers had no intention of trying to work up the cases, nor did they have the ability or finances to do it. Instead, they hoped to build an inventory of clients through advertising, and then settle the cases directly with the defense on the theory that the defense could get thousands of potential litigants to disappear by simply settling the cases.

Unfortunately, these newcomers were clueless regarding the complexities of mass tort litigation. They simply had no idea how difficult and costly it is to mount a successful mass tort campaign against a large corporation. It takes years of litigation, millions of dollars, and tens of thousands of hours of attorney and paralegal time. They also had no concept of how hard Papantonio had worked over a decade to build a legal team that could spend millions of dollars taking hundreds of depositions and reviewing millions of pages of documents in a single mass tort case without any realistic hope of a quick settlement. They perceived Papantonio as a competent salesman they could emulate. They didn't grasp the sophistication of his efforts, and the true nature of his legal and trial skills that was making all of this work.

Corporate America saw the tobacco and Fen-Phen settlements as huge mistakes. They saw these huge payouts of fees as funding their enemies, who could wage even larger and more protracted litigation. They saw their enemies, with their new wealth, becoming players in funding state and national politics. They concluded that reaching settlements with plaintiff firms was no longer good business. Instead, they now chose to extend the litigation, costs, and staff demands as much as conceivably possible in the hope of driving the plaintiff firms under financially. Now the challenge has become a matter of financial staying power and willingness to commit to the long term before any potential payoff, which is a game relatively few can play.

Interestingly, and with the typical Levin luck, this change in strategy is working to the advantage of Levin-Papantonio. No longer do the small plaintiff firms believe they can play at mass torts without the assistance of Levin-Papantonio or the few other firms in their league. Levin-Papantonio became a giant in the field, with lawyers all over the country consulting them to handle their cases. The firm performs the work and extends the money, and the lawyer referring the case gets a piece of the action, if and when it ever works out.

Levin-Papantonio has also taken the lead to both clean up the mass torts practice and make it more cohesive—which has made them more money. The firm (along with John Morgan) started Mass Torts Made Perfect (MTMP), a conference held twice a year, usually in Las Vegas, to bring together mass tort lawyers from across the country. Papantonio came up with the idea during the Fen-Phen case as a takeoff of a program Morgan and Papantonio were already doing called Practice Made Perfect. During Fen-Phen, Papantonio needed a way to bring in 4,000 cases to put enough pressure on Wyeth, the drug's manufacturer, to resolve the suits. He wanted to start teaching other lawyers how to advertise for mass tort cases and sort through them. The strategy worked out so well that it has been significantly expanded. In essence, MTMP has created a national law firm without the infrastructure of a national law firm, but with all the muscle.

"We have taught people what we do, because there is a need to orchestrate and galvanize our attacks," explains Mark Proctor, president of the

Levin firm. "A big part of MTMP is that it gives us our own army. This allows us to launch a George Patton flank attack in these cases. The surrealistic beauty of it is that when it is time to declare war on a company, we tap into our MTMP participants and do it with 100 firms. We all try to file everywhere on the same day."

Levin-Papantonio is in it for the long haul. Gone are the days at the Levin firm when the single-event personal injury cases funded the firm, and mass torts was a small contributor. It's just the opposite today: Single-event cases are drying up. They don't exist any longer because air bags, the use of seat belts, and better-designed vehicles now limit injuries even in major motor vehicle accidents. Fred still pulls in a few major cases each year, which make up the bread and butter that covers the annual costs of the firm, but the real sugar comes from the mass torts cases that resolve by settlement or trial.

Ironically, all of the success Levin-Papantonio has enjoyed ended up running Martin out of practicing law. Over the years of practicing trial law and running the firm, Martin became disgusted with the legal process. At first his feelings were directed toward defense lawyers and how deceptive and callous he perceived they had become. Next his anger turned to the judges, many of whom he saw as unprepared, failing to timely rule, and failing to take control and discipline lawyers who were violating their ethical code in the name of zealous representation. Eventually his anger turned toward his own clients. Many were greedy and willing to lie if they thought it meant collecting more money. Last he became fed up with other plaintiff's lawyers who lazily thought they didn't have to try cases; they could just settle them on the coattails of others. So after the tobacco fees began coming in and as mass torts were paying off, Martin concluded that he was well enough off financially that he could quit.

"I knew he was depressed, but I didn't know the full extent," Fred says. "The breaking point came one afternoon. We had just won a $32 million verdict in a medical malpractice case that we had tried together, as we often did. As we were walking out of the courthouse, I put my arm around him and said, 'Let's go get a drink.' He stopped. 'No, Dad,' he said. 'It's too much money for a case like this.' My first thought was, damn, what's wrong with *my* son?"

It turned out that money also became one of the reasons for Martin quitting the practice. "I no longer knew if I was doing it for the good of the client and society, or for my one third," Martin says. "When I couldn't honestly answer that question, I decided it was time to walk away."

Not long after the $32 million verdict, Fred's brother Allen came to Fred and said that they and Martin were going to meet at Copeland's restaurant for cocktails. "Whatever you do, don't get upset," Allen warned Fred. "Martin is going to divinity school at Harvard. When he tells you that, the last thing you want to do is try and talk him out of it."

Fred was floored. "I asked if he was becoming a Jew for Jesus," Fred says. He wasn't; he was just opting for something radically different. When Martin told his father that he was leaving the practice that Fred had worked to build since 1961 and pass on to Martin, Fred did not resist.

"The truth is, I thought he was crazy as hell," Fred says. "Martin was already running the firm—the firm that would be his firm. He was very, very good at what he did. He was making millions of dollars per year. I daresay he was one of the best lawyers I have ever seen. But I also realized right away that he wasn't going to return."

Martin eventually graduated as a Master of Theological Studies from Harvard Divinity School, and as a Master of Public Health from the Harvard School of Public Health. Though Martin left the firm more than a decade ago, and now lives with his wife Terri and two young boys in Boston, he and his father are still best friends, talking business and personal matters two or three times every day, and occasionally going on gambling trips to shoot dice. Martin even litigated a personal insurance claim for Fred recently that dragged through the court system for years without any substantive offer ever being made. The judge ruled in Martin's favor on every single issue, and Fred was awarded $2.1 million.

Fred has become resigned to the fact that his son will not return to the law firm that Fred built to turn over to him. Instead, Martin now devotes his time providing free legal services to various charitable organizations, including the Robert F. Kennedy Center for Justice and Human Rights, where he serves as special counsel.

"To this day, I think he made a mistake," Fred says. "I can't say that I understand the decision fully, but on most days I've learned to accept it."

Epilogue

The Aging Elephant in the Circus

After spending a year researching and writing this book, I have a mixed perception of trial lawyers of Fred Levin's caliber. They can be heroes, yet vulgar. Their actions often are motivated by immense financial incentive, but also often result in colossal societal health benefits that could not be attained without them. They can be self-absorbed and egomaniacal, but at the same time unusually empathetic. Without question, they have been historically needed to preserve and protect individual liberties and freedom, and to promote universal safety improvements in all facets of commercial life.

If we step back and look at what has happened in this country, it becomes clear that the federal government does less and less for the people. The agencies designed to help people and to keep Big Business honest do not work properly. The Food and Drug Administration is unable to keep up with the drug companies and has practically become their functionary. The Consumer Product Safety Commission is overwhelmed. And all of the agencies tasked with protecting the financial system have had abysmal track records of late, which led to a catastrophic financial crisis in 2008. The central problem is that these agencies are all beholden to Big Business. For this reason, whether you love or hate them, trial lawyers are a necessary part of our society.

Despite decades of legislative and corporate attempts to destroy the plaintiff's trial lawyer, the Levin firm continues to prosper. It's the largest it's ever been since its founding in 1955. Its annual Mass Torts Made Perfect meetings in Las Vegas draw hundreds of lawyers from around the country interested in working with and emulating Levin-Papantonio.

"From our perspective, there is a wonderful aspect to being dedicated to leveling the playing field in some small way so that the little guy can do battle with the big guy," says Mark Proctor, who continues to serve as president of Levin-Papantonio. "Out of our success, a synergy has been developed between doing well while we are doing good. The lawyers in our firm believe very strongly in what they do. When you really try to objectively look at what has happened to individual rights in this country in the last twenty years, it is clear that people need a voice, and a powerful one at that. We try to be that voice. But we've come to realize in the last twenty years that just being that voice in the courtroom is not enough. There is also a larger social agenda at play."

Law Partners Mike Papantonio, Fred, and Mark Proctor.

Papantonio has taken very seriously to advocating the larger social and political agenda, which he believes in and which also clearly benefits the firm. Along with Robert Kennedy Jr. and Sam Seder, Papantonio owns Ring of Fire radio, which broadcasts to 315 stations across the country every day. Papantonio hosts nearly every show from a state-of-the-art studio in the firm's building. He always chooses a topic that will get under the skin of conservatives, government, or Big Business. The radio show has a weekly TV broadcast on Free Speech TV. Papantonio also regularly appears on MSNBC and other national and international stations to express his dogmatic views.

"Mike does this extremely well, and there is a pure beauty about that because he doesn't care about the repercussions, much the same way I never have when I speak out for what I believe," Fred says. "Most businessmen can't take strong positions because they are afraid to put their economic interests on the line. That isn't an issue at our firm."

One of the areas the firm moved into two decades ago that fit hand in glove with the mass torts practice and the social agenda it advocates was environmental law. Levin-Papantonio's environmental practice has taken the lead in national cases that have affected hundreds of thousands of people. Papantonio led a large class action against Conoco concerning massive groundwater contamination on the Panhandle and obtained a settlement of nearly $100 million for the affected residents. Along with Kennedy, Papantonio also won a $400 million verdict in a case against DuPont on behalf of 8,000 West Virginia residents whose land was contaminated by the company.

The firm's lengthy history with environmental law positioned it to be one of the leaders in recovering damages for business after the BP oil spill. After the unprecedented spill in April 2010, which resulted in more than 200 million gallons of oil gushing into the Gulf of Mexico, Levin-Papantonio was judicially appointed as one of only four law firms in the entire country to serve as executive counsel in the multibillion-dollar national civil litigation pending against those responsible.

Additionally, thousands of individual businesses along the Gulf Coast retained the services of the Levin firm to sue BP individually for their damages. Ironically, many of these businesses have been sued by the Levin firm in the past, yet chose to hire the firm when they were harmed.

It's rare that any major mass tort in the country does not present itself to Levin-Papantonio. The firm clearly is considered one of the very few

800-pound gorillas in the field. It has earned that reputation over many decades of not being scared to go to trial, not being afraid to invest millions of dollars in a single case, and not accepting settlement offers when its lawyers believe the clients can do better—whether the money offered was $2 million in the 1980 *Thorshov* train derailment case or more than $100 million in the 2001 Fen-Phen diet drug litigation. Whatever the combination—incredible lawyering, hubris, or both—it seems to work well for the relatively small firm operating out of the "Redneck Riviera."

"The firm really is a mirror image of the personalities, and because of that it doesn't have any hard-and-fast rules," Proctor explains. "What I tell these young lawyers is that you need to have the entrepreneurial spirit to be here. We're cowboys. We're a high-wire circus act without any net. We are going for it. We do everything on a contingency fee. We are the consummate dice throwers, and we back up our desire with our money and our investment in cases."

Fred Levin is still kicking and doing what he does best. In 2006, *Super Lawyers* magazine ran a headline that read: "The Pugilist: The three biggest things to hit Pensacola just might be Jesus, Hurricane Ivan, and Fred Levin." While Hurricane Ivan is long gone, and the debate rages over whether or not Jesus will return, Fred is still there to this day, as he has been his entire life.

Steve Yerrid, one of the Dream Team lawyers from the tobacco case, attributes Fred's longevity to his achieving the ideal balance for a trial lawyer. "Is Fred a tough guy? Fred's a tough guy," Yerrid says. "Is Fred a kind guy? Fred's a kind guy. Fred shows that you can be tough and kind at the same time without betraying either talent. It takes a tough guy to win in court. It takes a kind guy to represent people that you love and carry their cross even when you think all hope is lost."

Fred has admittedly mellowed somewhat. He's seventy-seven years old at the time of this writing. His wife of fifty-plus years has died, and he has no interest in remarrying. He has no real hobbies, and he doesn't like to travel. He's not really interested in gambling anymore, rarely drinks, and never smokes. He only goes to a casino with friends and then only if it is a social outing. Most nights, he comes home from the office by 6 P.M., sits down with a friend or two for dinner, and then retires to his room early to watch reality television and read the *National Enquirer*.

Fred also has begun to show much more interest in his Jewish heritage, something he always was proud of, but didn't focus on. Recently, he donated $1 million in Marilyn's name to the Lubavitch/Chabad Student & Community Center at the University of Florida. "Of all the donations I have made, this is the one I believe that Marilyn would be most proud of," Fred says. "At the dedication, there were Jews of all ages and all levels of spiritual beliefs from agnostic to Hasidic. Everyone was together as one, eating, drinking, dancing, and just celebrating life. This center provides all Jews at University of Florida, and throughout the Gainesville area, a place to eat incredible kosher food, work out, do laundry, socialize, pray, attend services, or just get some much-needed spiritual advice. They are so open and accepting of every Jew, without exception or judgment. Marilyn would have been overwhelmed with joy to know we were doing something to help college kids make one of the most significant transitions in their lives, yet have the comfort and assistance of Judaism."

Fred openly acknowledges his faults, but makes no excuses and carries few regrets. "All of these guys say, 'If I had to do it again, I wish I would have spent more time with my family,'" he says. "But here I was winning these huge cases, being with all these incredible people, getting involved with things that saved lives and changed the law. And boxing! There are not many people who've had the opportunity to be on national TV in the middle of the ring of a title fight with the camera on them and experience that excitement, that rush.

"I did not spend time with my wife, Marilyn, or my children when they were young. I missed out, and they missed out," he continues. "My kids are much better parents than I ever was, but I did provide for them so they can afford to be good parents. I regret I didn't do more for Marilyn. I wish I had understood the physical pain she truly was in, and that it could have turned out differently. I hope one day to see her again and apologize, and of course dance with her. I'm obviously pleased that the kids turned out so great. It certainly wasn't because of my fathering skills."

He pauses for a rare moment of introspection. "I want to be remembered for two things: my family and the law," he says. "As for my family, my children have left their own legacy that I could not be more proud of, and I know their kids will continue the same. As for my career, my name is going to be on that University of Florida law school forever, so in fifty or a hundred years people may stop to look me up. Hopefully, history will be kind to me, but if not, I hope they at least spell my name right."

Fred continues to go to work at the firm every day, including Saturday and Sunday. He still finds himself involved in political controversies, both locally and on a state level. He continues to develop business ideas, which he may or may not follow through on (though likely not). The most recent one is an online video yellow page using BLAB-TV with the slogan of "Between Angie and Craig, there's BLAB's List. It's as easy as A-B-C."

He still takes on single-event cases, preferably ones that have a special challenge. "From a conceptual perspective, I think I'm a better lawyer now than I've ever been," he says. "If something happens to my health, I can still be the rainmaker. They can prop me up on television and make me look like I can still do it, like Dick Clark on New Year's Eve."

In 2013, when he was seventy-six, Fred proved that he still could win a seemingly unwinnable case. The case stemmed from an accident that occurred in July 2007. A woman named Jackie McMahon, who lives in Pensacola, was in Alabama driving an all-terrain vehicle (ATV) called a Yamaha Rhino 660. She was on flat terrain making a turn when it tipped over, and she suffered severe leg and arm injuries.

Fred brought suit alleging a defective product and went to trial in October 2010. In a three-week trial, Fred pointed out what he found were defects in the Rhino 660. The defense retorted that this particular off-road vehicle had more safety features than any competitor. The case was tried in Alabama, where Fred was not intimately familiar with state law.

"The defense lawyers misled the court in a number of ways, and I really felt like I was getting 'hometowned' by the judge," Fred says. "I lost the case. Initially, I started simply to mark it off as a loss, since cases against Yamaha, as a result of the defective Rhino 660, had been lost throughout the country on every occasion. However, we were staying at the same hotel with the defense attorneys, and their celebration of their victory, as well as their press release, was terribly embarrassing to me. For those reasons, I appealed and the case was sent back for a new trial."

The retrial occurred in April 2013. On the first day, the judge called Fred into chambers with the defense counsel and told Fred that he should settle the case because he couldn't win it. Fred explained that his client wanted to go through with the trial. The judge asked to meet with Jackie McMahon, who agreed to see her.

"This was the first time in my career that a judge had called my client into chambers," Fred says. "The judge told my client there was absolutely no way that this case was going to be a plaintiff's verdict. The judge really pushed my client to accept a settlement that would have been somewhere between $200,000 and $350,000, which was approximately the costs that would be incurred by the defendant to try the case."

McMahon refused to settle, and the trial began. Fred changed tactics from the first trial and went after Yamaha, the company, rather than focusing on the design of the Rhino 660 itself. He presented a case that Yamaha had done a good job in initially producing the Rhino 660, but then pointed out that the company realized soon after it went on the market that it was having tip-over problems on flat terrain while in a curve. Fred further pointed out that Yamaha had, on a number of occasions in the past, recalled other products, but not the Rhino 660, which had become the fastest-selling off-road vehicle in the world. He then argued that his case was about Yamaha's failure to recall the Rhino 660 prior to McMahon's purchasing it. Rather than argue simple negligence (the failure to exercise reasonable care) in Yamaha's failure to produce a safe ATV, Fred argued that Yamaha actually acted with wantonness (the conscious doing of some act or omission with knowledge that injury likely will result), in failing to recall the ATV from the market after the company became aware of it tipping over.

While this sounded like a more difficult burden for Fred, and it was, it also provided him a unique benefit under Alabama law. It prevented Yamaha from arguing that McMahon's own negligence in operating the ATV was a contributing cause of her injuries, which under Alabama law would be an insurmountable obstacle to her recovering damages. Fred's new strategy worked better than anticipated.

In his closing argument, Fred told the jury they should find reasonable compensatory damages, but only $1,000 in punitive damages. After the trial, the jurors said that all twelve immediately determined they would find for the plaintiff, and then spent six hours arguing over the damages. Incredibly, they returned a verdict of $1.4 million in compensatory damages and $2 million in punitive damages.

Fred continues to come to work every day because, he says, he hopes in some small way that continuing to represent individual clients will keep the practice of law going, much the same way the millions of dollars he donated to the University of Florida help facilitate that same goal.

"I want the practice of law to continue," he says. "I want there to be lawyers. Less and less people are going to law school now. In 2013, applications to accredited law schools dropped for a third consecutive year. My son, Martin, left the practice of law because of its transformation from the personal—a lawyer representing one client—to a business where a lawyer represents thousands of clients in a mass tort or class action."

So is that why a multimillionaire lawyer who could be tooling around the Gulf of Mexico on his yacht still goes to the office? Is it really something as simple as Fred's desire to stimulate the practice of law that causes him to continue to work despite the fact that his son decided not to carry on the practice he built and that mass torts (in which he has no interest) are the future of the profession?

It sounds noble, but I tell Fred that doesn't sound very Fred Levin. He leans back in his chair and says there's one other reason. He asks if he can tell a story to illuminate his point.

The circus was in town, he begins, and the elephants were walking down the main street to get to the circus venue. Behind one of the elephants was a young man who pulled one of the elephants out of the line and shoved his entire arm into the elephant's behind. The young man then pulled his arm out and immediately was covered from head to toe with elephant crap. The young man was asked what was he doing, and he replied that it was his job to relieve constipated elephants. He was then asked why he didn't quit. The young man answered, "And give up showbiz?"

And so what is the real reason Fred Levin won't quit practicing law? He smiles. "And give up showbiz?"

Index

Acknowledgments

· ·

This book would not exist without Martin Levin. As the keeper of the Levin family archives and the institutional memory of his father's colorful life, Martin provided invaluable help with the book. Beyond that, his insights added depth and clarity to both the complex legal stories and the bittersweet personal ones.

A chain of events led me to Fred Levin's office. Wayne Rogers introduced me to Mike Papantonio, who in turn introduced me to Fred— handshakes that were all much appreciated. As a subject, Fred was a dream to work with. Rather than shying away from the less flattering events in his life, he insisted that they be included. Not to worry, Fred; any racy stories cut out will be in the movie.

The following people shared their insights and stories: Mark Proctor, Morris Dees, Reubin Askew, Rick Matasar, Phillip Morris, Dean Baird, Fred Vigodsky, Emmitt Smith, Roy Jones Sr., Marshall Criser, Roy Jones Jr., Chuck Kahn, Jimmy Kemp, Bob Kerrigan, John Morgan, Jerry Pate, James Rinaman Jr., Kay Stephenson, Leo Thomas, Terdema Ussery, Steve Yerrid, Ashton Hayward, Jim Schettler, Marci Goodman, Debra Dreyer, Kim Brielmayer, and Teri Levin. Fred's secretary, Donna Gilbert, made sure that Fred had time for me. Mark O'Brien conducted some of the initial interviews, and Samuel Proctor's oral history added context to several stories.

Andrew Stuart, agent extraordinaire, offered clear guidance through all steps of the process and put together the deals with his usual precision. Nancy Young provided some helpful analysis of the first draft. Dorianne Perrucci edited the manuscript with a sharp pencil and refined the narrative, with an assist from copyeditor James Fraleigh. Brian Feinblum at Media Connect enthusiastically handled the publicity.

And thanks most of all to publisher Glenn Yeffeth and his amazingly professional team at BenBella Books—Debbie Harmsen, Vy Tran, Jenna Sampson, Jennifer Canzoneri, Sarah Dombrowsky, Adrienne Lang, Alicia Kania, Monica Lowry, and Jessika Rieck—for nurturing the book and bringing it to life.

About the Author

· ·

JOSH YOUNG is a best-selling author whose work spans entertainment, business, politics, science, and natural history. He has coauthored five *New York Times* best sellers and two additional national best sellers.

He is the coauthor of comedian Howie Mandel's *Here's the Deal: Don't Touch Me*; of Dr. Sam Parnia's *Erasing Death: The Science That Is Rewriting the Boundaries between Life and Death*; and *The Link: Uncovering Our Earliest Ancestor* with Colin Tudge, which has been translated into five languages. He is also the coauthor with movie mogul Mike Medavoy of *You're Only as Good as Your Next One*, and coauthor with actor and entrepreneur Wayne Rogers of the iconoclastic business book *Make Your Own Rules: A Renegade Guide to Unconventional Success*. Josh also wrote *Dino Gangs*, the story of renowned paleontologist Phil Currie's quest to uncover the mystery of how dinosaurs behaved.

Among the other books he cowrote are Bob Newhart's comedic memoir *I Shouldn't Even Be Doing This!*; actor and comedian Jay Mohr's *Gasping for Airtime: Two Years in the Trenches of* Saturday Night Live; Jim Belushi's *Real Men Don't Apologize*; and Sir David Attenborough's *First Life: A Journey Back in Time*. He also contributed to the No. 1 *New York Times* best seller *The Right Words at the Right Time*, edited by Marlo Thomas.

As a journalist, Josh served as a contributing editor at *George* magazine and a contributing writer to *Entertainment Weekly* and *LIFE* magazine. Prior to that, he was the movie writer for *Esquire* and a contributing writer to the *New York Times* Sunday Arts & Leisure section. His writing has appeared in numerous other publications, including *Talk, New Republic,*

Details, *Allure*, the *Sunday Telegraph* (London), the *Independent* (London), and *Los Angeles* magazine. He has also has written "as told to" magazine articles for former First Lady Laura Bush and CNN's Anderson Cooper.

He has appeared on several national and international television programs, including *ABC World News*, NBC's *Today*, Fox News' *The O'Reilly Factor*, CBS' *Entertainment Tonight*, CNBC's *Rivera Live*, *EXTRA*, and the MSNBC *Morning Show*. He also hosted *Screening Room* on the Discovery Times Channel.